Marriage and the Common Good

Marriage and the Common Good

Proceedings from
the Twenty-Second Annual Convention of
The Fellowship of Catholic Scholars

September 24–26, 1999
Deerfield, Illinois

Kenneth D. Whitehead
Editor

ST. AUGUSTINE'S PRESS
South Bend, Indiana
2001

Manufactured in the United States of America.

1 2 3 4 5 6   07 06 05 04 03 02 01

Library of Congress Cataloging in Publication Data
Fellowship of Catholic Scholars. Convention (22nd : 1999 : Deerfield,
Ill.)
    Marriage and the common good : proceedings from the Twenty-
    Second annual Convention of the Fellowship of Catholic
    Scholars, September 24–26, 1999, Deerfield, IL / Kenneth D.
    Whitehead, editor.
      p. cm.
    Includes bibliographical references.
    ISBN 1-890318-88-4 (alk. paper)
    1. Marriage – Religious aspects – Catholic Church –
    Congresses. 2. Family – Religious aspects – Catholic Church –
    Congresses. I. Whitehead, K. D. II. Title.
BX2250 .F45 1999
261.8'358 – dc21   00-010655

∞ *The paper used in this publication meets the minimum requirements of the*
American National Standard for Information Sciences – Permanence of Paper
for Printed Materials, ANSI Z39.48-1984.

Contents

INTRODUCTION
Dr. Mary Shivanandan,[1] Program Chair

As program chair, I would first like to acknowledge my fellow program committee members, Dr. Michael Healy of the Franciscan University of Steubenville, and Dr. William E. May of the John Paul II Institute for Studies on Marriage and the Family. It was in every sense a team effort to bring you this fine program.

And now to turn to the program itself: almost every day, we open a newspaper and we see yet another assault on the institution of marriage. In July, Rutgers University released the report of the National Marriage Project. Among the gloomy news, about half of all adults under 40 years of age have lived with a partner before marriage. The divorce rate has soared by 30 percent in 30 years, and nearly half of all marriages are expected to end in divorce or permanent separation. In August, feminist Barbara Ehrenreich urged that we acknowledge the disappearance of fatherhood and provide increased welfare benefits to single mothers. She argues that the state is less bothersome to deal with than men, who are hard to manage.

In September, two leading candidates for the presidency came out in favor of domestic partner protection for gays and lesbians, while saying that they oppose same-sex marriage for religious reasons.

"Nobody is focusing on marriage. It is not in the national debate." Such is the pessimistic conclusion of David Popenoe, co-director of the National Marriage Project.

But that is what this meeting of the Fellowship of Catholic Scholars is all about: inserting marriage into the national debate. As Catholics and Christians, we offer the good news of Jesus Christ. Cardinal Francis George, O.M.I, ordinary of this illustrious Archdiocese of Chicago, and our banquet speaker tomorrow evening, states that: "Evangelizing means speaking in the public forum." He proposes that we begin "by offering our vision of what the world can be: a vision founded on faith, but also one that is persuasive in the public square."

So we begin this meeting with "the Theology of Marriage and Celibacy," presented by Dr. Alice von Hildebrand. Understanding that the destiny of the human person is to participate in divine Trinitarian union, of which sacramental marriage is an efficacious sign, provides the vision.

While preparing the publicity material for this program, our FCS Executive Secretary, Fr. Tom Dailey – who has done a magnificent job! – sent me a draft program in which he described Dr. Alice von Hildebrand as the "wisdom" of her late husband, the philosopher Dietrich von Hildebrand. Indeed she is! (The more prosaic term, of course, is "widow.") But Dr. Alice von Hildebrand is a distinguished scholar in her own right. Fr. Paul DeLadurantaye of the Diocese of Arlington, Virginia, ably responds to her presentation.

We are very fortunate to have Dr. David Blankenhorn, founder and director of the Institute on American Values, to share with us his pioneering work on fatherhood in the session devoted to "Fatherhood and Society." Dr. Philip Sutton, a licensed psychologist and counselor, provides a response.

Professor Robert P. George, who redeems the reputation of Princeton University sullied by the hiring of consequentialist Dr. Peter Singer, brings to us an indispensable perspective on "Homosexuality and the Law" in the session devoted to that topic. The current president of the Fellowship of Catholic Scholars, Professor Gerry Bradley of the Notre Dame Law School, responds.

Dr. Jean Bethke Elshtain of the University of Chicago, author of *Public Man, Private Woman: Women in Social and Political Thought*, among other books and innumerable articles, is uniquely qualified to address the issue of "Women's Roles and Family Policy." Dr. Patricia Donohue-White of the Franciscan University of Steubenville provides a response.

Our last two main speakers are much concerned with the contemporary "culture of death." Ambassador Alberto Piedra, currently at the Catholic University of America, discusses the consequences for a population that is not reproducing itself, while fellow economist Dr. Guillermo Montes responds with a discussion of the contribution child care makes to the economy.

Also concerned with the "culture of death," Professor William E. May discusses a topic that is hardly ever mentioned in the public square as a major contributor to the breakdown of marriage and the family – namely, contraception. The availability of abortion and hormonal contraception since the late 1960s has been described – as constituting a "technology shock" from which our culture is still reeling. Marquette's Dr. Monica Migliorino Miller responds.

Finally, not to be overlooked, is our keynote speaker from Oxford, England, Stratford Caldecott, director of the Center for Faith and Culture there. He reminds us of another English Catholic, G. K. Chesterton, who was able to speak persuasively in the public square.

As Cardinal George says, "we have reasons for hope." Without further ado, then, I turn the microphone over to the first of our speakers – who are not the least among those "reasons for hope."

Note

1. Mary Shivanandan, S.T.D., is Associate Dean and Professor of Theology at the John Paul II Institute for Studies on Marriage and the Family in Washington, DC. She is author of the recent *Crossing the Threshold of Love: A New Vision of Marriage in the Light of John Paul II's Anthropology* (The Catholic University of America Press, Washington, DC, 1999). She is currently a member of the Board of Directors of the Fellowship of Catholic Scholars.

KEYNOTE ADDRESS

THE DRAMA OF THE HOME: MARRIAGE, THE COMMON GOOD AND PUBLIC POLICY
Dr. Stratford Caldecott[1]

When we defend the family we do not mean that it is always a peaceful family; when we maintain the thesis of marriage we do not mean that it is always a happy marriage. We mean that it is the theater of the spiritual drama, the place where things happen, especially the things that matter. It is not so much the place where a man kills his wife as the place where he can take the equally sensational step of not killing his wife.

G. K. Chesterton[2]

Most of us here are too old and cynical – or I should say too sophisticated and mature – to believe what we read in the newspapers. Whenever you are personally acquainted with some person in the news, you can be sure that you will be able to detect a distortion taking place. If the story is not a flat lie, it is only a partial truth, presented in a way that leads to a conclusion you know is wrong.

Nowhere is this more apparent than in the way the mass media deal with the Catholic Church. During the last twenty years, we have been privileged to witness one of the most remarkable pontificates in history. Pope John Paul II is not only a philosopher, a poet, a linguist, an actor, and a sportsman, who turned the tide against communism when it seemed unbeatable, but he is also a holy man, maybe a saint. The media occasionally acknowledge his extraordinary popularity by giving him a few minutes of air time. But no one actually *listens to what he says*. In the media, it is only *image* that is important, and for many people the pope is an image – perhaps *the* image – of conservatism and rigidity. The reason for this is not so much that he represents a Church which has survived two thousand years of human history unchanged in essence and still vibrant with life (for they are mostly not aware of this fact or of its significance). Nor is it the pope's political views that particularly strike them as "conservative" – for most, when pressed, will acknowledge that he has preached consistently against dictatorships and in favor of democracy and human rights. The reason is first and foremost his support of *Humanae Vitae* and his defence of the traditional Catholic teaching on marriage and sexuality.

Yet it is precisely here, where in the popular mind he is on the weakest ground, defending the indefensible, ignoring the true facts of human nature, wanting to preserve his authority and power at all costs, that the pope is actually at his most courageous, his most intelligent, his most well-informed, and his most original. The richness and rounded human wisdom of his teaching on marriage has been brought out in a book by Professor Mary Shivanandan, *Crossing the Threshold of Love*).[3]

By mentioning this book here I intend not only to honor the gracious lady who invited me here, but to draw attention at the outset to the context in which a Catholic group such as this meets to explore the rich theme of the family and public policy. For that context has been set largely by the pope, in documents such as *Familiaris Consortio*, the *Letter to Families* and *Evangelium Vitae*. There, and elsewhere in his writings, he has contrasted a "culture of life" with a "culture of death": characteristic phrases of this tremendous pontificate which refer to two opposing tendencies present throughout human history since the Fall, and in a particularly intense way in our own society on the eve of the Great Jubilee.

Since I am by trade a publisher, to help to set a direction for my remarks I will recommend to you another book to read. It is John Saward's *The Way of the Lamb*.[4] This book is important because it bears eloquent witness to the physical, psychological, and ultimately spiritual assault that has been waged for over a century now against the spirit of childhood – that is, against human life in its most innocent and vulnerable form, and in this way against the very heart of the Christian family. The book draws our attention to St Therese, G.K. Chesterton, Charles Peguy, Georges Bernanos and Hans Urs von Balthasar as prophetic agents raised up by divine Providence to confront this evil.

It is Chesterton in particular that I will draw upon in this paper to help highlight some aspects of the pope's teaching on the family. As for the evil itself, the evil of the culture of death, we see it everywhere prevalent not only in the abuse and killing of children by adults but, increasingly, in the killing of *children by children*. The massacre at Columbine High School in Littleton, Colorado, provides one vivid example (although there are others I might have chosen from my own country). The event provoked the following judgment by Denver Archbishop Charles J. Chaput:

> Violence is now pervasive in American society – in our homes, our schools, on our streets, in our cars as we drive home from work, in the news media, in the rhythms and lyrics of our music, in our novels, films and video games. It is so prevalent that we have become largely unconscious of it. But, as we discover in places like the hallways of Columbine High, it is bitterly, urgently real. The causes of this violence are many and complicated: racism, fear, selfishness. But in another, deeper sense, the cause is very simple: we're losing God, and in losing him, we're losing ourselves. The complete contempt for human life shown by the young killers at Columbine is not an accident, or an anomaly, or a freak flaw in our social fabric. It is what we create when we live a contradiction. We cannot systematically kill the unborn, the infirm and the condemned prisoners among us; we cannot glorify brutality in our entertainment; we cannot market avarice and greed . . . and then hope that somehow our children will help to build a culture of life. We need to change. But societies only change when families change, and families only change when individuals change. Without a conversion to humility, non-violence and selflessness in our own hearts, all our talk about "ending the violence" may end as pious generalities. It is not enough to speak about reforming our society and community. We need to reform ourselves.[5]

The archbishop is right about the pervasiveness of violence, and of the violent *imagination* nourished by the entertainment industry. His comments, as I suggested, apply much more widely than in America. He is also right about the loss of a living relationship with God, even where the trappings of religion may survive. People often speak as though they believed in God, without *living* as though God truly existed.[6]

The archbishop's third point is also valid: there is a profound inconsistency between society's espousal of humanity and its manifest brutality, especially towards its most vulnerable and least visible members. Now, as G. K. Chesterton pointed out long ago, the reformer is always right about what is wrong, but he is generally wrong about what is right. The archbishop, however, is right about the need for a radical and far-reaching conversion: first of all the conversion of our own hearts and lives, and, only through this primary and ongoing interior reform, the transformation of families and society. There is no doubt that he and Chesterton would be in agreement about this. Everything starts with the heart.

Nevertheless, I am sure that Chesterton would add that there is also a lesser but important effect in the opposite direction. Our society does not take love seriously enough; consequently the images and values it projects and imposes do anything but facilitate the healing of the heart, and it fails to support the dignity and integrity of the family by protective legislation. "If we wish to preserve the family," he concluded, "we must revolutionize the nation" (*BNF*, p. 24).[7]

In what follows, I want to explore something of what lies behind this rather striking remark in the light of our overall theme. I hope, with Chesterton, to avoid falling into the trap of being either *conservative* or *progressive* in the modern sense of those words. For as he remarks somewhere, "The whole modern world has divided itself into conservatives and progressives. The business of progressives is to go on making mistakes. The business of conservatives is to prevent the mistakes from being corrected."[8]

The Gifts of the Family

One of my favorite serious passages from Chesterton comes from the first chapter of his book *Chaucer*. He writes:

> There is at the back of all our lives an abyss of light, more blinding and unfathomable than any abyss of darkness; and it is the abyss of actuality, of existence, of the fact that things truly are, and that we ourselves are incredibly and sometimes almost incredulously real. It is the fundamental fact of being, as against not being; it is unthinkable, yet we cannot unthink it,

though we may sometimes be unthinking about it; unthinking and especially unthanking. For he who has realized this reality knows that it does outweigh, literally to infinity, all lesser regrets or arguments for negation, and that under all our grumblings there is a subconscious substance of gratitude. That light of the positive is the business of the poets, because they see all things in the light of it more than do other men.

In these few lines is the essence of his book on St. Thomas Aquinas, which Etienne Gilson praised as the greatest book on Thomas ever written; for Thomas was above all the philosopher of creation, who showed by the distinction of existence from essence that the created world was indeed a free and wonderful gift.[9]

This theme or understanding runs all the way through Chesterton's writing. It certainly seems appropriate, therefore, to frame his vision of the family in terms of "gift." And one way of doing so is to reflect on some of the particular gifts that God gives to us through the family.

1. Life. Firstly, of course, the family is "the sanctuary of life: the place in which life – the gift of God – can be properly welcomed and protected against the many attacks to which it is exposed, and can develop in accordance with what constitutes authentic human growth" (*Centesimus Annus*, 39). But if life is not understood or regarded as *gift*, what takes over is the mentality of *control:* including the desire to manipulate others for our own ends. To respect life as something given is to respect its inner mystery, and particularly the mystery of otherness and freedom present in every human person. The difference between these two positions is profound, indeed it could not be more so, since each determines in a different way the attitude we take to our own existence in the world and the relationships that alone can give a meaning to our lives.[10] That is why the popes have spoken so emphatically and repeatedly on the subject of contraception, John Paul II underlining and deepening Paul VI's teaching in *Humanae Vitae* (1968).

In sexual intercourse a fundamental attitude to life and to the other person is inevitably embodied. When we take steps to render infertile an act that might otherwise be fertile, we are not simply rejecting the new life that might otherwise come to be (as John

Finnis, William May and others have rightly pointed out), but effectively attempting to close off the spiritual dimension of the act in which new life is created, reducing it thereby to a merely biological and psychological process. The employment of barrier or chemical contraceptives (in this respect fundamentally unlike simple self-restraint) tends to change the nature of the sexual act from a form of true self-giving into a form of mutual use – an attitude which logically extends itself into surrogate motherhood, *in vitro* fertilization, and ultimately human cloning, where the living being is treated as the result of a mechanical process and therefore potentially as a commercial product.[11]

This is a recurrent theme in Chesterton's writing, for he saw the intellectuals of his generation taking the road towards eugenics and denounced them for it. As for "birth control," he wrote, "it is a name given to a succession of different expedients (the one that was used last is always described as having been dreadfully dangerous) by which it is possible to filch the pleasure belonging to a natural process while violently and unnaturally thwarting the process itself" (*BNF*, p. 199).

2. Love. Gratitude for existence is only conceivable where there is some sense, however obscure, that existence is a gift and that somewhere there must be a Giver. Thus intimately linked to the gift of life is the gift of love. The pope writes in this connection not simply of love, but of "fairest love": that love which is rooted in the Trinity and flows into the world through the Incarnation, through the Holy Family with Mary at its heart, and through the sacraments. "*For love to be truly 'fairest,'*" he adds, "*it must be a gift of God,* grafted by the Holy Spirit on to human hearts and continually nourished in them (cf. Rom. 5:5). Fully conscious of this, the Church in the sacrament of marriage asks the Holy Spirit to visit human hearts. If love is truly to be 'fairest love,' a gift of one person to another, it must come from the One who is himself a gift and the source of every gift" (*Letter to Families*, 20).

Hans Urs von Balthasar lays great stress on the "mother's smile" as the first revelation to the child of this love at the heart of being. It *personalizes* the cosmos that confronts us, gives it a human face, reveals its interior life, awakens the freedom of the subject.

Perhaps I do not need to labor this point. It is clear enough that the dawning realization that I am a person in a world of persons is the first step in the birth of love, the breaking open of the closed circle of the self.

3. Adventure. The third great gift God gives us through the family is *adventure*. At the simplest level, we are all aware that we do not make or choose our brothers and sisters, our parents and children. Chesterton writes: "The supreme adventure is being born. Our father and mother . . . lie in wait for us and leap out on us, like brigands from a bush. Our uncle is a surprise. Our aunt is, in the beautiful common expression, a bolt from the blue. When we step into the family, by the very act of being born, we . . . step into a world that is incalculable, into a world that we have not made. In other words, when we step into the family we step into a fairy-tale" (*BNF*, p. 44).

The same applies to marriage itself. While, in contrast to being born, we generally choose the person we marry, the experience is no less adventurous and unpredictable for that (quite apart from the surprises we will receive from our children). The marriage vow is intrinsically adventurous, as Chesterton showed in an essay called "A Defence of Rash Vows." For

> the man who makes a vow makes an appointment with himself at some distant time or place. The danger of it is that he should not keep the appointment. And in modern times this terror of one's self, of the weakness and mutability of one's self, has perilously increased, and is the real basis for the objection to vows of any kind. A modern man refrains from swearing to count the leaves on every third tree in Holland Walk, not because it is silly to do so (he does many sillier things), but because he has a profound conviction that before he had got to the three hundred and seventy-ninth leaf on the first tree he would be excessively tired of the subject and want to go home to tea. In other words, we fear that by that time he will be, in the common but hideously significant phrase, another man. . . . And this is the condition of the decadent, of the aesthete, of the free-lover. To be everlastingly passing through dangers which we know cannot scathe us, to be taking oaths which we know cannot bind us, to be defying enemies who we know can-

not conquer us – this is the grinning tyranny of decadence
which is called freedom.

Let us turn, on the other hand, to the maker of vows. . . .
It is the nature of love to bind itself, and the institution of marriage merely paid the average man the compliment of taking
him at his word. Modern sages offer to the lover, with an ill-
favored grin, the largest liberties and the fullest irresponsibility; but they do not respect him as the old Church respected
him; they do not write his oath upon the heavens, as the record
of his highest moment...All around us is the city of small sins,
abounding in backways and retreats, but surely, sooner or later,
the towering flame will rise from the harbor announcing that
the reign of the cowards is over and a man is burning his ships"
(*BNF*, pp. 49–52).

4. History. The person who is born into a family receives another
gift. The adventure into which he or she enters has already been
going on for quite some time. By being born we are grafted into a
history, and into relationships that extend not just around us in the
present but into the far past and the far future. Just as each of us is,
as the ancients saw, a microcosm or tiny cosmos, so each human life
story is the history of a world within a world, woven into a much
larger tapestry. The Providence which shapes our ends (though never
without taking our free acts into account) is the same Providence
that shapes the whole pattern of earthly time into a *history of salvation*.

Being born into a family we receive, then, not merely parents,
but grandparents and ancestors extending back to Adam himself. We
inherit the legacy of our family: a legacy of sins and virtues, of
choices made long before we were born. We pass that legacy on to
others, transformed perhaps, but part of a single pattern of events.

5. Name. Implicit here, but deserving of more attention, is the mys-
terious fifth gift. It is our family that gives us a name. And the act of
naming plays an important part in the whole of Scripture. We recall
Adam's naming of the animals and of his wife, God's naming of
Abraham and Israel; we recall (in the New Testament) the naming of
John the Baptizer, and Jesus' naming of Peter. Names in Holy

Scripture are rarely if ever accidental. A true name is no mere label attached to a piece of luggage, but something almost sacred, almost sacramental. A personal name is supposed to depict and crystallize a particular *mission* or *vocation*. In fact, in traditional societies the family name often derives from the family trade or profession (which in such societies is viewed as a "vocation" indeed, and not a mere "job") – examples would be Fletcher, Smith, Thatcher and so on. The name may also derive from that of the father (Barabbas, Johnson, Peterson), or a saint whose care for the child the family wishes to invoke. In cultures less traditional, it is still common to choose a name that "runs in the family." Why is this?

To be given a family name is to be accepted as a member of that family. In Jewish culture, and many others, it is the custom for the father to name the child. This is part of what it means to be a father. It was Joseph's job to give Jesus his name, thereby recognizing him as belonging to the family of David, the family of Abraham, the family of Adam. Through the name that one receives from the family, one possesses more than a place in history (for even a child unnamed or disowned has that). The father or the family that names a child performs a ritual that in its original significance is supposed to reveal something of the *identity* of that person within history: their role in the unfolding drama. Archetypally, if not in practice actually, my name is a *revelation of myself* – or at least it is a sign that I have a self which will one day stand revealed in God's kingdom (hence the "white stone" of Rev. 2:17). And that is because who I am is essentially other-directed, *in missio*, "sent" into the world to accomplish a task. I am what the Lord gives
me to do.

6. Education. Gift number 6 I will call *education*. By this I mean much more than the conveying of information or practical skills, to which the word is often reduced in a world which measures all value in pragmatic terms. The family is not merely the most efficient means yet devised of initiating new citizens into the jobs they must perform, and of inculcating the civic virtues. True, if these things are not learnt in the family, or if the foundations of the moral life are not laid there, it is unlikely they will be picked up on the streets or in the workplace. But the Church has all these things in perspective, and sees education not primarily as service to the State but as belonging intrinsically to the adventure of the family.

The pope writes in the *Letter to Families*: "To give birth according to the flesh means to set in motion a further 'birth,' one which is gradual and complex and which continues in the whole process of education." He relates this to the Fourth Commandment (Ex. 20:12): to say that children must "honor" their parents is to imply also that parents must honor their children, for the *"principle of giving honor,"* which means the recognition and respect due to man precisely because he is man, "is the basic condition for every authentic educational process."

The process is an extension of the self-giving which is at the heart of the sacrament of marriage (I will return to this theme later). It is a process of exchange in which the parents are continually educated by the child even as they lead the child towards maturity in love. The pope calls it a *reciprocal "offering" on the part of both parents:* "Together they communicate their own mature humanity to the newborn child, who gives them in turn the newness and freshness of the humanity which it has brought into the world. This is the case even when children are born with mental or physical disabilities. . . . The 'communion of persons,' expressed as conjugal love at the beginning of the family, is thus completed and brought to fulfillment in the raising of children." All of this applies in a specially intense way to the role of the mother, about which the pope has much to say. But both parents share in God's *"paternal and at the same time maternal way of teaching,"* which is revealed in Christ.

Parents, according to the Church, are "the first and most important educators of their own children," and "they are educators because they are parents." This idea is echoed, need I add, in the writings of Chesterton. In fact, he says that:

> The idea of a non-parental substitute is simply an illusion of wealth. The advanced advocate of this inconsistent and infinite education for the child is generally thinking of the rich child; and all this particular sort of liberty should rather be called luxury. It is natural enough for a fashionable lady to leave her little daughter with the French governess or the Czecho-Slovakian governess or the Ancient Sanskrit governess, and

know that one or other of these sides of the infant's intelligence
is being developed; while she, the mother, figures in public as
a money-lender or some other modern position of dignity.

But among poorer people there cannot be five teachers to
one pupil. Generally there are about fifty pupils to one teacher.
There it is impossible to cut up the soul of a single child and
distribute it among specialists. It is all we can do to tear in
pieces the soul of a single schoolmaster, and distribute it in
rags and scraps to a whole mob of boys. And even in the case
of a wealthy child it is by no means clear that specialists are a
substitute for spiritual authority. . . . The millionaire could, no
doubt, hire a mahatma or mystical prophet to give his child a
general philosophy. But I doubt if the philosophy would be
very successful even for the rich child, and it would be quite
impossible for the poor child. In the case of comparative
poverty, which is the common lot of mankind, we come back
to a general parental responsibility, which is the common sense
of mankind. We come back to the parent as the person in
charge of education (*BNF*, pp. 155–56).

Associated with this is Chesterton's strong view of the supreme
importance of mothers, and of their work in the home, and particularly with children in the home, as not only supremely important but
supremely *interesting*. He could not understand, and frequently
mocked, the tendency of the modern woman to perceive the world
outside the home as somehow more exciting, more adventurous and
more challenging than the world of the home:

> I remember my mother, the day that we met,
> A thing I shall never entirely forget;
> And toy with the fancy that, young as I am,
> I should know her again if we met in a tram.
>
> But mother is happy in turning a crank
> That increases the balance at somebody's bank;
> And I feel satisfaction that mother is free
> From the sinister task of attending to me.[12]

Elsewhere Chesterton spoke of "the simple truth that the private
work is the great one and the public work small. The human
house is a paradox, for it is larger inside than out" (BNF, *p. 157*).

*"The place where babies are born, where men die, wh*ere the drama of moral life is acted, is not an office or a shop or a bureau. It is something much smaller in size and much larger in scope. And while nobody would be such a fool as to pretend that it is the only place where women should work, it has the character of unity and universality that is not found in any of the fragmentary experiences of the division of labor" (*BNF*, p. 148).

At the same time, Chesterton perceived that the real reason for the appeal of feminist emancipation – remember he lived at the time of the suffragettes – was an entirely legitimate one: "The generation in revolt fled from a cold hearth and a godless shrine" (*BNF*, p. 75). They fled from the hearth because they saw through the great Victorian hypocrisy, which was an exaltation of tradition and respectability and domesticity masking the destruction of tradition and of the adventure of the home. The home that had once, perhaps, been larger inside than out had become a prison from which it was understandable and inevitable that woman should want to escape.

7. Society. The seventh gift is simply *society*. The family is, according to the Second Vatican Council, "the first and vital cell of society"; and, according to the pope's *Letter to Families*, "the primordial and, in a certain sense, 'sovereign' society." One aspect of the educative process that takes place within the family is an initiation into acceptable and responsible social behavior. It even lays the foundations of later political behavior. For a genuinely democratic spirit to prevail, citizens must be actively engaged *as citizens*, and not merely as consumers, wishing to be indulged and entertained. Genuine democracy is learned, somewhat paradoxically, in the family home where children are subject to the natural monarchy of father and mother. There we learn the humility of children which goes with dependence; but if we are loved we also learn the freedom and responsibility of citizens. This brings me fairly neatly to the next part of my paper, where I intend as best I can to address more directly the themes first of public policy and then of the common good.

Public Policy
Pope John Paul II writes, "*A family policy must be the basis and the*

driving force of all social policies" (*Evangelium Vitae*, 91). He believes that for there to be a culture of life, families must live out the implications of the sacrament that joins them to Christ, but governments and public institutions must by the same token find ways to support that way of life. It might be done through differential taxation to assist larger families; through salaries and working hours that make it possible for one partner to remain with the children; through transport policies that encourage stability instead of mobility; through legislation on weekend trading that would preserve Sundays for rest and prayer and "family time"; through restrictions on advertising to curb the rising levels of moral pollution – the list is endless, and it is a very different list from those which make up the manifestos of most of the major political parties, whether in your country or mine.

The philosophy or attitude that Chesterton espoused under the name of "Distributism" was an attempt to put families right at the center of society, where they belong. The point, as he and Hilaire Belloc originally explained, was to devolve as much economic power as possible to families and to individual workers working cooperatively through guilds and other intermediate institutions. I am one of those who happen to believe that Distributism is not so impractical as it has been made out to be – even by many of the Distributists themselves.

But perhaps a broader and more acceptable name for the social policy I have in mind would be "the Family Way," as described by Allan C. Carlson in his book *From Cottage to Work Station* (Ignatius Press, 1993). Carlson emphasizes the need to bring work back to the family, to "relearn and recommit to the deeper meanings of the ancient words *husbandry* and *housewifery*" (p. 168) if Western civilization is to survive. He writes that "the core requirements of family reconstruction are, at once, reactionary and radical, involving the recovery of human character and immediate community. The American republic presupposed the necessary character type: persons who cherish their economic autonomy, rooted in stable families and the possession of land and property" (p. 168). He concludes that:

> In the 1990s, to be sure, the modern system of state capitalism, combining personal liberation from traditional ties and an

obsession with equalitarianism with an economy predicated on mass consumption and common dependence on the welfare state, has no meaningful rivals. Rather than a return to natural human community, the more predictable future is another round of futile social and political engineering in which Americans will continue their elusive quest for an artificial harmony between the domain of modern industry and the domain of nurture and reproduction. Failing society-wide renewal, families may, of necessity, fall back on the more modest, but more perilous, strategy of simply protecting their small communities of virtue from extinction. In the footsteps of Benedict of Nursia, they will strive to weather the social and cultural storms gathering in the "post-family" era (pp. 170–71).

Carlson's words are confirmed by the rapid growth of the home-schooling movement in North America, with which you are familiar. Nor is this the only movement of the Spirit in our time that is creating conditions favorable for the practical revival of a "Family Way." In May 1988, there took place in St. Peter's Square in Rome an enormous "meeting of the movements" from around the world. More than 300,000 people came, representing more than 50 movements. These are the new communities, ranging from Focolare to Regnum Christi, which are rediscovering the spiritual and cultural power of the Gospel applied directly in everyday life. In bringing them together, the pope was concerned to bring these movements into the heart of the Church and into closer relation to the parishes and to each other, in such a way that the temptation for them to turn inwards and become a "cult" or "sect" might be avoided.

In his *Ecclesia in America*, published in the wake of the Synod of the Americas, John Paul II referred to his vision that the large urban parish might increasingly become a "community of communities and movements," restoring the experience of life on a human scale so that personal relationships may flourish (n. 41). In many of the movements, even in those which are not explicitly directed to the family (such as Family Encounter), it is very often the family which benefits from the renewal of faith that comes through this experience of personal encounter with Christ, and from a fresh and vibrant vision of the Church and the sacraments. I use the word "vision" here advisedly, because it seems we are witnessing a phenomenon less of intellectual synthesis or theological development (as yet) than of the *moral imagination*, moving us beyond what Russell Kirk called the Age of Discussion, beyond the Age of Sentiments, towards a "reassociation of sensibility" and the possibility of a new Christian culture through the Family Way.

Chesterton's own Distributist movement had little effect on public policy at the time (with the possible exception of Ireland). His followers were divided amongst themselves on a variety of intellectual and practical matters, and the movement declined after his death in 1936. A few communities (such as Ditchling and Laxton) survived until recent times, but the movement tended to eschew politics and its influence was mainly indirect, through the ideas conveyed by the generally eloquent writings produced by the leaders of the movement.

Of course, this influence has been considerable in Catholic circles, wherever those writings have penetrated: in Canada, the Southern States, Australia, India and even Eastern Europe. I gathered recently from a native of Barcelona that the Christian Democratic Party there owed its existence partly to Chesterton, and others have testified that the circulation of his writings in Russia in *samizdat* form helped to keep the ideal of freedom alive in communist times. But the further influence of his work is impeded partly by the fact that Chesterton, although a profound thinker, was also something of a caricaturist. You can see this in his drawings, but I would suggest this carries over into his writings. It is one reason why his books of literary biography are seldom taken seriously by scholars. While it is linked to his ability to capture the essence of an idea or insight in a bold stroke of the pen, making him enormously quotable, it also helps to account for many of the crudities and dangerous short-cuts in his writing and thinking – most notoriously in his comments about the Jews (but also on occasion about Chinamen, and even Australians). It shows up partly in his remarks about Distributism as the alternative to Capitalism and Communism, as the following passage may illustrate:

> It cannot be too often repeated that what destroyed the Family
> in the modern world was Capitalism. No doubt it might have

been Communism, if Communism had ever had a chance, outside that semi-Mongolian wilderness where it actually flour-
ishes. But, as far as we are concerned, what has broken up
households, and encouraged divorces, and treated the old
domestic virtues with more and more open contempt, is the
epoch and power of Capitalism. It is Capitalism that has forced
a moral feud and a commercial competition between the sexes;
that has destroyed the influence of the parent in favor of the
influence of the employer; that has driven men from their
homes to look for jobs; that has forced them to live near their
factories or their firms instead of near their families; and,
above all, that has encouraged, for commercial reasons, a
parade of publicity and garish novelty, which is in its nature the
death of all that was called dignity and modesty by our mothers and fathers (*BNF*, p. 191).

In the United States, especially, such talk may raise hackles. Yet
if we are prepared to look beyond the rhetorical facade, we find that
Chesterton is still saying something valid about aspects of what
today we might prefer to term "consumerism," or "industrialism," or
the "cult of growth." For Distributism interpreted broadly and sym-
pathetically is in fact simply an uncompromising attempt to apply
Catholic social teaching, which itself originated in Pope Leo XIII's
concern for the family.[13] In terms of public policy, Distributism
highlights the link between freedom, personal responsibility and the
ownership of private property. But it has a special interest, as we
should all have, in the family. In the final section I want to probe a
bit more deeply into the foundations of this particular institution,
and its relationship to the common good.

The Family and the Common Good

Ours may be the last generation in which we can still refer openly to
"the family" and be understood as referring to a social group formed
by a married man and woman, with their own children. The acceptance in law of the "equal rights" of gay couples to marry, and any
commercial application of the new reproductive technologies on a
large scale, will inevitably undermine this understanding. Even in
the past it was, of course, often something of an ideal, abused in
practice. Other cultures have departed from it to a greater or lesser

extent, and even where monogamy was the rule kings have often made exceptions for themselves.

But the Christian tradition represents monogamy as more than one among many equally valid ways of organizing human society. Christ spoke of restoring something that had been lost, an original unity between man and woman that existed in the beginning. It is becoming increasingly clear to Catholic theologians that the sacrament on which our ideal of "family" is founded, the sacrament of marriage, cannot be based on any questionable generalizations about human nature or psychology. It is not founded, for example, on the assumption that women are better off when protected by men, or that the most lasting and wholesome friendships are between members of the opposite sex, or even that having both a mother and a father is essential for mental health. The true foundation for Christian marriage is a revelation of the purpose and destiny of human beings.

Why do animals reproduce sexually? Naturalists and evolutionists will explain it a hundred ways, none of which is in conflict with the deeper reason known only to Christians. The deeper reason is theological, and it is this: human nature attains its ultimate goal only in becoming united with God through the Incarnation. The union of divine and human nature in Christ, and by extension the union of Christ with his Church, is the archetype that underlies the cosmic and biological division of the sexes. Unbelievable as it may seem, that is the reason why that division actually exists in nature.

We can go even deeper. The archetypal union of divine and human, of which the union of the sexes on earth is a symbol and manifestation, is itself rooted in the *unity without confusion* of Self and Other in the divine Trinity. The three divine Persons are One, and yet eternally distinct. It is their infinite self-giving love that almost requires the existence of the sexes to give it expression in the creation. It is no wonder, then, that Christianity always made such a "thing" about monogamy. The Incarnation and the revelation of the Trinity *make sense of it* in a way that no other tradition has, or perhaps ever could do.

I want now to try to see what went wrong in our history that so quickly blighted the common understanding of marriage in our tradition, and the implications of this for Western society. For that understanding had, it seems, only just begun to dawn when it began to fail – in the centuries of the Black Death and the fragmentation of Christendom through and after the Crusades. It is very much as though there were something about *modernity as such* that was built on a rejection of this understanding. These days criticisms of "the Enlightenment project" are rife, and perhaps I can presuppose familiarity with the tradition of scholarship from Richard Weaver to Louis Dupre that identifies *nominalist philosophy* as lying at the root of "the modern."[14]

For if, as the nominalists taught, only individual things exist, not universals, then what the ancient and medieval world understood by *metaphysics* is dead in the water. Philosophy moves rapidly through dualism to positivism, until it finally dissolves into the language games played by the analytic school on one side of the English Channel and the postmodernists on the other. The sophisticated barbarians, the "cyberpunks" of intellectual endeavor, play in the rubble of a city that once stood on metaphysical foundations. In parallel with philosophy, science – having proved that only material particles exist in the framework of space and time – now quickly dissolves these further into subatomic elements and then into something much more ambiguous (often strangely resembling a kind of Pythagorean mathematics).

At the social level, to those living in the long shadow of nominalism, the world "society" itself can mean little more than an aggregate of individuals, bonding through self-interest and joined together by contract. If there are only individual existents, then (as Margaret Thatcher is notorious in our country for saying) "there is no such thing as society," except as an umbrella we decide to erect over the mob. Stripped down to this atomic level, even the "nuclear" family of children and parents is quickly split into its elementary particles, and we are told that most marriages begun in the late twentieth century will end in divorce. Over in England you may have heard that we have a declining and aging population: but this is coupled with a housing boom, due to the fact that increasing numbers of families no longer wish to live under one roof. The splitting of the nuclear family releases hugely destructive energies, vented very often on children, on the unborn, on the aged – and on a culture that no longer makes imaginative (or any other kind of) sense to its inheritors.

The concept of the "common good" has suffered a similar fate to that of the family. The reason is obvious. To someone of a nominalist cast of mind, it must be hard to conceive of any intrinsic link between the good or *telos* of an individual and that of a whole community. How can there be a "common good," except as a composite of individual goods – as, for example, in the standard utilitarian calculus? Adam Smith's "invisible hand" may have been an attempt to reinvent it, but the idea itself was gone.[15] Gone, that is, from the mainstream culture. In Catholic culture it survives a while longer. For Catholicism is a kind of *mystical realism*, in which God is as truly the Creator of mankind and of families and of nations, as he is of individual persons. The perfect community is a "whole composed of wholes"; that is, of persons, each of which transcends all nonspiritual reality.[16]

In the moral life, justice is that cardinal virtue through which the others are directed towards the common good of "all and each."[17] Individualism would reduce this to a sum of goods to be enjoyed by individuals, but Christian personalism claims that the well-being of persons is achieved only in relationship, literally, then, in a *common* good or goal. In a forthcoming important study on chastity and the common good,[18] Patrick Riley defines the term under discussion as follows: "The common good is the end or purpose common to a society's individual members and their actions." He goes on to say that a "society" only exists as long as that common purpose is respected, for society itself is "a sort of permanent common seeking, a permanent common striving after a good." Society is an "accidental" rather than a "substantial" entity in Thomistic terms, since it is held together or comes into being through the will – the will to belong to that society, to seek the common good. However, this *will to belong* depends on love. Human society is therefore a union brought about by love, the love for a common good of persons. Since love, St. Paul tells us, "will never come to an end," our earthly society – to the extent it is genuinely founded on love – opens onto an eternal horizon, in a heavenly Kingdom.

The key to reclaiming the notion of the common good from the shadows to which nominalism and individualism have consigned it lies close at hand. It lies as close as the experience of *family life and human love*, which (notwithstanding the decline I have described) more than all other experiences is still capable of introducing us to the truth of our own nature as persons, and the reality of a community that is more than the sum of its parts. This is roughly how I want to relate marriage and the family to the common good.

I find, however, that in the pope's *Letter to Families* most of the work has already been done. For as he says there (n. 7): "The family has always been considered the first and basic expression of man's *social nature*." It is a community of persons living together in that *communion* of which only persons are capable. This communion is a reality that originates not in a mere "contract" but in a *covenant*, which is a sharing of life founded on self-gift.[19]

I want to emphasize this idea of covenant. Britain's Chief Rabbi, Jonathan Sacks, contrasts the (explicit or implicit) "social contract" that underpins the modern state, and which depends on force to hold it together, with the social or kinship bonds created by "covenant" (*brit*). As he puts it: "A social contract gives rise to the instrumentalities of the state – governments, nations, parties, the use of centralized power and the mediated resolution of conflict. It is the basis of political society. A covenant gives rise to quite different institutions – families, communities, peoples, traditions, and voluntary associations. It is the basis of civil society."[20]

Civil society, which develops organically in the realm of intermediate institutions and overlapping associations, pertains directly to the "common striving after a good" (the good of social life). What Sacks calls "political society" exists to serve and protect civil society, and in modern society is governed mainly by types of contract, as is the "market" within economic life. For nominalism – which is inherently reductionistic, analytic, divisive, fissiparous – there are only contracts, because the bonds which hold things together can only be extrinsic and temporary. A covenant, on the other hand, creates a new entity (for example, the "two in one flesh" of marriage), whose existence is more than the sum of its parts. The essence of a covenant is the *gift of self*, which is why it is capable of establishing kinship.

In sections 10 and 11 of the *Letter to Families*, the pope goes on to say that the common good of the couple and of the family is defined by the words of consent that bring the marriage into existence, "embodied" or "realized" in the newborn child. That common good comprises love, fidelity, honor, continuity until death – all of which is to be given in such a way that it is shared also with the children, and in this way the communion of the family opens out into a *communion of generations.*

It is therefore not merely the "nuclear" family that the pope has in mind – although the covenant of marriage is certainly a kind of nuclear force at the heart of it – but rather the extended community of generations, and even the spiritual extension of the family's love to others in society. Today there seems to be "a shortage of people with whom to create and share the common good; and yet that good, by its nature, demands to be created and shared with others."

It is therefore not surprising that it is in the *Letter to Families* that we find some of the pope's most profound and even lyrical words on the subject of the common good:

> *A child comes to take up room, when it seems that there is less and less room in the world.* But is it really true that a child brings nothing to the family and society? Is not every child a "particle" of that common good without which human communities break down and risk extinction. Could this ever really be denied?

He is a "common good," the pope emphasizes, not in the sense that he is a means to an end (even to the end of preserving the species), but in the first place because he is an individual. "God the Creator calls him into existence 'for himself'; and in coming into the world he begins, in the family, his 'great adventure,' the adventure of human life."

Conclusion

How are these two things to be reconciled: the existence of the person for himself, and as a "common good"? This takes us back to the nub of the whole question – the question concerning the One and the Many, the Self and the Other, individuality and personality. According to the pope and the whole Christian tradition, it is only through the *sincere gift of self* that the human being can ultimately find and fulfill itself. The human person is designed in such a way that its true center lies *outside itself in the Other*: most profoundly, of course, in the transcendental Other that is God.

This is the key to the reconciliation of each and all in a common good, whether in a particular family or in society as a whole. In a loving family, I cannot be truly happy as long as you are sad. I cannot be rich if you are poor. But this does not mean that I lose my identity and my own goods. The point about love is that it creates a kind of unity that deepens distinction and even difference. It is for being *you* that I love you, not for being an extension of myself (though I may love you *as myself* – and indeed Jesus commands me to do so). Thus the common good depends on the development of the good of the individual. And, as the pope reminds us, "the more *common* the good, the *more properly one's own* it will also be: mine – yours – ours. This is the logic behind living according to the good, living in truth and charity. If man is able to accept and follow this logic, his life truly becomes a 'sincere gift.'" And that, ladies and gentlemen, is the real "drama of the home."

Notes

1. Stratford Caldecott, M.A. Hons (Oxon.), FRSA, is director of the Centre for Faith and Culture, which he founded in 1994, at Plater College in Oxford. A tutor in Christianity and Society at Plater College, he also works as a senior editor and publisher for T & T Clark, the Scottish Christian academic press. He is assistant editor of *The Chesterton Review*, and writes regularly for a variety of journals; together with his wife, edits the "Second Spring" section of *The Catholic World Report*. He was educated at Hertford College, Oxford, and at Dulwich College in London.

2. From "The Home of the Unities," first published in *The New Witness* in 1919, and cited in Alvaro de Silva (ed.), *Brave New Family* (Ignatius Press, 1990), p. 24.

3. Mary Shivanandan, *Crossing the Threshold of Love: A New Vision of Love in the Light of John Paul II's Anthropology* (T &T Clark and Catholic University of America Press, 1999).

4. John Saward, *The Way of the Lamb: The Spirit of Childhood and the End of the Age* (Ignatius Press and T&T Clark, 1999).

5. Cited from *L'Osservatore Romano*, English Weekly Edition, 5 May 1999, p. 10.

6. On the roots and implications of this 'practical atheism,' see David L. Schindler, *Heart of the World, Center of the Church* (Eerdmans and T&T Clark, 1996).

7. On occasion it made Chesterton quite angry to be labeled "conservative." "Because I want almost anything that doesn't exist; because I want to turn a silent people into a singing people; because I would rejoice if a wineless country could be a wine-growing country; because I would change a world of wage-slaves into a world of freeholders; because I would have healthy employment instead of hideous unemployment; because I wish folk, now ruled by other people's fads, to be ruled by their own laws and liberties; because I hate the established dirt and hate more the established cleanliness; because, in short, I want to alter nearly everything there is, a cursed, haughty, high-souled, well-informed, world-worrying, sky-scraping, hair-splitting, head-splitting, academic animal of a common quill-driving social reformer gets up and calls me a *Conservative!*. Excuse me!" (Cited in *Chesterton Society Newsletter*, No. 32)

8. Yielding to severe temptation, I have revised this paper slightly in the light of reflections provoked by the meeting of the Fellowship of Catholic Scholars in which it was presented as a keynote address. To be more specific, I have expanded from four to seven the "gifts of the family," and brought into the main text some considerations on the common good that were originally relegated to the Notes.

9. On the metaphysics of gift see Kenneth L. Schmitz, *The Gift: Creation* (Marquette University Press, 1982) and *At The Center of the Human Drama: The Philosophical Anthropology of Karol Wojtyla/Pope John Paul II* (Catholic University of America Press, 1993).

10. See Kenneth L. Schmitz, *ibid.*

11. See Mary Shivanandan, op. cit.; Paul Quay S.J., *The Christian Meaning of Human Sexuality* (Ignatius Press, 1985); David S. Crawford, "*Humanae Vitae* and the Perfection of Love," *Communio*, Fall 1998.

12. This poem by Chesterton is cited by Sheridan Gilley in "Chesterton, Catholicism and the Family," *The Chesterton Review* (November 1997), p. 428.

13. This being a point that was made by Cardinal Francis George to participants at the Fellowship of Catholic Scholars convention.

14. Richard Weaver, *Ideas Have Consequences* (University of Chicago Press, 1948); Etienne Gilson, *History of Christian Philosophy in the Middle Ages* (Sheed & Ward, 1955); Louis Dupre, *Passage to Modernity* (Yale University Press, 1993). See also Kenneth L. Schmitz, *op. cit.* A retrospective on Weaver's book recently appeared under the title *Steps Toward Restoration: The Consequences of Richard Weaver's Ideas*, edited by Ted J. Smith, III (ISI Books, 1998): see especially the essays by Robert A. Preston and Marion Montgomery.

15. This thought might be pursued with reference to Thomas R. Rourke, *A Conscience as Large as the World* (Rowman & Littlefield, 1997). For example, in Adam Smith, "No longer guided by natural law or teleology, practical reason renounces its Aristotelian function as a virtue to take up a new task as the servant of desire in the midst of a world of competing desires" (p. 64). Rourke believes that contemporary Catholic neoconservatives participate in modernity to the extent that they follow Smith and "loose practical reason from its moorings in the realization of natural finalities" (*ibid.*), and freedom from the good (pp. 124–28). This is connected to their separation of the "form" from the "matter" of the common good, rendering the latter essentially unknowable and excluding the possibility of any kind of objective judgment concerning its instantiation or achievement. The result is a reduction of politics and economics to a competition between individual wills (pp. 111–24).

16. Jacques Maritain, *The Person and the Common Good* (University of Notre Dame Press, 1966), pp. 57, 61. Maritain's notion of the common good presupposes the distinction between "individual" and "person": for nominalism, the distinction rapidly becomes meaningless.

17. John Paul II, in *Fides et Ratio,* has recalled us to recover our confidence in "the power of human reason" and our "passion for ultimate truth" (n. 56). With that recovery will come a recovery of the precious concept of the common good. In order to fulfill its mission, the pope writes, "moral theology must turn to a philosophical ethics which looks to the truth of the good, to an ethics which is neither subjectivist nor utilitarian" (98). The point had already been made in *Veritatis Splendor.* As one reads these encyclicals, one can almost hear the warm water of the post-nominalist "jacuzzi" theologians swilling away down the drain, and the comforting *slap* of the soft, dry towel of Catholic sanity preparing us to step out into the real world.

18. Patrick Riley, *Civilizing Sex* (T&T Clark, forthcoming).

19. According to Rourke (*ibid.*), the Thomist thinker Yves R. Simon defines the common good as "not an addition of individual goods but a good that is enjoyed by all members and that is brought about by their community of intention" (p. 94). A community is more than a partnership (p. 92), and requires an authority to engage in common action (p. 96). Rourke does not discuss the development of the concept of authority in relation to *marriage* as distinct from civil society. In the former, which is a sacrament, we may talk of "mutual subjection" in the love of Christ (Eph. 5:21). Despite the distinction of levels, there are implications here for the ways authority should manifest itself in a civilization of love, and certainly within both Christian marriage and the Church (*Mulieris Dignitatem*, 24). The family has the mission to "guard, reveal and communicate love" to the whole of society (*Familiaris Consortio*, 92).

20. J. Sacks, *Education, Values and Religion* (Center for Philosophy and Public Affairs in the University of St. Andrews, 1996), p. 15.

SESSION I
THEOLOGY OF MARRIAGE AND CELIBACY

MARRIAGE: *MAGNA RES EST AMOR*
Dr. Alice Jourdain von Hildebrand[1]

Magna res est amor: Love is a great thing. So is marriage – this bastion of every sane society, which God has elevated to the dignity of a sacrament. That this noble institution is today under constant attack, and has even been sapped in its very foundations, is a plain indication of the fact that we are facing moral disaster. Not only is the rate of divorce appalling, but a large segment of the population has opted for co-habitation without commitment. As it is most unlikely that the lovers will remain together for any length of time, it is, according to contemporary wisdom, much more desirable to create no bond. After all, every one should be free to "pursue happiness" in his own way.

In his great educational work, *The Republic,* Plato writes that "great things are never easy." This truth applies to marriage. To have a happy and successful marriage, i.e., a marriage that the spouses without hesitation *would choose to repeat* if they were given a chance to live their lives over again, is an art that few people have mastered. Cardinal Newman writes: "No two persons perhaps are to be found, however intimate, however congenial in taste and judgments, however eager to have one heart and one soul, but must deny themselves, for the sake of each other, much which they like or dislike, if they are to live together happily."[2]

In his own inimitable style, Chesterton writes in the same vein: "If Americans can get a divorce for incompatibility of temper, I cannot conceive why they are not all divorced. I have known many happy marriages, but never a compatible one."[3] We need not endorse this last statement, but we must acknowledge that a truly successful marriage is one in which *both spouses work daily* for its realization, never assuming that a marriage which has started on the right course will necessarily arrive at its completion without the full, awakened collaboration of husband and wife.

When a person enters a religious order, he knows that he is

choosing self-renunciation, that daily he will have to die to himself, to carry the cross of obedience, chastity, and poverty. Many people enter into marriage animated by the *illusion* that the ravishing experience of falling in love will be endlessly repeated until cruel death separates the lovers.

We are dealing here with a paradox. On the one hand, it is true (and should never be forgotten) that marriage is a unique source of human happiness. Only a hopelessly slumbering individual does not even wish to fall in love (it would disturb his circles); he fears the "adventure" of falling in love, for it involves responsibility, continuity, and faithfulness; indeed it belongs to the very essence of marriage to be a lasting bond. Deep down in the human soul, there is an *ardent longing* to meet another soul that we can truly call our own – someone with whom we have one heart, one mind, one soul. This truth has been powerfully expressed in Schiller's *Ode to Joy:*

> Yea, if any hold in keeping
> Only one heart all his own,
> Let him join us, or else weeping
> Steal from our midst, unknown.[4]

Deep down, every man knows that *he alone who loves is fully alive*. To remain imprisoned in one's own ego, to feel nothing but indifference toward others, is to vegetate, spiritually and humanly. Such people fit the description that Dante gives of some of the damned:

> These unfortunate ones,
> Who were never even alive.[5]

Why should this noble desire so deeply ingrained in the human soul so often remain unfulfilled? Why should something so beautiful that God has implanted in human nature be so rarely realized? One cannot help but think of the pessimistic words of Leopardi:

> O Nature, Nature, why do you refuse to give
> What you promise?[6]

A bit of self-knowledge and humility, however, teaches us that human nature is subject to a law of psychological gravity which constantly pulls us downward, and against which we must wage a ceaseless war.

A person entering into a religious order must first go through the Novitiate – a period of trials during which the postulant's vocation is constantly tested. Many are those who, realizing how narrow is the way leading to holiness, leave – and they are wise to do so.

But there is no Novitiate for marriage. The engagement period, however important – and which for many people is unclouded bliss – is widely different from the full sharing of another person's life, culminating in the bodily union of the spouses. The *constant intimacy* which binds the spouses creates a totally different situation; and those well prepared for marriage know that, much as they love their spouses, they will have to *wage war against their own will*. The will, usually dormant during the engagement period, will resurge after marriage, and loudly make its claims. It was Kierkegaard who wrote that, much as the spouses love each other, they are tempted to love their own will more.[7]

Spouses must be willing to renounce themselves in small ways which, however insignificant, are nevertheless sacrifices which many people are reluctant to make day in and day out. Many things which in themselves are morally irrelevant gain, in marriage, a certain moral relevance because they can become expressions of selfless love. Some people prefer to sleep with the window open; others prefer it closed. Some like a very warm room; others prefer a cool one. Some enjoy Italian cooking; others prefer American cooking. Innumerable are the occasions in which the spouses' wishes will differ, and this often leads to disagreements which can degenerate into conflicts. The one who yields out of love is the stronger one, even though he seems to be defeated; but he is in fact the victor.

All of us have cherished habits: some good, some not so good. Some people do not mind living in total disorder; they are used to it. They cannot leave a kitchen or a bathroom without having created a state of chaos. Others are orderly and suffer from the unaesthetic quality of disorder. Obviously, order is better than disorder, but the orderly spouse will have to practice *patience*, for to change an ingrained habit is not easy. As Plato remarked at the end of his life:

people are not very eager to improve themselves. And yet the true lover will constantly try to avoid doing things which are displeasing to his spouse.

One thing, however, is unshakably certain: man and woman are made for each other. Genesis could not be clearer: "God created man . . . male and female he created them." The plenitude of human nature is to be found in both man and woman; they belong together. Moreover, "it is not good that man should be alone." Being a person, he is made for communion. Let us recall Adam's joy upon seeing Eve: ". . . bone of my bones and flesh of my flesh." He who chooses to isolate himself from others, nay, refuses any sort of communion, is in fact an "idiot," a crippled person, because he has chosen to remain imprisoned in the narrow limits of his ego.

That man and woman complement and enrich each other was admirably sketched out by Edith Stein in a lecture she gave in Salzburg in 1930. Woman, according to her, is more geared toward the concrete than toward the abstract – a domain in which men excel. She is more drawn to the personal than to the impersonal; to the living than to the non-living; to the whole than to its isolated parts. Whereas her male partner's mind is more analytic, her mind is more intuitive. Her heart is the beacon of her life and the deep words of Pascal, "the heart has its reasons that reason does not know of," find a deep echo in her soul.

She is awed by man's intellect, and can, through him, learn intellectual discipline; she deeply appreciates his creative gifts, but she does not envy his superior inventiveness. She knows that her *charism* is empathy, compassion, self-giving – i.e., to bring *fire* to a human life which, deprived of these qualities, should be desperately frigid and lifeless. It would lack glow and warmth.

We might add that the great charism of woman is her *receptivity*, which is not to be confused with passivity – a confusion which Aristotle is somewhat guilty of. Creatures are essentially receptive because, whatever they have, is a gift from above. But the very core of femininity is precisely this openness to receiving, to spiritual, intellectual, and biological *fecundation*. The perfect model of receptivity is the Holy Virgin who accepted to become the mother of the Savior by uttering the words: "Be it done to me according to thy word." Mary accepts to receive, and in this "fiat" she opens the door to the salvation of the world. Receptivity is a religious category *par excellence.*

The male and female talents *combined* constitute the plenitude of human nature – a nature so noble that, as it is said in the Psalms, God has created it just a little below the angels. But alas, Original Sin has disrupted the harmony, joy, and peace that reigned between our first parents. There is one great law that most people forget nowadays, namely, that sin creates a chasm between the sinners. The very moment that Adam and Eve sinned, they realized they were naked, and felt shame. Their sweet union was disrupted; having cut themselves off from God, they had severed the bond that God had created between them. The physical proximity experienced between two people committing adultery is an optical illusion; their sin has cut them off from each other.

In this brief talk, we need not mention the metaphysical and religious consequences of the Fall. Our concern here is to shed light on the disharmony that was created between the culprits. How right St. Augustine was when he wrote that every sin brings about its own punishment (*Confessions*, I, 12).

The admirable gifts that had been granted to Adam as head of the human race – nobility, courage, strength, consciousness of his responsibility, spirit of chivalry, etc. – now threatened to degenerate into their caricature. How often in the sad history of mankind have men abused their strength and not only failed to protect the "weaker sex," but treated it brutally.

But women's sensitivity, modesty, gentleness, openness to others, and self-giving were also clouded by sin. The female sex is now tempted to use her woman's charm to manipulate others and use them for her own self-centered purposes. Her sensitivity can now easily degenerate into sentimentality and an unhealthy concern about herself. She protects herself from the superior strength of her husband by learning the dangerous art of craftiness. Adam failed to use his authority and yielded to the tempting words of Eve; Eve used her powerful influence over her husband, and led him to his (and our) downfall.

It should be clear that, because of Original Sin, the beautiful union that God has established between man and woman, now stands badly in need of mending. No doubt sin has separated them and this split calls for repair. We are far from endorsing the words of Simone de Beauvoir, the mother of French feminism, in which she claims that a man can never understand a woman. As a matter of fact, following my husband, I would defend the thesis that a man can understand a woman better than another woman could and vice versa – but provided that the rift between them has been repaired. No doubt St. Clare understood St. Francis better than any of his beloved friars. St. Jeanne Françoise de Chantal had deeper insights into St. Francis de Sales than anyone else. But these are relationships that have been healed and transfigured by grace. We shall say more about this later.

Human nature has been wounded by Original Sin, but it has not been completely corrupted as some people have claimed. Great literature is rich in examples of great loves between man and woman. Every time we read about the tenderness of such loves, we are deeply moved and we know that "this is how it should be." My husband used to call human love "a remnant from the earthly paradise."

But what is love? It is appropriate to say a few words about this most sublime of human emotions – which, in the case of man and woman, usually finds its fulfillment in marriage.

Love is primarily a "response to value," i.e., to qualities and characteristics that are perceived in the beloved and touch one's heart. These qualities are objectively important, independently of whether or not they are perceived and appreciated. They are important in and by themselves: kindness, loveableness, generosity, intelligence, charm, beauty. Tristan expresses his love for Isolde in uttering the words: "How beautiful thou art!" There is an abysmal difference between a burning interest in another person because of her loveableness, and an interest triggered by the fact that the other person can be "useful" to us. In one case, there is a response to value; in the other case, the other person is viewed as a means that we can put to good use.

Once our heart is touched, we inevitably wish "to do good to the other person," to shower him with benefits; whatever lies in the line of his true interest becomes our concern, and we nourish the ardent desire to be the one giving him every possible gift (*intentio benevolentiae*). This attitude of fluid goodness toward the loved one leads further to the desire to be *united* to him. The paradox of love is that – from one point of view – we ardently long for union with the loved one; on the other hand, we are awe-struck by his beauty, and we feel unworthy of him; we can only hope that he will favor us by requiting our love.

All of this is uniquely expressed in several of Shakespeare's plays. Let me just quote the following lines from *The Tempest*; they are words that Miranda addresses to Ferdinand:

> At my unworthiness that dare not offer
> What I desire to give, and much less to take
> What I shall die to want...
> I am your wife if you will marry me;
> If no I shall die your maid . . . (Act III, Scene 2)

The person who falls in love wishes to overwhelm the loved one with every possible gift; and, at the very same time, he discovers how poor he is. Just as his words are incapable of conveying the depth of his love, so he is too "poor" spiritually, intellectually, and psychologically, to be able to meet the demands that love makes on him.

Marriage is the most complete, the most perfect of all purely natural communities. It aims at a union, a closeness, an intimacy which cannot be matched in other natural communities, beautiful as these can be. Not only does it mean sharing one name, one roof, common possessions, but it aims at the physical union of the spouses as well; indeed, they become one flesh.

But beautiful and profound as the union between the spouses can be, it is bound to meet with trials. Not only the adjustments we have alluded to will have to be made, but – more than that – a purely human marriage carries within itself the seeds of tragedy. For love longs for infinity, and yet the lover discovers that he is terribly finite. Love longs for eternity (forever), and yet man is the prisoner of time, which keeps flowing forward and cannot be stopped. The lover would like the most beautiful moments to be extended forever (*"Verweile doch! Du bist so schoen!"* – Goethe, *Faust*, I, 1700), but is incapable of stopping the course of time.

Every moment brings the lovers closer to death – the fearful moment when human love seems irretrievably doomed. The tragedy of *Tristan and Isolde* illumines the drama of a purely human love: it is death that unites them, but *can* death unite?

In his book on marriage, my husband has powerfully shown that human love can only be redeemed by the supernatural. The overwhelming experience of discovering the sublime teaching of the Holy Catholic Church opened his eyes to a totally new dimension of love and marriage, even though prior to his conversion he always considered love to be the greatest gift that man can aspire to.

First, the supernatural opens our eyes to the sacredness of the sexual sphere – so tragically desecrated today. Freud has convinced the "experts" that sex is a purely biological instinct – like hunger and thirst – and that this instinct craves for fulfillment and severely damages the psyche of those who refuse to obey its demands. How, though, can Freud explain the radiance, the joy, of those who have chosen "to remain eunuchs for the Kingdom of Heaven"? Innumerable male saints have led celibate lives; innumerable young maids have consecrated their virginity to God and thrived spiritually, intellectually, and even physically. Virginity certainly cannot cause death. Who would dare assert that a St. Clare of Assisi, a St. Teresa of Avila, St. Therese of Lisieux, a Mother Teresa of Calcutta are crippled individuals?

Alas, the spirit of the times is infectious, and many are those even within the Catholic Church who now claim that the *kairos* calls for abolishing the law which prevents the Catholic clergy from marrying. Some modern psychologists defend the thesis that the canceling of this "outdated" law would bring about a series of salutary consequences. Married priests would be better equipped to deal with marital difficulties among their parishioners; and, of course, it would solve the grave crisis of a lack of priestly vocations.

But what is left unmentioned is that the sexual sphere symbolizes a mystery, a self-donation; and it is only proper and just that those called to the priesthood – those who wish to consecrate their lives to God – should seal this mysterious domain for the sake of the Kingdom: "Let him hear who has ears to hear." Those who renounce paternity or maternity out of love for Christ will be blessed by a plenitude of children that the most fruitful marriage cannot even imagine. In a way, we can say that he or she chooses celibacy or virginity as an expression of ultimate love for Christ, and declares that twelve children are too few. The heart of such is open to all children who will cross their path. Indeed, a Mother Teresa has received the centuple by joyfully accepting not to have children of her own flesh.

For it is the supernatural which opens our eyes to the greatness and mystery of the sexual sphere. *Sex is always deep.* Many of us will eat a meal and forget what we have eaten, but sex calls for a full presence: it involves a closeness to another human being, made in God's image and likeness, a being that we should approach with reverence and should never view as a tool for our own satisfaction. Catholic moral theology teaches us that the sexual sphere is always "serious matter." This is why, if it is in any way abused, with full knowledge and full consent of the will, it constitutes mortal sin.

Sex constitutes a unique self-donation to another person, and this is why St. Paul puts to shame (cf. I Cor 6:16) those who become one with a harlot. This self-donation is simultaneously a "self-revelation." In the marital act, the spouses chastely unveil themselves; this is powerfully expressed in Genesis: "Adam knew Eve his wife." The word "knew" is eloquent, so much so that no more needs to be said. It hints at the nobility of the marital embrace when it takes place "*in conspectu Dei*." That sex is both a self-donation and a self-revelation sheds light on its essential link to *faithfulness.* Just as one "cannot serve two masters," so one cannot "give" oneself to several persons. Fornication and adultery cannot be authentic self-donations; they are necessarily counterfeits, or worse, they are an irreverent playing with another person, "just for fun."

Any abuse of this mysterious sphere constitutes not only a grave offense to God, but also stains what is meant to be beautiful. Inevitably, the sexual sphere will elevate a person higher – or pull him downward toward an abyss.

What a terrible desecration takes place when one partner or both of them simply wishes to use the other for his or her own satisfaction, and this without any love, any commitment, any reverence. Once again, how profound are the words of St. Augustine when he wrote that "every sin brings about its own punishment" (*Confessions*, I, 12). The punishment of those who approach the sexual sphere with irreverence is that, whereas they will experience lust, they will (like Alberich in the *Ring of the Niebelungen*) never expe-

rience the sweet happiness given to those who live this great
moment *in conspectu Dei.*

By elevating marriage to the dignity of a sacrament, Christianity
has radically transformed the relationship existing between husband
and wife. How many Christians today – in our secularized society –
think that the marital embrace is a means of grace which brings us
closer to God? How many thank God for this amazing privilege?
How many understand that the physical closeness between the
spouses can lead to the creation of another human person, made in
God's image and likeness? How overwhelming it is that man can
collaborate so closely with his Creator – Who is Life itself – in the
procreation of another human life.

The parents' embrace can lead to the creation of a child's body,
but then God creates the soul in the mystery of the female womb,
thereby sanctifying this organ that two thousand years ago sheltered
the Savior of the universe.

We are now in a position to see why the sexual sphere can only
be understood by those who approach it with reverence, with God's
permission, in marriage. The essence of purity is not satisfactorily
explained by temperance and self-discipline. It is more than that: it
is a reverent response to the mystery of sex. Reverence enables us to
understand the greatness of the divine plan in marriage, and shuns
with horror any abuse of this mysterious domain.

The supernatural life infused in us through baptism enables us to
re-conquer the beauty that marriage had before the Fall. We desperately need this help, because the sexual sphere has been particularly
damaged by the fault of our first parents. It is a domain in which lazy
devils have a field day; but, alas, rare are those who resist the siren
call of isolated sex.

Grace enables us to live marriage as God intended us to live it. It
constantly reminds us of our frailty, and the impossibility of our living love as it should be lived without the help of prayer and the
sacraments. It teaches us that before reforming others, we should try
to reform ourselves. The union between the spouses is so deep that
if one comes closer to Christ, it is bound to benefit the other. Grace
helps us to remain awakened, and to thank God for the gift of our
loved one. Alas, how often do we take things for granted? How often
do we forget to say, "Thank you," for small deeds of love? How

often do we lose sight of the Tabor vision that was granted to us when we fell in love, because we are irritated by small faults and mistakes of our loved one?

Habit is a great danger in human life. Useful as it is for practical purposes, it is deadly when it leads us to spiritual sleepiness, and dulls our perception. Kierkegaard expressed this powerfully when he wrote: "Let the thunder of a hundred cannons remind you daily to resist the force of habit."[8] Let us recall the ardor we felt when we fell in love, and how spiritually listless and unmindful we have become; the dull refrain of *routine* has replaced the song of young lovers. It is a well known fact that widows and widowers shed bitter tears when recalling how often they failed to give the response of loving gratitude for the gift of their spouses.

Love transfigured by grace renders us humble; indeed, there is no authentic love without humility. This is why in a truly Christian marriage, the forgotten words (today) are so often heard: "Forgive me!" It is a sad fact that, because in marriage we are so close to our spouse, we can hurt him more than we can possibly hurt any other person. Just as a saint begs God for forgiveness every single day of his life, so spouses should realize how imperfect their love is, how easily they make mistakes. The perfect marriage is not the one in which there is no conflict, but rather the one in which every conflict is resolved before the sun goes down, through humility and contrition.

We have seen that love longs for eternity, and that purely human love inevitably betrays its deepest longing. But in a truly Christian marriage, love can reach the perfection to which it aspires. We have all been told that there are two categories of love: human love (love between spouses, between siblings, between friends, etc.); and supernatural love (love of God and love of neighbor). But the conclusion that we have now reached is that every single type of love must be transformed by and in Christ; every love must be "baptized" to reach its fulfillment. Every love must partake of Christ's love for the beloved. And the most beautiful spousal love is the one in which both spouses feed their love in the Sacred Heart of Jesus, *"fornax ardens caritatis."*

By this we do not mean to say that husband and wife should love one another as they love their neighbor. Far from it. That would be a betrayal of spousal love. To "baptize" a love does not mean to deprive it of its ardor, of its tenderness; on the contrary, such a "baptized" love will teach us to be more ardent, more tender. But these qualities will be purified, transfigured because of the supernatural. St. Augustine expressed this well when he wrote: "*Quanto notiores, tanto cariores*" ("the better known, the more loved").

This type of love has found its most perfect expression in the marriages between *saints*. Let us think, for example, of a St. Henry and a St. Cunegonde. This kind of marriage should remain the ideal for every Christian marriage because it will reflect the love of Christ for His Holy Bride, the Roman Catholic Church!

Notes

1. Alice Jourdain von Hildebrand holds a Ph.D. in philosophy from Fordham University. She is a Professor Emeritus at Hunter College of the City University of New York. Widow of the renowned philosopher Dietrich von Hildebrand, she is herself the author of numerous books and articles, including *An Introduction to a Philosophy of Religion; By Love Refined; By Grief Refined*; "Von Hildebrand and Marcel: A Comparison"; and "Edith Stein: Philosopher and Saint."

2. J. H. Newman, *The Idea of a University* (Doubleday Image Book), p. 63.

3. G. K. Cheserton, *What's Wrong with the World?* (Sheed and Ward), pp.67–68.

4. Translated by Natalie MacFarren for the *Chorale Symphony* of Beethoven, (New York: H. W. Gray).

5. Dante, *Divina Commedia*, Hell, Canto 3, Verse 64.

6. "To Sylvia"; translated by Giuseppe Tusiani (The Baroque Press), p. 163.

7. Cf. Kierkegaard, *Discourses* (Oxford University Press), p. 86.

8. Kierkegaard, *Works of Love* (Harper and Row), p. 51.

THE DRAMA OF LOVE: A RESPONSE TO ALICE VON HILDEBRAND
Rev. Paul F. DeLadurantaye, S.T.D.[1]

The story of each human life is different, because each human person is unique and irrepeatable. No one else shares in exactly the same way my history, my experiences, my thoughts and desires. At the same time, however, there is a fundamental sense in which it can be said that each human life is the same. As Dr. von Hildebrand has rightly noted, "Deep down in the human soul, there is an ardent longing to meet a soul which we can truly call our own. . . . Deep down, every man knows that he alone who loves is fully alive."

Every human life, then, despite its singular uniqueness, is, in microcosm, a drama of love. My task in responding to Dr. von Hildebrand's presentation, then, is simply to explore further some of the insights of her paper with the aim of shedding light on the "drama of love" as it is lived in the married state and in the celibate, virginal state.

The word "love" is used in many different ways and with a variety of meanings today.[2] Love can be thought of in the lyrical, romantic way found in novels and poetry. In these, the ecstatic quality of love is portrayed. Beautiful as this is, though, it is imperfect when applied to conjugal love, which is not primarily a passion renewed over and over again, but a lasting and enduring development.

Another way of speaking about love is the scientific or empirical one that sees love as a biological activity, a natural function to be examined solely on a physiological level. This perspective, however, overlooks the fact that love has an ethical dimension because the biological act is permeated by the spirit.[3] Furthermore, in such a view, love itself is reduced to the act of love.

As Dr. von Hildebrand has pointed out, using the example of Tristan and Isolde ("How beautiful thou art," Tristan exclaims to her), in every experience of love there is an attraction. This is what is meant by the *amor complacentia* of the medieval theologians.[4] Saint Thomas Aquinas notes that love is something pertaining to the appetite, and that the object of the appetite gives the appetite a certain adaptation to itself, which consists in complacency in that object: "Accordingly, the first change wrought in the appetite by the desirable object is called love, and is nothing else than complacency in that object."[5] For something to attract means it is apprehended as a good. In the case of persons, as Dr. von Hildebrand has stressed in the course of her presentation, what is good must be the whole person and not simply one particular quality. Pope John Paul II makes the same point:

> It is essential to stress that the attraction must never be limited to partial values, to something which is inherent in the person but is not the person as a whole. There must be a direct attraction to the person: in other words, response to particular qualities inherent in a person must go with a simultaneous response to the qualities of a person as such.[6]

From this attraction *(amor complacentia)* arises a movement of desire which culminates in the joy of possessing the person who is loved.

Dr. von Hildebrand has reminded us of the truth that Original Sin has wounded our human nature. Man and woman, created by God for harmonious interpersonal union, often now experience a deformation of their original vocation. Love, and the joy of possessing another, can turn into the threat of one person using another for his or her own selfish motives. Saint Thomas saw this problem very well when he distinguished two kinds or species of love: the love of desire *(amor concupiscentiae)* and the love of benevolence or goodwill *(amor benevolentiae)*.[7]

The love of desire is the expression of the longing one person experiences for something else (which may or may not be a person) as ordered to the one desiring. In the case of persons, there is an awareness of a lack within oneself that can only be filled by the desirable qualities possessed by another: "I want/need/love you because you are good for me." In this type of love, the partners do not feel affection for one another *per se* but in terms of the good accruing to each from the other.[8]

For Saint Thomas, the higher, more perfect form of love is *amor benevolentiae/amicitiae*; its peculiar characteristic is that its object is loved simply and for itself, whereas that which is loved with the love of desire is loved, not simply and for itself, but for something else.[9] Love between man and woman would be incomplete and even degrading if it went no farther than *amor concupiscentiae*, because we are dealing with persons, and persons cannot be merely the means to an end. It is not enough to long for a person as good for oneself; one must also long for that person's good.

Amor benevolentiae, then, is the same as selflessness in love: "I long for that which is good for you."[10] This love is an unconditional love that perfects the person who experiences it and brings the greatest fulfillment to both the subject and the object of that love. The love that exists between man and woman, and most especially husband and wife, must be a love that treats the other not as an object (a "good for me") but as a subject (a "good in and for himself/herself"). In Dr. von Hildebrand's words (expressing the same theme), "There is an abysmal difference between a burning interest in another person because of her loveableness, and an interest triggered by the fact that the other person can be 'useful' to us. In one case, there is a response to value; in the other case, the other person is viewed as a means that we can put to good use."

Love fails to reach its fullness if it is reduced merely to the sensory enjoyment of another's body or to an emotional attachment that is directed at certain values associated with a person, but not to the total value of the person as such. The reason for this is the fact that the value of a person is bound up with the whole being of the person and not with his or her sex: sex is only an attribute of that being. Therefore, as Pope John Paul II has noted:

> [I]n every situation in which we experience the sexual value of
> a person, love demands integration, meaning the incorporation
> of that value in the value of the person, or indeed its subordi-
> nation to the value of the person. This is where we can see
> clearly expressed the fundamental ethical characteristic of
> love: it is an affirmation of the person or else it is not love at
> all.[11]

Love in the full sense of the word is a virtuous act, not just an emotion or a sensory stimulation. This virtuous act is produced in the will and has at its disposal the resources of the will's spiritual potential: in other words, it is an authentic commitment of the free will of one person (the subject), resulting from the truth about another person (the object).[12]

Love as a virtue is, as we have seen, oriented to the value of the person. This is the *amor benevolentiae* of Saint Thomas: the person is loved simply and for himself or herself.[13] This does not mean that emotional or sensual aspects are absent from the notion of love as a virtue, but rather that these aspects are linked closely to the value of the person as such. Once again, we find a confirmation of this truth in the words of the pope:

> [I]t is only when it directs itself to the person that love is love. It cannot be called love when it directs itself merely to the body of a person, for we see here only too clearly the desire to use another person, which is fundamentally incompatible with love. Nor yet is love really love when it is merely an emotional attitude to a human being of the other sex. As we know, this feeling which relies heavily on an emotional response to "femininity" or "masculinity" may in time fade in the emotional consciousness of a man or a woman if it is not firmly tied to affirmation of the person.[14]

Love, however, affects not only the "object" (the other person), but it affects the "subject" as well. Love seeks to be united with its object.[15] Thus, love impels, as it were, the lover to give of himself – to surrender himself to the one he loves. This is the case above all in conjugal love, where one person no longer wishes to be his own exclusive good, but to join with another with a willingness to give himself to his spouse in realizing the common end of their life together. In such self-giving, the existence of the persons involved is enriched and fulfilled.[16]

Moreover, a love that is a gift of self commits a person's will in a profound way. In marriage, husband and wife choose to belong to each other in a permanent, faithful, and, God willing, fruitful way. They make a voluntary, reciprocal gift of themselves which creates

between them a genuine *communio personarum*. Such a communion, as Dr. von Hildebrand indicates, implies not only the sharing of
"one name, one roof, common meals, common possessions, but
aims at the most amazing form of oneness: for husband and wife
become one flesh."[17] At the same time, this kind of communion, this
intimacy, calls for self-renunciation and self-sacrifice. Dr. von
Hildebrand is surely right in noting that "the one who yields out of
love," i.e., the spouse who is willing to deny himself, "is the stronger
one." He "wins" because he is willing to lay down his life (cf. Jn
15:13) and make the sacrifices necessary to build up a fruitful nuptial communion, expressed not only spiritually but bodily also.[18]

The fact of Original Sin leads to the danger that the body of a
man or a woman can so thoroughly obscure the person that it
becomes an impediment to interpersonal communion.[19] The body of
the woman ceases to be expressive of that woman as person and so
ceases to invite the man to self-donation. In this lustful perception,
men see women – and in an analogous way women see men – as an
object of selfish consumption rather than as a person to be loved.[20]
Hence there is an absolute need, as Dr. von Hildebrand reminds us
in the last part of her presentation, for love to be redeemed and res-
cued from selfishness by the supernatural.[21]

To accomplish this redemption of human love, or as Pope John
Paul II refers to it, the "redemption of the body," God sent His Son,
who as God could offer the ultimate sacrifice in reparation for sin,
and as man could act for the whole human race. On the Cross, Jesus
Christ accomplished the redemption of the body and in His flesh
won for us again the possibility of functioning the way we were created to do as images of God both in our interior structures and in our
bodies. In the ethos of the redemption of the body, the original ethos
of creation is again taken up and renewed.[22]

The effort to overcome the temptation to use another person for
one's own gratification requires the imperative of self-mastery, that
is, the necessity of immediate continence and habitual temperance in
which the human heart remains bound to the nuptial meaning of the
body. Self-mastery is not something that diminishes man or deprives
him in some way. Rather, self-mastery leads to a two-fold freedom:
the freedom from the power of lust in order to make of oneself a free

gift to another. Self-mastery enables a person to place his sexual passions in the service of his love and thus truly to respect the dignity
of the person who is loved.

The result of self-mastery is the possession of the gift and the
virtue of purity. Dr. von Hildebrand has spoken of the desacraliza-
tion of sexuality in our contemporary culture, and certainly one of
the signs of such a moral decay is the belief that purity is either
somehow unhealthy for modern men and women, or that it represents some unattainable ideal. Pope John Paul takes a much different view. For him, purity is a matter of control of one's passions and
abstention from actions that contradict a person's ability to give of
himself and thus love in an authentic manner. At the same time, purity is the fruit of the indwelling of the Holy Spirit, and therefore purity is not only a capacity and a potential, but a virtue.[23]

Purity connotes a mode of being proper to the person, in which
the person realizes the nuptial meaning of the body and expresses
the freedom of the gift of self. By means of Christ's redemptive act,
and through participation in the grace that flows from that act, it is
possible for man and woman to live in accord with God's will and
become again what they were created to be: enfleshed persons who
manifest their personhood in a bodily way through acts of mutual
and loving self-donation.

Clearly the union of person with person in this life takes place
within the covenant of marriage, in accordance with the human
being's bodily-spiritual nature and the natural effects of the sexual
drive. Nevertheless, the need to seek a loving union with another
person has profounder origins than the sexual instinct and is connected above all with the spiritual nature of the human person.[24] This
need to give oneself to and unite with another person is not finally
and completely satisfied simply by union with another human being.
Dr. von Hildebrand reminds us that those who choose celibacy or
virginity "for the sake of the kingdom" (cf. Mt 19:12) include in
their self-donation "the gift of the mystery that sex embodies."
Those consecrated to God do not turn away from the body with all
its nuptial meaning. The voluntary renunciation of marriage does not
lead to a "neutering" of human beings, for the masculinity and femininity of the body, and its nuptial meaning, are more fundamental
than marriage and can serve love in other than marital ways.[25]

What Pope John Paul II calls "spiritual virginity" is another attempt to respond to our desire for lasting personal union. Spiritual virginity, lived out in the consecrated life or the celibate priesthood, is a total and exclusive gift of self to God which results from a spiritual process occurring within a person under the influence of grace. As the Holy Father puts it:

> The movement towards final union through love with a personal God is here more explicit than in marriage, and in a sense spiritual virginity anticipates that final union in conditions of the physical and temporal life of the human person.[26]

It may seem that the life of consecrated virginity presupposes values quite opposite to those of marriage. In particular, it may seem that this life rejects the values of sexuality for the sake of higher values. These appearances are misleading, for the two vocations are complementary. Pope John Paul II explains:

> Virginity or celibacy for the sake of the Kingdom of God not only does not contradict the dignity of marriage but presupposes it and confirms it. Marriage and virginity or celibacy are two ways of expressing and living the one mystery of the covenant of God with his people. When marriage is not esteemed, neither can consecrated virginity or celibacy exist; when human sexuality is not regarded as a great value given by the Creator, the renunciation of it for the sake of the Kingdom of Heaven loses its meaning.[27]

Marriage with Christ is the authentic end for every person. The unique abandonment of oneself to one's spouse, the life of love which one lives and should live, opens the heart and enables it to love more and more.[28] Virginity consecrated to God actualizes this nuptial marriage within its own status. In this regard, Dietrich von Hildebrand writes: "In virginity, God does not call us to a stoic ideal of apathy, but to fill our hearts with the most intense and vital love."[29] Those who answer the call to the life of consecrated virginity or celibacy in no way repudiate the goods of married life, because such goods are perfectly realized in the Kingdom of Christ to which their virginal, celibate lives attest.[30]

Moreover, such persons stand as a constant reminder that we can come into full possession of our sexuality without engaging in genital activity, and that we can reasonably engage in sexual activity only within a vocation in which the precious goods of human sexuality are fostered and respected.

The mystery of love constitutes one of the greatest dramas of human existence. Whether this drama is lived out in the married state or in the virginal, celibate state, it lies at the heart of every person's life. No one can be indifferent to the question of love, for we are called to, and made for, communion, and thus for love, viewed not as mere sentiment or emotion, but as a real, mutual self-donation.[31] Dr. von Hildebrand has admirably shown us this truth throughout her presentation, not only on the natural plane, but also on the supernatural one. Perhaps the words of our Holy Father, spoken by the character Adam in his play *The Jeweler's Shop*, can serve as a fitting conclusion to our reflections on the theme of the theology of marriage and celibacy:

> Sometimes human existence seems too short for love. At other times it is, however, the other way around: human love seems too short in relation to existence – or rather too trivial. At any rate, every person has at his disposal an existence and a love. The problem is how to build a sensible structure from it. But this structure must never be inward-looking. It must be open in such a way that, on the one hand, it embraces other people, while, on the other, it always reflects the absolute Existence and Love; it must always, *in some way*, reflect them. That is the ultimate sense of your lives.[32]

Notes

1. Father Paul F. DeLadurantaye holds the S.T.D. degree from the John Paul II Institute for Studies on Marriage and the Family. He currently serves as Diocesan Secretary for Religious Education and the Sacred Liturgy in the Diocese of Arlington, Virginia. He also teaches at the Notre Dame Graduate School of Christendom College.

2. For what follows, see the reflections offered by Jean Guitton, "Eros and Agape," in *Christian Married Love*, ed. Raymond Dennehy (San Francisco: Ignatius Press, 1981), pp. 75–77.

3. Consider the difference between an act of rape and an act of conjugal love: in both cases, the same biological act and material behavior is present, but vastly different spiritual attitudes are revealed (e.g. violence and oppression in the former; mutual self-surrender and communion in the latter).

4. Karol Wojtyla, *Love and Responsibility* (New York: Farrar, Straus and Giroux, 1981), p. 76.

5. Saint Thomas Aquinas, *Summa Theologiae* I-II, Q. 26, a. 2: *"Prima ergo immutatio appetitus ab appetibili vocatur amor, qui nihil est aliud quam complacentia appetibilis"* The English translation is made by the Fathers of the English Dominican Province (Westminster, Maryland: Christian Classics, 1981).

6. Wojtyla, *Love and Responsibility*, p. 79.

7. Saint Thomas Aquinas, *S.Th.* I-II, Q. 26, a. 4: *"Sic ergo motus amoris in duo tendit, scilicet in bonum quod quis vult alicui, vel sibi, vel alii; et in illud cui vult bonum. Ad illud ergo bonum quod quis vult alteri, habetur amor concupiscentiae; ad illud autem cui aliquis vult bonum, habetur amor amicitiae."*

8. Aristotle had already noted this centuries before Aquinas: "So we see that when the useful is the basis of affection, men love because of the good they get out of it, and when pleasure is the basis, for the pleasure they get out of it. In other words, the friend is not loved because he is a friend, but because he is useful or pleasant. Thus, these two kinds are only friendship incidentally, since the object of affection is not loved for being the kind of person he is, but for providing some good or pleasure." See Aristotle, *Nicomachean Ethics*, Book VIII, ch. 3, 1156a13–56a17, trans. Martin Ostwald (Indianapolis: The Bobbs-Merrill Co., Inc., 1963), p. 218. It should be noted that Aristotle does not claim that these friendships are bad or wrong; he only states that the motive for friendship based on use or pleasure is not the most noble of motives.

9. Saint Thomas Aquinas, *S.Th.* I-II, Q. 26, a. 4: *"Nam id quod amatur amore amicitiae, simpliciter et per se amatur; quod autem amatur amore concupiscentiae, non simpliciter et secundum se amatur, sed amatur alteri."*

10. Wojtyla, *Love and Responsibility*, p. 83.

11. Ibid., p. 123.

12. Ibid.

13. See note 8 above.

14. Wojtyla, *Love and Responsibility*, pp. 123–24.

15. This truth is at work in those cases where a man seeks union with a woman because of her perceived sexual value or because of an emotional attachment. The same is true in the case of *amor concupiscentiae*: a man desires union with a woman in order that she might become a good for him.

16. See for instance Adam's words upon discovering that God had created a suitable partner for him: "This at last is bone of my bones and flesh of my flesh" (Gen 2:23). Adam rejoices in the fact that he can now enter into a personal relationship with Eve, something he could not do with other animals (cf. Gen 2:20 – "But for the man there was not found a helper fit for him").

17. See also the comments made by Saint Thomas Aquinas when arguing against divorce in Book III of the *Summa contra Gentiles*: "Now there seems to be the greatest friendship between husband and wife, for they are united not only in the act of fleshly union...but also in the partnership of the whole range of domestic activity" (*Summa contra Gentiles*, trans. Anton Pegis [Garden City, New York: Image Books, 1956], Book III, ch. 123, p. 6).

18. In marriage, this communion of persons expressed by the nuptial meaning of the body assumes a particular significance. Pope John Paul puts it thus: "The persons – man and woman – become for each other a mutual gift. They become that gift in their masculinity and femininity, discovering the spousal significance of the body and referring it reciprocally to themselves in an irreversible manner: in a life-long dimension." See Pope John Paul II, General Audience of January 5, 1983, in *The Theology of Marriage and Celibacy* (Boston: St. Paul Editions, 1986), pp. 305–6.

19. John F. Crosby, "The Mystery of 'Fair Love,'" *The Catholic World Report* (April 1999), p. 55. In his *Love and Responsibility*, Karol Wojtyla examines the psychological dimension of love, focusing on the experiences of sensuality and affectivity. These traits characterize love in its subjective dimension, yet however powerfully and explicitly love is connected to the body and the senses, it is not the body and the senses alone that impart to human love its unique character. Love essentially involves the spirit of man, and to the extent to which love ceases to

be a spiritual matter, it ceases to be love. Thus, love, to be authentic and fully personal, must concern itself with freedom and truth, which are the primary elements of the human spirit. See *Love and Responsibility*, pp. 101–18.

20. Crosby, "The Mystery of 'Fair Love,'" p. 56.

21. See Dietrich von Hildebrand, *Marriage: The Mystery of Faithful Love* (Manchester, New Hampshire: Sophia Institute Press, 1991), especially pp. 41–77.

22. The redemption of the body is intimately connected with the spousal union of Christ and the Church, which itself encompasses an election of the members of the Church to holiness and their filial adoption in Christ. See Georges Chantraine, "La relation homme-femme selon Jean Paul II," in *Karol Wojtyla: Filosofo, Teologo, Poeta* (Vatican City State: Libreria Editrice Vaticana, 1984), pp. 211–14.

23. Pope John Paul II, General Audience of March 18, 1981, in *Blessed Are the Pure in Heart* (Boston: St. Paul Editions, 1983), p. 249: "Purity, as the virtue, that is, the capacity of 'controlling one's body in holiness and honor,' together with the gift of piety, as the fruit of the dwelling of the Holy Spirit in the 'temple' of the body, brings about in the body such a fullness of dignity in interpersonal relations that God Himself is thereby glorified. Purity is the glory of the human body before God. It is God's glory in the human body, through which masculinity and femininity are manifested. From purity springs that extraordinary beauty which permeates every sphere of men's mutual common life and makes it possible to express in it simplicity and depth, cordiality and the unrepeatable authenticity of personal trust."

24. Wojtyla, *Love and Responsibility*, p. 253.

25. Crosby, "The Mystery of 'Fair Love,'" p. 56.

26. Wojtyla, *Love and Responsibility*, p. 254.

27. Pope John Paul II, *Familiaris Consortio*, 16 (Boston: St. Paul Editions, 1981). See also Pope John Paul II, General Audience of May 5, 1982, in *The Theology of Marriage and Celibacy*, pp. 128–33.

28. Dietrich von Hildebrand, Marriage: *The Mystery of Faithful Love*, p. 75.

29. Ibid., p. 76.

30. This same idea is expressed, with reference to cloistered nuns, in the recent Instruction issued from the Holy See on the contemplative life

and the enclosure of nuns. See The Congregation for Institutes of Consecrated Life and Societies of Apostolic Life, *Verbi Sponsa: Instruction on Contemplative Life and the Enclosure of Nuns* (May 13, 1999), p. 4: "Their [nuns'] life is a reminder to all Christian people of the fundamental vocation of everyone to come to God [citing *Gaudium et Spes,* 19]; and it is a foreshadowing of the goal toward which the entire community of the Church journeys, in order to live forever as the bride of the Lamb."

31. This is the profound meaning of the words of the Second Vatican Council: "if man is the only creature on earth that God has wanted for its own sake, man can fully discover his true self only in a sincere giving of himself" (*Gaudium et Spes,* 24).

32. Karol Wojtyla, *The Jeweler's Shop*, Act 3, Scene 5 in Karol Wojtyla, *The Collected Plays and Writings on Theater*, ed. Boleslaw Taborski (Berkeley: University of California Press, 1987), p. 321.

SESSION II
FATHERHOOD AND SOCIETY

TEN SHORT REFLECTIONS ON THE RELATIONSHIP BETWEEN DIVINE AND HUMAN FATHERHOOD
Dr. David Blankenhorn[1]

ONE

Because this question takes us to the heart of Christian faith and our understanding of the nature of God, the question is necessarily inexhaustible and ultimately mysterious. *(Psalm 39: "Such knowledge is too wonderful for me; it is high, I cannot attain unto it.")*

But let us begin by recalling one of Jesus' clearest and most startling instructions to us, which is his teaching that we address God as "Father." This teaching represents an important shift in our understanding of God. For Jesus teaches us to call God, "Abba," an intimate and personal form of address, similar to the way in which a child might call his or her father "Daddy" or "Papa."

And so, on many Sundays at my church in New York, the pastor begins the service by saying, "Don't be afraid. You are a child of God in your Father's world." And, as a child growing up in Jackson, Mississippi, I learned to sing the song, "This is my Father's world. I rest me in the thought."

Therefore, we might begin to consider this inexhaustible topic – this mystery of the relationship between human and divine fatherhood – by asking ourselves: Why did Jesus teach us to call God "Father" or "Abba"?

TWO

As regards the growth and development of the human infant, the human father is often described by psychologists and other experts as "the first other" – that is, the child's first source of love, protection, and nurture that is outside of, and in important ways separate from, the physical and emotional unity, initially symbiotic, of the mother-child dyad. The child thus meets his or her father as the first loving person, who is not "me/my mother." In this sense we might say that the human father is the child's first encounter with an "intimate other."

This may give us a clue as to why we most often call God "Father," instead of "Mother," or alternatively, a name that is non-familial, and therefore more impersonal, less intimate, and less associated with generativity.

For we know from the scholarship of John W. Miller and others that in those religions that speak of God as maternal or female, there is a marked tendency to neglect or ignore the "otherness" of God, and instead to view God as that which is natural or immanent, as in the tendency to view God as identified with nature, or with the natural process of human procreation, birth, and death.

On the other hand, if our language or metaphors for understanding God became *too* "other" – *too* abstract, *too* impersonal, *too* distant, *too* undefinable – we run the risk of losing our understanding that our God is a *personal* God, a God who is, as the Scriptures say, "merciful and gracious, slow to anger, rich in goodness and faithfulness."

Now, we know that all our words for God are imperfect and partial; they are but a shadow of the reality. We know, for example, that God subsumes, and is infinitely larger than, male or female sexual embodiment, or human maternity or paternity. And we know that our experience of Yahweh, and of God as Abba, is an experience of a Heavenly Father whose caring, as Miller reminds us, is often felt by us as mother-like in its tenderness and compassion.

And yet surely there is a beauty and truth in our calling God "Father" or "Abba," the intimate "Other" who is both the pattern of all parenthood, and is also the source of love: a love that is *intimated* to the human infant *early*, especially when that infant first looks outside the bond or fusion of "me/my mother" to see and say, "Abba," "Daddy," "Papa," my first intimate other.

THREE

Our understanding of God as "Father" also corresponds beautifully and naturally with young children's images of God and of mothers and fathers, as revealed by wide-ranging, cross-cultural research. Children's images of "mother" suggest a cluster of similar and closely related traits, including intimacy, love, belonging, closeness, compassion, and immanence – at times approaching ideals of symbiosis. In contrast, children's images of "father" *partly* include these "intimacy" traits, while at the same time reflecting a cluster of somewhat *opposing* traits that suggest dissonance, distance, and even negation, with their clear suggestions of challenge, endurance, coaching, limits, rules, and, generally, the push outward, beyond here and now, toward strangers and risks, or what we might call, in a phrase, early steps in the search for transcendence.

FOUR

We must frankly admit, I believe, that when we call God "Father," we may, in our shortsightedness, tend wrongly to divinize – to improperly privilege – the human male as a by-product of our God-language. Many of us have done this in the past and many of us may do so today. It is important, therefore, to understand that God's love for us – his paternity – is intimated to the child through motherhood as well as fatherhood. We certainly do *not* call God "Father" because fathers are more important than mothers, and not because men are more important than women. On the contrary, I want to venture that part of the reason we are taught to call God "Father" may be related, not to paternal prowess or strength, but instead, and perhaps paradoxically, to the tendency of males toward paternal waywardness, and to the demonstrated fragility of the father-child bond as compared to the mother-child bond.

Moreover, as with any scriptural revelation – and surely this revelation about "Abba" is among the most stunning of them all – we must first and foremost endeavor to become its disciples. And so ultimately, above and beyond the search for reasons, we call God "Father" because Jesus *reveals* God to us as "Our Father." Similarly, we cannot project human fatherhood onto God. Rather, we believe that human paternity, at its best, can be a partial mirroring of the divine paternity.

FIVE

Across time and cultures, men abandon their children much more frequently than do mothers. The mother-child bond is the most robust bond in the human species. The father-child bond is significantly more fragile. It becomes an existing reality only when it is supported, taught, and expected by the surrounding society, especially by the society's basic moral codes and religious teachings.

And so, this may be another clue as to why we are taught to call God "Father." It is not because fathers are stronger or better than mothers, and it is not because men need God more than women do. In this regard, the Judeo-Christian revelation has contributed crucially to the gradual establishment of a cultural narrative or story that actively participates in this reminding, enshrining the ideal of the human father who is nurturantly involved with his biological children and their mother in a permanent way. Yet in our time, this narrative has begun seriously to unravel, with dramatic consequences, both religious and social. Calling God "Father" *today*, then, may be more important than *ever* as a means of cultural reminding: communicating a powerful message to the men of today regarding their sacred covenant with, and their unbreakable and loving responsibility to, their children and the mothers of their children.

SIX

In practical sociological terms, if you want to see what happens to human fatherhood in those societies which increasingly fail to recognize God as our Heavenly Father, look around. The evidence is everywhere around us.

SEVEN

As some modern societies become weaker in their understanding of God as Abba or Father, one important social consequence is the tendency toward a reductionist or minimalist understanding of human fatherhood, in which fatherhood is viewed in strictly natural or biological terms.

Consider a highway billboard near Dallas, Texas. It reads "Who's the Father?" and then the telephone number to call: "1-800-DNA-TYPE." The idea is for mothers to call a toll-free number so that a genetics laboratory can help identify the fathers of their children. There are at least two private companies now displaying such billboards in the U.S.

These signs give us an important insight into our current understanding of what a father is. They are telling us that we can answer the question, "Who's the father?" by obtaining the results of a DNA test. Could our understanding of fatherhood possibly get any smaller?

Here are our choices. We can see fatherhood as a bare biological act, in which case it is very small indeed: no larger than a drop of semen. Or we can see fatherhood as essentially a spiritual calling or vocation, in which case it is very large indeed; one of the largest things a man can do; indeed, it is one of the most important ways that a human male, even in his weakness and short-sightedness, can participate with God in creation.

And here is what will ultimately guide these two choices. Whether we view fatherhood as fundamentally a biological act, or fundamentally a spiritual vocation, depends *decisively* on whether or not men seek to know and love God. For true human fatherhood – fatherhood that is loving and strong, consisting of the sincere gift of the self – must necessarily point beyond itself, allowing itself to become ordinated toward something larger and better than the fragile human male. In this sense, true human fatherhood must always consist of what the Holy Father, when he was the playwright Karol Wojtyla, once called the "radiation" of fatherhood – that is, seeking to let the perfect paternity of God radiate through the frail man, and understanding that the human father is genuinely authoritative only to the degree that he himself is under authority, recognizing himself as God's obedient son.

EIGHT

It has been beautifully said that mothers are not made by children, but by fathers. Similarly, I want to suggest that fathers, in this sense, are likewise made by mothers. A man can become an inseminator through sex alone – through mere assertion, as it were – but he typically can become a nurturant father only with the permission and active support of the mother. In this sense, the man *auditions* for fatherhood, *offers* himself for fatherhood. The woman must say "I choose and accept you as the father of our child." Thus, the reality of fatherhood extends well beyond the individual man and becomes much more than a purely male vocation. Fatherhood thus becomes clearly *metaphysical*, in that it becomes inextricably reciprocal and relational, embracing and requiring for its fulfillment not only the child, but also the mother.

This understanding of the father's vocation again militates against our misunderstanding of human paternity as the mere unilateral claim and assertion of male power and privilege. It also points to the certainty of the couple – the union of persons in marriage – as the caretaker and nurturer of the child. And, finally, this understanding underscores again the fact that fatherhood is ultimately a metaphysical idea, intimately linked to religious faith and to the search for transcendence.

NINE

We are living in this generation through what might be called "the great unraveling" of our understanding of personhood and of fatherhood, in which various aspects of the truth are separated from one another, and even pitted against one another, often leading to crude reductionisms and other forms of short-sightedness, especially as regards the connection of the natural and biological to the spiritual. In these remarks I have focused perhaps one-sidedly on the spiritual dimension or culmination of authentic fatherhood, but I hope that in the near future, inspired by the great synthetic work on the family done by Aquinas and others, including the Holy Father, John Paul II, we might strive to pass beyond the great unraveling, once again integrating, for our time, the natural and biological basis of human fatherhood with its spiritual center and culmination.

TEN

As a Protestant, a Presbyterian who is indebted to Catholic teaching and who believes that the Holy Father, Pope John Paul II, is in many important ways the leader on earth of all Christians, I want to conclude with an observation based on my admittedly partial understanding of current Catholic teaching and theological reflection on marriage and the family.

I personally have been deeply moved and instructed by the Church's teachings regarding marriage, women, and children. But I am not aware of similarly rich and socially profound teachings and reflection from the Church regarding fatherhood. And since fatherhood as a social role for men is disintegrating before our eyes in so many modern societies, leaving in its wake a vast array of harmful social consequences, my hope is that all of us, in the Church and in the larger society, will do everything we can, in our time, to turn the hearts of the fathers toward their children.

For example, might it be appropriate for the Catholic Church, and for all Christians, to renew and deepen our examination of *Saint Joseph* as an important model of the spiritual core of fatherhood? And more generally, might it not be appropriate, for the Year of the Father, to hope for an encyclical from the Holy Father on the subject of human fatherhood?

Note

1. Dr. David Blankenhorn is founder and president of the Institute for American Values, a private, non-partisan organization devoted to research, publication, and public education on issues of family well-being and civil society. The Institute is located at 1841 Broadway, Suite 211, New York, NY 10023. In 1994 he also helped found the National Fatherhood Initiative. Author of *Fatherless America* (1996), he has also co-edited four books, including *Promises to Keep* (1996) and *The Fatherhood Movement* (1999).

THE FATHERHOOD MOMENT: THE REST OF THE STORY[1]
Dr. Philip M. Sutton[2]

I. The Fatherhood Moment

I would like to begin my response by thanking David Blankenhorn and his colleagues at the Institute for American Values for their contributions to what I call the "fatherhood moment." The last thirty years have seen an unprecedented rise in volitional fatherlessness due to divorce and unwed childbirth. As the second millennium comes to a close, there finally is a recognition – all too reluctant – by many of the liberal voices in the social sciences, politics, and popular culture that the state and future of fatherhood are at a critical, defining moment.

By the 1990s, it had become too difficult to ignore that escalating, volitional fatherlessness is the "single major force lying behind many of the attention-grabbing issues that dominate the news."[3] Social issues such as poverty, chronic welfare dependency, juvenile delinquency and adult crime, violence among youth and adults, premature sexual activity and out-of-wedlock child-bearing by teens, deteriorating academic achievement, depression, drug sales and abuse, and alienation among teenagers and young adults may be seen as direct or indirect effects of fatherlessness. Also, there has been a small but growing, "politically incorrect" recognition that a significant number of persons who experience homosexual attractions or who live a gay lifestyle have had psychologically or physically absent fathers.[4]

The undeniable consequences of volitional fatherlessness have made it more possible, if not more popular, to consider publicly whether fatherhood may be more necessary for the happiness of children and adults than many professionals in academia and the media had assumed. The 1990s spawned a significant increase in scholarly study of, and popular communication about, the importance of fatherhood. David Blankenhorn, his colleagues Maggie Gallagher,[5] David Popenoe,[6] Barbara Dafoe Whitehead,[7] and others[8] have contributed immensely to our understanding of the significance of physical and psychological father presence and absence, and of how well – and how poorly – men are fulfilling their paternal roles; of what it means to be a good enough father; and of how to help men become the fathers they are called to be.

In *Fatherless America*, David Blankenhorn expresses well some of the "good fruit" borne by the fatherhood moment. First, is the recognition that "the most urgent domestic challenge facing the United States at the close of the twentieth century is the recreation of fatherhood as a vital social role for men."[9] Next is the awareness that what is needed first and fundamentally is not passing new laws, creating new social programs, or commissioning more research, but a change in our "philosophy." We need to change our ideas about what constitutes the "good family man" and "good-enough" fatherhood. These notions reset on two propositions: "The first is that marriage constitutes an irreplaceable life-support system for effective fatherhood. The second is that being a real man means being a good father. The first proposition aims to reconnect fathers and mothers. The second aims to reconnect fatherhood and masculinity."

It should be acknowledged that the fatherhood moment has included popular as well as scholarly movements. Although the 1990s have seen overtly non-religious associations, such as the modern "men's movement,"[10] and the 1995 "Million Man March" in Washington, DC, attempt to promote fatherhood and to support fathers, most of the recent movements and associations by and for fathers in the United States have arisen among Christians. These groups include Promise Keepers and the National Center for Fathering among Protestants, and an even more recent groundswell of initiatives among Catholics.

II. The Rest of the Story: The Catholic Moment

As valuable as his insights from *Fatherless America* are, David Blankenhorn's comments in today's paper highlight that fundamental questions and truths are missing from the secular approach of the social sciences to the problem of confronting fatherlessness and restoring fatherhood. David Blankenhorn writes and speaks today not only as a social scientist, but also as a Christian. In reflecting on the relationship between divine and human fatherhood, he opens his own contributions to the fatherhood moment to what I call "the rest of the story" about modern fatherhood.

The fatherhood moment has occurred simultaneously with another movement or moment in modern history called the "Catholic moment."[11] By the Catholic moment, I mean the opportunity, challenge and activities of the Catholic Church since the Second Vatican Council. During the last 35 years, the Church's greater openness to putting the discoveries of the modern sciences at the service of the Gospel, and to putting revealed truth at the service of empirical truth, has been sorely needed in scholarship, public activism, and the practice of fatherhood.

The Church may learn much from a more discerning study of the fatherhood moment in the social and behavioral sciences, as well as from the Christian fatherhood movements among Protestants. But both the secular and Christian fatherhood movements have much to learn from Catholic teaching as well if their efforts are to have lasting value.

What the Church Can Learn from the Secular and Christian Fatherhood Moments

From the secular fatherhood moment, the Church can learn to be more courageous about recognizing, respecting, and asserting the truth about gender complementarity, including the unique worth of men and fathers. As devoted as Church leaders have been to affirm the truth about the vocation of women and their equality of dignity with men, I think that Church leaders have been not assertive enough about reminding and challenging men about their own vocation and dignity.

This omission is more pastoral than doctrinal, for Church teachers at various levels have acknowledged the unique worth of men and fathers. For example, Pope John Paul II has called for efforts "to restore socially the conviction that the place and task of the father in and for the family is of unique and irreplaceable importance."[12] And the U.S. Bishops have written that a couple who accept their equality as sons and daughters in the Lord "will honor and cherish one another. They will respect and value each other's gifts and uniqueness."[13]

The Church also will benefit in learning from the non-Catholic Christian father movements, especially the way men are challenged and supported as husbands and fathers to be "male servant leaders." I think it is time for Church leaders to be less cautious about encouraging men to develop the unique and complementary gifts that they bring to Christian marriage and fatherhood. I believe that today more men need to be challenged to actualize their innate masculinity, including their proclivity for servant leadership, than to be warned to restrain or suppress it.

Also the Church may learn from largely Protestant movements like Promise Keepers the pastoral importance of men-only ministries, of developing more worship, fellowship, and service groups just for men; and of challenging men more clearly and firmly to become the husbands and fathers God calls them to be.

What the Secular and Christian Fatherhood Moments Can Learn from the Church

The Catholic moment offers secular and Christian fatherhood moments a valid anthropology or philosophical understanding of human nature and the understanding of Gospel revelation interpreted by the *magisterium*, the teaching authority of the Catholic Church. In particular, studying the contemporary fatherhood crisis from the perspective of the Natural Law reveals causes and effects of fatherlessness which secular researchers and Christian advocates of fatherhood either have overlooked or have misunderstood. Specifically, these causes and effects include *childless divorce, artificial contraception, artificial conception,* and *abortion.*

Childless Divorce: Some prominent family scholars propose that "marriages between adults without minor children (remain) easy to dissolve."[14] It is inconsistent – and ultimately self-defeating – to support the continuation of easy divorce laws for spouses without children as if divorce among childless couples is "elective, cosmetic surgery," instead of "last chance, life-saving surgery."[15]

Divorce among couples without children is hardly "easy," for even then, the psychological, medical, financial, material, and spiritual costs of divorce may be quite high. And tolerating divorce for childless marriages inevitably undermines the value and durability of all marriages.

Easy divorce for childless marriage also denies the intrinsic truth that marriage is, and ought to be treated as, a permanent relationship (i.e., a covenant). For the Church teaches that marriage is permanent and that a husband is a perpetual and exclusive partner of his wife until one of them dies. When a man freely chooses to marry, he makes his wife his "unique, irreplaceable, and nonsubstitutable" partner.[16]

Chastity and Artificial *Contraception*: Unfortunately, most fatherhood scholars and advocates fail to discuss chastity and how the methods and intentions of family planning affect fatherhood. Some advocates actually offer misguided and harmful advice, for example, encouraging young adults to delay the age of marriage in order to reduce the frequency of divorce and to avoid out-of-wedlock pregnancy through the use of "contraceptives."

Bishop John J. Myers of Peoria has criticized the widespread use of contraceptives for invigorating "a culture of utility: the use of women and men as objects of sexual pleasure, the use of children as objects of personal fulfillment to be enjoyed or avoided. The contraceptive society provides neither men nor women with the incentive to take personal responsibility or to mature in the life-giving commitment of faithful marriage. Rather, it encourages a chronic adolescence which balks at commitment. Whatever the motives for practicing contraception, its use has clearly impaired the permanence of marriage."[17]

The consequences of artificial contraception have been devastating for marriages and families. "The rates of abortion, divorce, family breakdown, wife and child abuse, venereal disease and out-of-wedlock births have all massively increased" since the widespread use of chemical contraception began in the 1960s. Although contraception is not the only cause of these problems, "easy access to reliable contraception" is a major cause,[18] largely unnoticed by most academics and community activists concerned about the causes and effects of fatherlessness.

Artificial *Conception*: This is another cause and effect of father-lessness substantially ignored by academics and advocates in the fatherhood moment. Advances in reproductive technology and medical science have enabled the conception of a child to occur apart from sexual intercourse between the parents. Social scientists have not overlooked the problem of artificial conception entirely. For example, both Blankenhorn and Popenoe have criticized "sperm-donor fatherhood" (i.e., anonymous artificial insemination) and the harm caused by the commercial "production of radically fatherless children."[19]

But the Church teaches that not only anonymous artificial conception is wrong, but that every other form is wrong also. Even "homologous artificial insemination," in which the husband's sperm is brought into contact with the wife's egg outside of sexual inter-course, is a rejection of responsible fatherhood, and of the right and need of every child to be born through the sexual intercourse of his or her parents.[20] A father who participates in such a conception fails in his role as his child's protector, puts his child at grave risk of harm and degradation; he also allows his child to be treated as a com-modity to be created or destroyed at whim.[21]

Abortion and the "Culture of Death": Unfortunately, scholars and advocates of the fatherhood moment too often have ignored not only the deaths of so many children, but also the way that abortion harms fathers and fatherhood. Men who comply with the abortion decision regarding their children, whether through pressuring their child's mother to abort, or not supporting her adequately, fail in their essential roles as providers, protectors, nurturers, and sponsors of their children.[22]

Men whose children were aborted may experience "broken rela-tionships, sexual dysfunction, substance-abuse, self-hate, risk taking and suicidal behavior . . . and feelings connected to a sense of lost manhood."[23] Other surviving relatives of an aborted child, including his or her grandparents, siblings (older and younger), aunts, uncles, and cousins may also experience psychological difficulties. In turn these difficulties may become problems for the men either directly or by hindering these relatives from providing social and emotional support.[24] Many other problems also may ensue.[25] And whether or not a father of an unborn child is aware of or consents to his child's death, abortion involves a rejection and betrayal of his fatherhood.

Unfortunately, abortions may occur not only intentionally but also unintentionally, or at least without knowledge that a conception has occurred. This may happen during the use of the "abortifacient contraceptive" methods, which include intrauterine devices or IUDs; chemical "contraceptives" whether taken orally, injected or implant-ed,[26] and post rape "D & C" (dilation and curettage). The annual number of unintentional or anonymous abortions through the use of such "contraceptives" has been estimated at five to eight times the number of intentional abortions,[27] and the use of so-called "emer-gency contraception" or "morning after pills" will only increase the number of such unknown chemical abortions.

Moreover, the process of artificial conception commonly involves the destruction of newly conceived human beings. The methods for "selective reduction" of human embryos that are genet-ically unwanted or judged otherwise less desirable than one or more of their embryonic brothers or sisters result in the abortion of such tiny unwanted humans.

III. Spiritual Causes ad Remedies for Fatherlessness
The Root of Fatherlessness

Beyond the scope of philosophical anthropology and the Natural law, the Catholic moment provides the fatherhood moment with an understanding of the fundamental spiritual cause and remedy for fatherlessness. *"The vanishing of fathers from the American scene"*[28] (emphasis in the original) is not simply a sociological, psychologi-cal, or political crisis. The causes and effects of physically absent, emotionally uninvolved, and psychologically inaccessible fathers are also spiritual. "The crisis in fatherhood is only one in a network of problems about family life today, none of which can be solved in isolation from the others. Sexual promiscuity, rape, divorce, pornog-raphy, homosexuality, contraception and abortion are grave evils that are linked together and have to be dealt with together. They all result from the abandonment by a large part of the American people of the moral bases of family life,"[29] and a loss or failure to develop a relationship with God as a loving father.

John Paul II writes that a "wound deep in the very fiber of human existence" that causes and is caused by fatherlessness is rooted "in the obscure but real fact of Original Sin." He asserts: *"Original Sin attempts, then, to abolish fatherhood . . .* placing in doubt the truth about God who is Love and leaving man only with a sense of the master-slave relationship." As a result, man loses (or perhaps never develops) the sense of God's being his father and his being God's son, and instead battles against God, "the master who kept him enslaved."[30]

And in *Evangelium Vitae*, the Holy Father writes: "The heart of the tragedy being experienced by modern man [is] *the eclipse of the sense of God and of man*, typical of a social and cultural climate dominated by secularism. . . . A sad vicious cycle [results]: *when the sense of God is lost, there is also a tendency to lose the sense of man*, of his dignity and his life; in turn the systematic violation of the moral law, especially in the serious matter of respect for human life and its dignity, produces a kind of progressive darkening of the capacity to discern God's living and saving presence."[31] For "where God is denied and people live as though he did not exist, or his commandments are not taken into account, the dignity of the human person and the inviolability of human life also end up being rejected or compromised."[32]

Repentance and Conversion

The fundamental remedy for the sins underlying the rejection of human and divine fatherhood is repentance and conversion. For there can be no reconciliation of husbands with their wives – or with the mothers of their children, of fathers with their children or of human beings with God without genuine repentance and conversion.

"The demands of discipleship and fatherhood" require men "to live virtuous lives." Virtues important for a man to be a responsible husband, father and disciple include: humility, faith, fidelity to one's word, and compassion.[33] And in order to become virtuous: "Men need to be evangelized to assume their dignity as sons of God, brothers of Christ, faithful spouses of their wives, and committed fathers of their children. Without this dignity, men become sterile, unwilling, or even unable to assume the dignities of spiritual fatherhood at the service of the human community."[34] Growth in these and other virtues such as trust, compromise, communication and a sense of humor is necessary if husbands and fathers are to persevere through a family's experiences of "hurt and forgiveness, failure and sacrifice."[35]

Fatherhood as Vocation

In today's talk, David Blankenhorn is in harmony with the Catholic moment when he calls fatherhood "essentially a spiritual calling or vocation." In *Familiaris Consortio*, Pope John Paul II describes the vocation to fatherhood in similar terms. In living out "his gift and role as husband and father," a man is called to reveal and to relive "on earth the very fatherhood of God." The Holy Father regards "love for the wife as mother of their children and love for the children themselves as the "natural way" in which a man understands and fulfills his vocation to fatherhood.

Grace

The Catholic moment has much to say about how men may find the wisdom, courage, and strength to embrace moral and spiritual conversion, and to answer their vocations to be authentic husbands and fathers. The Holy Father teaches that the Church contributes to the enrichment of fathers and the dignity of all people when she "proclaims God's salvation *to humanity*, when she offers and communicates the life of God through the sacraments, [and] when she gives direction to human life through the commandments of love and neighbor."[36]

The U.S. Bishops offer husbands and fathers guidance and encouragement when they advise spouses to: "Seek God's help and the support of the church. The church's treasures of prayer and worship, learning and service, contemplation and spiritual guidance are always available to you. The grace of the sacrament of matrimony and the power of the commitment which you have made to one another are continuing wellsprings of strength."[37]

Pope John Paul II likewise exhorts fathers: "Do not be afraid of the risks (of marriage, fatherhood and family life)! God's strength is always far more powerful than your difficulties!"[38] Every person, and each father in particular, needs to be reminded: "The growth of the inner man in strength and vigor is a gift of the Father and the Son in the Holy Spirit."[39]

And the Church offers the Communion of Saints for our inspiration and reminds us that the saints themselves actively intercede for us so that we may know Christ and do His will. David Blankenhorn suggested today that St. Joseph is a fitting model for fatherhood. In addition to St. Joseph, my patron saints of married or spiritual fatherhood include St. Thomas More, St. Louis, St. Paul, St. Barnabas and St. Maximilian Kolbe.

Final Remarks

In *Familiaris Consortio*, Pope John Paul II asserts that each family *is*, and ought to *become* an "intimate community of life and love" and that each family has been given "*the mission to guard, reveal and communicate love*."[40] This means that every man, and especially every father, is charged with the responsibility to promote and to preserve marital and family love and to seek the common good and the personal well-being of every family member. The dignity of marriage and family life may be summed up in John Paul II's assertion: "*The future of humanity passes by way of the family*."[41] And as both the fatherhood moment and the Catholic moment show, the future of the family – and thus the future of humanity – is passing by way of fatherhood. Such is the intrinsic dignity and awesome responsibility of fathers.

Every man is called to fatherhood. All men have the opportunity and the duty to serve better the children (and adults) in their lives, as biological, psychological, or spiritual fathers. The Catholic moment shows the fatherhood moment why it is necessary and how it is possible to honor and to fulfill human fatherhood through honoring and imitating divine fatherhood. It is my hope and prayer along with Dr. Blankenhorn, that "all of us, in the Church and in the larger society," especially everyone who participates directly in the fatherhood or Catholic moments, may be open to the Holy Spirit. May we "do everything we can, in our time, 'to turn the hearts of the fathers toward their children'" (cf. Malachi 3:23–24; Luke 1:17) and the hearts of all people to Our Father in heaven.

Notes

1. This paper is a condensed version of a manuscript under revision by Philip M. Sutton, entitled *Fathers, Become Who You Are: Social Science and Magisterial Teaching on What Causes Fatherlessness and How to Strengthen the Fatherhood of All Men.*

2. Dr. Philip M. Sutton holds a Ph.D. from Purdue University, and is a licensed psychologist in Michigan and Ohio. Currently he works as a counselor/social worker in Catholic schools and is also supervising psychologist for a Christian counseling center; he was the inaugural director of the graduate counseling program at the Franciscan University of Steubenville. He has authored several articles on psychology and a book.

3. David Popenoe, *Life without Father: Compelling New Evidence that Fatherhood and Marriage Are Indispensable for the Good of Children and Society* (New York:The Free Press, 1996), p. 6.

4. Cf. Conrad Baars, *The Homosexual's Search for Happiness* (Chicago: Franciscan Herald Press, 1976); Joseph Nicolosi, *Reparative Therapy of Male Homosexuality: A New Clinical Approach* (Northvale, NJ: Jason Aronson, 1991); Gerard van den Aardweg, *The Battle for Normality: A Guide for (Self-)Therapy for Homosexuality* (San Francisco: Ignatius Press, 1997); and John Harvey, OSFS, *The Truth About Homosexuality* (San Francisco: Ignatius Press, 1996), especially Chapters 3, 4, & 5. Fr. Harvey discusses the work of additional therapists whose therapeutic approaches also have proven helpful to men and women struggling with issues of same sex attraction as well as chastity. In helping homosexual men and women resolve the unmet need for "father love," therapeutic efforts have made it possible for some men and women to lead chaste lives and, in some cases, change to a heterosexual orientation.

5. Maggie Gallagher, *The Abolition of Marriage: How We Destroy Lasting Love* (Washington, DC: Regnery Publishing, 1996).

6. D. Popenoe, *Life Without Father.*

7. Barbara Dafoe Whitehead, "Dan Quayle Was Right," *The Atlantic Monthly* (April 1993), pp. 47–84; *The Divorce Culture* (New York: Alfred Knopf, 1997).

8. Cf. Alan Hawkins and David Dollahite, eds., *Generative Fathering: Beyond Deficit Perspectives* (Thousand Oaks, CA: Sage Publications, 1997); John Snarey, *How Fathers Care for the Next Generation: A*

Four-Decade Study (Cambridge, MA: 1993); Ross Parke, *Fatherhood* (Cambridge, MA: Harvard University Press, 1996); Ken Canfield, *The 7 Secrets of Effective Fathering: Becoming the Father You Want to Be* (Wheaton, IL: Tyndale: House, 1992); idem, *The Heart of a Father* (Chicago: Northfield Publishing, 1996).

9. David Blankenhorn, *Fatherless America: Confronting Our Most Urgent Social Problem* (New York: Harper Perennial, 1996), p. 222.

10. Robert Bly's *Iron John: A Book About Men* (Reading, MA: Addison-Wesley, 1990) is a clear example of the secular men's movement.

11. This phrase is inspired by the title and message of Rev. Richard John Neuhaus's book, *The Catholic Moment: The Paradox of the Church in the Postmodern World* (San Francisco: Harper & Row, 1987). Fr. Neuhaus asserts that since Vatican II, the Roman Catholic Church in the United States has had an unprecedented opportunity and obligation to "be the lead Church in proclaiming and exemplifying the Gospel . . . [and in assuming] its rightful role in the culture-forming task of constructing a religiously informed public philosophy for the American experiment in ordered liberty." How well the Church achieves its task of informing and transforming American culture will depend on how well the Church proclaims and exemplifies the Gospel (p. 283).

12. Pope John Paul II, *Familiaris Consortio*, 25.

13. National Conference of Catholic Bishops, "Follow the Way of Love: Pastoral Message to Families," *Origins*, 23 (25); (Dec 2, 1993): 439.

14. Whitehead, "Dan Quayle Was Right," p. 71; also Popenoe, *Life Without Father*, pp. 222–23.

15. Many family scholars and mental health professionals seem not to realize that a divorce with remarriage is like a "heart transplant," and that too many divorces are like "elective" heart transplants. In addition to making lifestyle changes regarding exercise, diet and stress management, as with anyone with a "heart condition," a person who undergoes a heart transplant also must deal with the complications of rejection of the new heart. It is more difficult to maintain the health of a "new," transplanted heart than to improve the health of one's own, "old" heart. People with mortal "heart conditions" may be able to live well enough after a transplant, but the difficulties are much greater than if their original hearts could have been "reconditioned."

16. William May, *Marriage: The Rock on Which the Family is Built*

(San Francisco: Ignatius Press, 1995), pp. 20–22.

17. Bishop John J. Myers, "Fathers Make Known to Children Your Faithfulness: A Pastoral Letter on Fathers and Fatherhood" (March 19, 1997). Published in *The Catholic Post*, Peoria, IL (Diocese of Peoria), March 23, 1997), B–2, 3.

18. Archbishop Charles Chaput, O.F.M. Cap., "Paul VI was Right," *Inside the Vatican* (August-September 1998, pp. 40–43), nos. 4, 40. This Pastoral Letter is dated July 22, 1998.

19. Blankenhorn, *Fatherless America*, p. 233.

20. Even the simplest case of artificial conception, "homologous artificial insemination," when the sperm is extracted through means that are not immoral (i.e., without masturbation) is problematic. Other forms, which may involve insemination by another man's sperm, insemination of another women's egg, and surrogate motherhood, involve additional problems. For further discussion of these issues, see *Donum Vitae: Instruction on Respect for Human Life in its Origin and on the Dignity of Procreation* (Boston: Pauline Books and Media, 1987); and also William May, "Begotten, Not Made": Catholic Teaching on the Laboratory Generation of Human Life, in *Marriage: The Rock on Which the Family Is Built* (San Francisco: Ignatius Press, 1995), pp. 85–99.

21. For example, a recent article in *The Catholic World Report* talked about the plight of "over 6,000 embryonic human beings held in refrigerators in in-vitro fertilization (IVF) units" in England. By law, "unless both parents asked for an extension, all human embryos created and frozen before August 1, 1991" were to be "allowed to perish" (actually "deliberately destroyed" by being "taken out of the freezers and killed by having water or alcohol poured on them.") Reportedly, parents of 2,800 of the embryos "indicated that they did not want their offspring to be preserved any longer," while "the parents of over 3,000 of these offspring could not be traced."

Fathers who chose not to be traceable or who chose not to have the embryos "preserved" were guilty of their deliberate destruction. Simply putting their child(ren) at the risk of such decisions was unconscionable, and I believe ultimately must have undermined the personhood and fatherhood of the men co-responsible for their embryonic children's conception and frozen state. Moreover, allowing their frozen, embryonic children to be destroyed, whether directly by so choosing or indirectly by being untraceable, is a denial not only of their biological father-hood, but also of their children's and their own humanity.

22. Cf. Blankenhorn, *Fatherless America*, pp. 212–21.

23. Thomas Strahan, "Portraits of Post-Abortive Fathers Devastated by the Abortion Experience," Association for Interdisciplinary Research in Values and Social Change, 7/3, Nov/Dec 1994.

24. Vincent Rue, "The Psychological Realities of Induced Abortion," in *Post-Abortion Aftermath: A Comprehensive Consideration,* ed. Michael Mannion (Kansas City, MO: Sheed & Ward, 1994), pp. 24–28.

25. Vincent Rue, a psychologist and expert on post-abortion syndrome, has noted the following consequences of abortion on fathers: "Induced abortion reinforces defective problem solving on the part of the male by encouraging detachment, desertion, and irresponsibility. . . . Abortion rewrites the rules of masculinity. While a male is expected to be strong, abortion makes him feel weak. A male is expected to be responsible, yet abortion encourages him to act without concern for the innocent and to destroy any identifiable and undesirable outcomes of his sexual deci-sion making and/or attachments...Whether or not the male was involved in the abortion decision, his inability to function in a socially prescribed manner (i.e., to protect and provide) leaves him wounded and confused.

Typical male grief responses include remaining silent and grieving alone. In the silence, a male can harbor guilt and doubts about his abil-ity to protect himself and those he loves. . . . Some become depressed and/or anxious, others compulsive, controlling, demanding, and direct-ing. Still others become enraged, and failure in any relationship can trigger repressed hostility from their disenfranchised grief. . . . [The act of running from the grief process] fosters denial and forces a male to become a "fugitive" form life, loving, and healing. A guilt-ridden, tor-mented male does not easily love or accept love. Vincent Rue, "The Effects of Abortion on Men," *Ethics and Medics* 21/4: pp. 3–4, 1996; quoted in David Reardon, "Forgotten Fathers and Their Unforgettable Children," *The Post-Abortion Review* (Springfield, IL: Elliot Institute, 4/4, 1996), p. 3.

26. Tragically for fathers, mothers, and their unknowingly conceived babies, oral and other chemical "contraceptives" are designed to work in three ways: 1) To prevent sperm from reaching and egg to fertilize it; 2) To prevent ovulation of an egg that could be fertilized; and 3) to pre-vent and embryo (newly conceived person) from implanting in his or

her mother's uterus to receive food, water, air, etc. See Rudolf Ehmann, M. D., physician of obstetrics and gynecology (in *Abortifacient Contraception: The Pharmaceutical Holocaust* [Gaithersburg, MD: Human Life International, 1993]); and Bogomir Kuhar, Pharm. D., Executive Director, *Pharmacists for Life International* (in *Infant Homicides Through Contraceptives* [Bardstown, KY: Eternal Life, 1994]) have summarized research documenting that the "pill," as well as "contraceptive" implants and injections, really act as abortifacients, not just "contraceptives," in the ordinary use of the word. *The Physician's Desk Reference* (PDR), available at one's pharmacy, physician's office, or public library, also describes this common threefold – including abortifacient – action of the "pill."

27. It has been estimated that while approximately 1.55 million intentional abortions are performed in the United States every year, another 8.1 million to 12.7 million *unintentional* abortion occur annually through artificial "contraception," including 4.3 to 9.3 million through the use of oral, injected and implanted chemical "contraceptives" See B. Kuhar, *Infant Homicides;* and R. Ehmann, *Abortifacient Contraception.*

28. Edward O'Connor, C.S.C., "The Crisis in Fatherhood," in *Social Justice Review* (July/August 1996), p. 105.

29. *Ibid.,* p. 107.

30. Pope John Paul II, *Crossing the Threshold of Hope* (New York, Alfred Knopf, 1994), p. 228.

31. *Ibid.,* no. 21, pp. 37–38.

32. John Paul II, *Evangelium Vitae,* 96.

33. Bishop Myers, "Fathers Make Known to Children," B–7.

34. *Ibid.,* B–4.

35. "Follow the Way of Love," pp. 438–39. The Bishops explicitly address "spouses" and "parents" in their remarks.

36. Pope John Paul II, *Centesimus Annus: On the Hundredth Anniversary of Rerum Novarum* (Boston: St. Paul Books and Media, 1991), no. 55.

37. National Conference of Catholic Bishops, "Follow the Way of Love," p. 439.

38. Pope John Paul II, *Letter to Families,* no. 18.

39. *Ibid.,* no. 23.

40. *Ibid*, pp. 31–32. John Paul II's phrase, "intimate community of life and love," reads "intimate partnership" in Vatican Council II's Pastoral Constitution on the Church in the Modern World, *Gaudium et Spes*, in *Documents of Vatican II*, ed. Austin Flannery, 48, p. 950.

41. Pope John Paul II, *Familiaris Consortio*, 86.

SESSION III
HOMOSEXUALITY AND THE LAW

"SAME-SEX MARRIAGE" AND "MORAL NEUTRALITY"[1]
Dr. Robert P. George[2]

Frequently I hear students (and others) say: "I believe that marriage is a union of one man and one woman. But I think that it is wrong for the state to base its law of marriage on a controversial moral judgment, even if I happen to believe (on religious grounds, perhaps) that judgment to be true. Therefore, I support proposals to revise our law to authorize same-sex 'marriages.'" The thought here is that the state ought to be neutral as between competing understandings of the nature and value of marriage.

Of course, the claim that the law ought to be morally neutral about marriage or anything else is itself a moral claim. As such, *it* is not morally neutral, nor can it rest on an appeal to moral neutrality. People who believe that the law of marriage (and/or other areas of the law) ought to be morally neutral do not assert, nor does their position presuppose, that the law ought to be neutral as between the view that the law ought to be neutral and competing moral views. It is obvious that neutrality between neutrality and non-neutrality is logically impossible. Sophisticated proponents of moral neutrality therefore acknowledge that theirs is a controversial moral position whose truth, soundness, correctness, or, at least, reasonableness, they are prepared to defend against competing moral positions. They assert, in other words, that the best understanding of political morality, at least for societies such as ours, is one that includes a requirement that the law be morally neutral with respect to marriage. Alternative understandings of political morality, insofar as they fail to recognize the principle of moral neutrality, are, they say, mistaken and ought, as such, to be rejected.

Now, to recognize that any justification offered for the requirement of moral neutrality cannot itself be morally neutral is by no means to establish the falsity of the alleged requirement of moral neutrality. My purpose in calling attention to it is not to propose a retorsive argument purporting to identify self-referential inconsistency in arguments for moral neutrality. Although I shall argue that the moral neutrality of marriage law to embrace same-sex relationships is neither desirable nor, strictly speaking, possible, I do not propose to show that there is a logical or performative inconsistency in saying that "the law (of marriage) ought to be neutral as between competing moral ideas." It is not like saying "No statement is true." Nor is it like singing "I am not singing." At the same time, the putative requirement of moral neutrality is neither self-evident nor self-justifying. If it is to be vindicated as a true (correct, sound, etc.) proposition of political morality, it needs to be shown to be true (etc.) by a valid argument.

It is certainly the case that implicit in our matrimonial law is a (now controversial) moral judgment: namely, the judgment that marriage is inherently heterosexual – a union of one man and one woman. (In a moment, I'll discuss the deeper grounds of that judgment.) Of course, this is not the only possible moral judgment. In some cultures, polygyny or (far less frequently) polyandry is legally sanctioned. Some historians claim that "marriages" (or their equivalent) between two men or two women have been recognized by certain cultures in the past.[3]

However that may be, influential voices in our own culture today demand the revision of matrimonial law to authorize such "marriages." Indeed, the Supreme Court of the State of Vermont appears to be on the verge of requiring officials of that State to issue marriage licenses to otherwise qualified same-sex couples. If the Court does so, it will then fall to the federal courts, and, ultimately, to the Supreme Court of the United States, to decide whether the "full faith and credit" clause of the Constitution of the United States requires every state in the Union to recognize same-sex "marriages" contracted in Vermont.

Anticipating developments of this sort, Congress in 1996 passed the Defense of Marriage Act which guarantees the right of states to refuse to recognize same-sex "marriages." The Act went to the President to sign or veto in the course of the 1996 presidential campaign. After denouncing the Act as both mean-spirited and unneces-

sary, Clinton quietly – one might almost say "secretly" – signed it
into law literally in the middle of the night. Of course, a second
opportunity for a veto effectively rests with any five justices of the
Supreme Court of the United States. Although it is impossible to say
with confidence how the Supreme Court will ultimately rule on the
inevitable constitutional challenge to the Defense of Marriage Act,
the stated ground of the Court's decision in the 1996 case of *Romer
v. Evans* (the so-called Colorado Amendment 2 Case) will surely
inspire hope among homosexual activists whom Clinton disappoint-
ed by failing to veto the Act. In *Romer*, the Court invalidated an
amendment to the Constitution of the State of Colorado by which the
people of that state sought to prevent its municipalities from enact-
ing ordinances granting protected status or preferences based on
homosexual or bisexual orientation. Six justices joined in an opinion
written by Associate Justice Anthony Kennedy suggesting that
Amendment 2 could only have been motivated by constitutionally
impermissible "animus" against a politically vulnerable minority
group.

There are two ways to argue for the proposition that it is unjust
for government to refuse to authorize same-sex (and, for that matter,
polygamous) "marriages." The first is to deny the reasonableness,
soundness, or truth of the moral judgment implicit in the proposition
that marriage is a union of one man and one woman. The second is
to argue that this moral judgment cannot justly serve as the basis for
the public law of matrimony irrespective of its reasonableness,
soundness, or even its truth.

In the remarks that follow, I shall mainly be concerned with the
second of these ways of arguing. The task I have set for myself is to
persuade you that the moral neutrality to which this way of arguing
appeals is, and cannot but be, illusory. To that end, however, it will
be necessary for me to explain the philosophical grounds of the
moral judgment that marriage is inherently heterosexual and monogamous – a union of one man and one woman – and to discuss the
arguments advanced by certain critics of traditional matrimonial law
in their efforts to undermine this judgment.

Here is the core of the traditional understanding: Marriage is a
two-in-one-flesh communion of persons that is consummated and

actualized by acts which are reproductive in type, whether or not they are reproductive in effect (or are motivated, even in part, by a desire to reproduce). The bodily union of spouses in marital acts is the biological matrix of their marriage as a multi-level relationship: that is, a relationship which unites persons at the bodily, emotional, dispositional, and spiritual levels of their being. Marriage, precisely as such a relationship, is naturally ordered to the good of procreation (and to the nurturing and education of children) as well as to the good of spousal unity, and these goods are tightly bound together.

This distinctive unity of spouses is possible *because* human (like other mammalian) males and females, by mating, united organically – they become a single reproductive principle. Although reproduction is a single act, in humans (and other mammals) the reproductive act is performed not by individual members of the species, but by a mated pair as an organic unit. The point has been explained by Professor Germain Grisez:

> Though a male and a female are complete individuals with respect to other functions – for example, nutrition, sensation, and locomotion – with respect to reproduction they are only potential parts of a mated pair, which is the complete organism capable of reproducing sexually. Even if the mated pair is sterile, intercourse, provided it is the reproductive behavior characteristic of the species, makes the copulating male and female one organism.[4]

Although not all reproductive-type acts are marital,[5] there can be no marital act that is not reproductive in type. Masturbatory, sodomitical, or other sexual acts which are not reproductive in type cannot unite persons organically: that is, as a single reproductive principle.[6] Therefore, such acts cannot be intelligibly engaged in for the sake of marital (i.e., one-flesh, bodily) unity as such. They cannot be marital acts. Rather, persons who perform such acts must be doing so for the sake of ends or goals which are extrinsic to themselves as bodily persons: sexual satisfaction, or (perhaps) mutual sexual satisfaction, is sought as a means of releasing tension, or obtaining (and, sometimes, sharing) pleasure, either as an end in itself, or as a means to some other end, such as expressing affection, esteem, friendliness, etc. In any case, where one-flesh union cannot (or cannot rightly) be sought as an end-in-itself, sexual activity necessarily involves the *instrumentalization* of the bodies of those participating in such activity to extrinsic ends.

In marital acts, by contrast, the bodies of persons who unite biologically are not reduced to the status of mere instruments. Rather, the end, goal, and intelligible point of sexual union is the good of marriage itself. On this understanding, such union is not a merely instrumental good, i.e., a reason for action whose intelligibility as a reason depends on other ends to which it is a means, but is, rather, an intrinsic good, i.e., a reason for action whose intelligibility as a reason depends on no such other end. The central and justifying point of sex is not pleasure (or even the sharing of pleasure) *per se*, however much sexual pleasure is sought – rightly sought – as an aspect of the perfection of marital union; the point of sex, rather, is *marriage itself*, considered as a bodily ("one-flesh") union of persons consummated and actualized by acts which are reproductive in type.

Because in marital acts sex is not instrumentalized,[7] such acts are free of the self-alienating and dis-integrating qualities of masturbatory and sodomitical sex. Unlike these and other non-marital sex acts, marital acts effect no practical dualism which volitionally and, thus, existentially (though, of course, not metaphysically) separates the body from the conscious and desiring aspect of the self, which is understood and treated by the acting person as the true self which inhabits and uses the body as its instrument.[8] As John Finnis has observed, marital acts are truly unitive, and in no way self-alienating, because the bodily or biological aspect of human beings is "part of, and not merely an instrument of, their *personal* reality."[9]

But, one may ask, what about procreation? On the traditional view, isn't the sexual union of spouses instrumentalized to the goal of having children. It is true that St. Augustine was an influential proponent of something like this view, and there has always been a certain following for it in the Church. The strict Augustinian position was rejected, however, by the mainstream of philosophical and theological reflection from the late middle ages forward, and the understanding of sex and marriage that came to be embodied in both the canon law of the Church and the civil law of matrimony does not treat marriage as a merely instrumental good. Matrimonial law has traditionally understood marriage as consummated by, and only by, the reproductive-type acts of spouses; by contrast, the sterility of spouses – so long as they are capable of consummating their marriage by a reproductive-type act (and, thus, of achieving bodily, organic unity) – has *never* been treated as an impediment to marriage, even where sterility is certain and even certain to be permanent (as in the case of the marriage of a woman who has been through menopause or has undergone a hysterectomy).[10]

According to the traditional understanding of marriage, then, it is the nature of marital acts as reproductive in type that makes it possible for such acts to be unitive in the distinctively marital way. And this type of unity has intrinsic, and not merely instrumental value. Thus, the unitive good of marriage provides a non-instrumental (and thus sufficient) reason for spouses to perform sexual acts of a type which consummates and actualizes their marriage. In performing marital acts, the spouses do not reduce themselves as bodily persons (or their marriage) to the status of means or instruments.

At the same time, where marriage is understood as a one-flesh union of persons, children who may be conceived in marital acts are understood, not as ends which are extrinsic to marriage (either in the strict Augustinian sense, or the modern liberal one), but, rather, as gifts which supervene on acts whose central justifying point is precisely the marital unity of the spouses.[11] Such acts have unique meaning, value, and significance, as I have already suggested, because they belong to the class of acts by which children come into being – what I have called "reproductive-type acts." More precisely, these acts have their unique meaning, value, and significance because they belong to the *only* class of acts by which children can come into being, not as "products" which their parents choose to "make," but, rather, as perfective participants in the organic community (i.e., the family) that is established by their parents' marriage. It is thus that children are properly understood and treated – even in their conception – not as means to their parents' ends, but as ends-in-themselves; not as *objects* of the desire[12] or will of their parents, but as *subjects* of justice (and inviolable human rights); not as *property*, but as *persons*. It goes without saying that not all cultures have fully grasped these truths about the moral status of children. What is less frequently noticed is that our culture's grasp of these truths is connected to a basic understanding of sex and marriage which is not only fast eroding, but is now under severe assault from people who have no conscious desire to reduce children to the status of mere means, or objects, or property.

It is sometimes thought that defenders of traditional marriage law deny the possibility of something whose possibility critics of the law affirm. "Love," these critics say, "makes a family." And it is committed love that justifies homosexual sex as much as it justifies heterosexual sex. If marriage is the proper, or best, context for sexual love, the argument goes, then marriage should be made available to loving, committed same-sex as well as opposite-sex partners on terms of strict equality. To think otherwise is to suppose that same-sex partners cannot really love each other, or love each other in a committed way, or that the orgasmic "sexual expression" of their love is somehow inferior to the orgasmic "sexual expression" of couples who "arrange the plumbing differently."

In fact, however, at the bottom of the debate is a possibility that defenders of traditional marriage law affirm and its critics deny, namely, the possibility of marriage as a one-flesh communion of persons. The denial of this possibility is central to any argument designed to show that the moral judgment at the heart of the traditional understanding of marriage as inherently heterosexual is unreasonable, unsound, or untrue. If reproductive-type acts in fact unite spouses interpersonally, as traditional sexual morality and marriage law suppose, then such acts differ fundamentally in meaning, value, and significance from the only types of sexual acts which can be performed by same-sex partners.

Liberal sexual morality which denies that marriage is inherently heterosexual necessarily supposes that the value of sex must be instrumental *either* to procreation *or* to pleasure, considered, in turn, as an end-in-itself or as a means of expressing affection, tender feelings, etc. Thus, proponents of the liberal view suppose that homosexual sex acts are indistinguishable from heterosexual acts whenever the motivation for such acts is something other than procreation. The sexual acts of homosexual partners, that is to say, are indistinguishable in motivation, meaning, value, and significance from the marital acts of spouses who know that at least one spouse is temporarily or permanently infertile. Thus, the liberal argument goes, traditional matrimonial law is guilty of unfairness in treating sterile heterosexuals as capable of marrying while treating homosexual partners as ineligible to marry.

Stephen Macedo has accused the traditional view and its defenders of precisely this alleged "double standard." He asks:

> What is the point of sex in an infertile marriage? Not procreation: the partners (let us assume) know that they are infertile. If they have sex, it is for pleasure and to express their love, or friendship, or some other shared good. It will be for precisely the same reason that committed, loving gay couples have sex.[13]

But Macedo's criticism fails to tell against the traditional view because it presupposes as true precisely what the traditional view denies, namely, that the value (and, thus, the point) of sex in marriage can only be instrumental. On the contrary, it is a central tenet of the traditional view that the value (and point) of sex is the *intrinsic* good of marriage itself which is actualized in sexual acts which unite spouses biologically and, thus, interpersonally. The traditional view rejects the instrumentalization of sex (and, thus, of the bodies of sexual partners) to any extrinsic end. This does not mean that procreation and pleasure are not rightly sought in marital acts; it means merely that they are rightly sought when they are integrated with the basic good and justifying point of marital sex, namely, the one-flesh union of marriage itself.

It is necessary, therefore, for critics of traditional matrimonial law to argue that the apparent one-flesh unity that distinguishes marital acts from sodomitical acts is illusory, and, thus, that the apparent bodily communion of spouses in reproductive-type acts which, according to the traditional view, form the biological matrix of their marital relationship, is not really possible.

And so Richard Posner declares that Finnis's claim that "the union of reproductive organs of husband and wife unites them biologically" is unclear in its meaning and moral relevance, and cannot "distinguish sterile marriage, at least when the couple *knows* that it is incapable of reproducing, from homosexual coupling."[14] Turning to my own claim that "intercourse, so long as it is the reproductive behavior characteristic of the species, unites the copulating male and female as a single organism," Posner asserts that "[i]ntercourse known by the participants to be sterile is not 'reproductive behavior,' and even reproductive intercourse does not unite the participants 'as a single organism.'"[15]

On the question of "reproductive behavior" or, better, the idea of "reproductive-type" acts, it is important to see that identical behavior can cause conception or not depending entirely on whether the non-behavioral conditions of reproduction obtain. And the intrinsic, and not merely instrumental, good of marital communion gives spouses reason to fulfill the behavioral conditions of procreation even in circumstances in which they know the non-behavioral conditions do not obtain. This is true just in case the fulfillment of the behavioral conditions of reproduction is, in truth, unitive. So the question is whether Posner is right to deny what Finnis, Grisez, and I affirm: namely, that reproductive-type acts unite a male and female as a single organism, viz., make them "two-in-one-flesh."

It is, it seems to me, a plain biological fact that, as Grisez says, reproduction is a single function, yet it is carried out not by an individual male or female human being, but by a male and female as a mated pair. So, in respect of reproduction, albeit not in other respects (again, like locomotion or digestion) the mated pair is a single organism, the partners form a single reproductive principle, they become "one-flesh." So, I would ask Judge Posner, what is there not to understand?[16] The issue is not one of translating medieval Latin; it is a matter of simple biology. Of course, the question remains, is there any particular value to the biological (organic) union of spouses. And one will judge the matter one way or another depending, for example, on whether one understands the biological reality of human beings, as Finnis says, as part of, rather than a mere instrument of, their personal reality.

But as to the fact of biological unity, there is no room for doubt. As to its moral implications, I suspect that Posner's difficulty is simply a specific instance of his general skepticism regarding the possibility of non-instrumental practical reasons and reasoning. If pressed to deal with the question, Posner would no doubt deny that the biological reality of human beings is anything more than an instrument of ends which are themselves given by feelings, emotions, desire, or other subrational motivating factors. As I have elsewhere sought to show, the implicit operating premise of Posner's treatment of sex, and other moral questions, is the Humean non-cognitivist understanding of practical reason as the "slave of the passions."[17] Marital communion cannot be a non-instrumental reason so far as Posner is concerned, because, on this account, there are no non-instrumental reasons.

Steven Macedo, by contrast, is no Humean. He rejects Posner's instrumentalist understanding of practical reason. Still, Macedo claims that "the 'one-flesh communion' of sterile couples would appear . . . to be more a matter of appearance than reality." Because of their sterility such couples cannot really unite biologically: "Their bodies, like those of homosexuals, can form no 'single reproductive principle,' no real unity."[18] Indeed, Macedo argues that even fertile couples who conceive children in acts of sexual intercourse do not truly unite biologically, because, he asserts, "penises and vaginas do not unite biologically, sperm and eggs do."[19]

John Finnis has aptly replied:

> in this reductivist, word-legislating mood, one might declare that sperm and egg unite only physically and only their pronuclei are biologically united. But it would be more realistic to acknowledge that the whole process of copulation, involving as it does the brains of the man and woman, their nerves, blood, vaginal and other secretions, and coordinated activity is biological through and through.[20]

Moreover, as Finnis points out:

> the organic unity which is instantiated in an act of the reproductive kind is not, as Macedo . . . reductively imagine[s], the unity of penis and vagina. It is the unity of the persons in the intentional, consensual *act* of seminal emission/reception in the woman's reproductive tract.[21]

The unity to which Finnis refers – unity of body, sense, emotion, reason, and will – is, in my view, central to our understanding of humanness itself. Yet it is a unity of which Macedo and others who deny the possibility of true marital communion can give no account. For this denial presupposes a dualism of "person" (as conscious and desiring self), on the one hand, and "body" (as instrument of the conscious and desiring self), on the other, which is flatly incompatible with this unity. Dualism is implicit in the idea, central to Macedo's denial of the possibility of one-flesh marital union, that sodomitical acts differ from what I have described as acts of the reproductive type only as a matter of the arrangement of the "plumbing."

According to this idea, the genital organs of an infertile woman (and, of course, all women are infertile most of the time), or of an infertile man, are not really "reproductive organs" – any more than, say, mouths, rectums, tongues, or fingers are reproductive organs. Thus, the intercourse of a man and a women where at least one partner is temporarily or permanently sterile cannot really be an act of the reproductive type.

But the plain fact is that the genitals of men and women are reproductive organs all of the time – even during periods of sterility. *And acts which fulfill the behavioral conditions of reproduction are acts of the reproductive-type even where the non-behavioral conditions of reproduction do not happen to obtain.* Insofar as the point or object of sexual intercourse is marital union, the partners achieve the desired unity (i.e., become "two-in-one-flesh") precisely insofar as they mate, i.e, fulfill the behavioral conditions of reproduction; or, if you will, perform the type of act – the only type of act – upon which the gift of a child may supervene.[22]

The dualistic presuppositions of the liberal position are fully on display in the frequent references by Macedo and other proponents of the position to sexual organs as "equipment." Neither sperm nor eggs, neither penises nor vaginas, are properly conceived in such impersonal terms. Nor are they "used" by persons considered as somehow standing over and apart from these and other aspects of their biological reality. The biological reality of persons is, rather, part of their personal reality. (Hence, where a person treats his body as a subpersonal object, the practical dualism he thereby effects brings with it a certain self-alienation, a damaging of the intrinsic good of personal self-integration.) In any event, the biological union of persons – which is effected in reproductive type acts but not in sodomitical ones – really is an interpersonal ("one-flesh") communion.

Now, Macedo considers the possibility that defenders of the traditional understanding are right about all this: that marriage truly is a "one-flesh union" consummated and actualized by marital acts; that sodomitical and other intrinsically non-marital sexual acts really are self-alienating and, as such, immoral; that the true conception of marriage is one according to which it is an intrinsically heterosexual (and, one might here add, monogamous) relationship. But even if the traditional understanding of marriage is the morally correct one – even if it is true – he argues, the state cannot justly recognize it as such. For, if disagreements about the nature of marriage "lie in . . . difficult philosophical quarrels, about which reasonable people have long disagreed, then our differences lie in precisely the territory that John Rawls rightly marks off as inappropriate to the fashioning of our basic rights and liberties."[23]

And from this it follows that government must remain neutral as between conceptions of marriage as intrinsically heterosexual (and monogamous), and conceptions according to which "marriages" may be contracted not only between a man and a woman, but also between two men, two women (and, presumably, a man or a woman and multiple male and/or female "spouses"). Otherwise, according to Macedo, the state would "inappropriately" be "deny[ing] people fundamental aspects of equality based on reasons and arguments whose force can only be appreciated by those who accept difficult to assess [metaphysical and moral] claims."[24]

It seems to me, however, that something very much like the contrary is true. Because the true meaning, value, and significance of marriage are fairly easily grasped (even if people sometimes have difficulty living up to its moral demands) where a culture – including, critically, a legal culture – promotes and supports a sound understanding of marriage, both formally and informally; and because ideologies and practices which are hostile to a sound understanding and practice of marriage in a culture tend to undermine the institution of marriage in that culture, thus making it difficult for large numbers of people to grasp the true meaning, value, and significance of marriage – it is extremely important that government eschew attempts to be "neutral" with regard to competing conceptions of marriage and try hard to embody in its law and policy the soundest, most nearly correct conception.

Moreover, any effort to achieve neutrality will inevitably prove to be self-defeating. For the law is a teacher. And it will teach *either* that marriage is a reality that people can choose to participate in, but whose contours people cannot make and remake at will (e.g., a one-flesh communion of persons consummated and actualized by acts which are reproductive in type and perfected, where all goes well, in the generation, education, and nurturing of children in a context – the family – which is uniquely suitable to their well-being); *or* the law will teach that marriage is a mere convention which is malleable in such a way that individuals, couples, or, indeed, groups, can choose to make it whatever suits their desires, interests, subjective goals, etc. The result, given the biases of human sexual psychology, will be the development of practices and ideologies which truly do tend to undermine the sound understanding and practice of marriage, together with the pathologies that tend to reinforce the very practices and ideologies that cause them.

Joseph Raz, though himself a liberal who does not share my views regarding homosexuality or sexual morality generally, is rightly critical of forms of liberalism, including Rawlsianism, which suppose that law and government can and should be neutral with respect to competing conceptions of morality. In this regard, he has noted that:

> monogamy, assuming that it is the only valuable form of mar-
> riage, cannot be practiced by an individual. It requires a culture
> which recognizes it, and which supports it through the public's
> attitude and through its formal institutions.[25]

Now, Raz does not suppose that, in a culture whose law and public morality do not support monogamy, someone who happens to believe in it somehow will be unable to restrict himself to having one wife or will be required to take additional wives. His point, rather, is that even if monogamy is a key element of a sound understanding of marriage, large numbers of people will fail to understand that or why that is the case – and will therefore fail to grasp the value of monogamy and the intelligible point of practicing it – unless they are assisted by a culture which supports, formally and informally, monogamous marriage.

And what is true of monogamy is equally true of the other marks or aspects of a morally sound understanding of marriage. In other words, marriage is the type of good which can be participated in, or fully participated in, only by people who properly understand it and choose it with a proper understanding in mind; yet people's ability properly to understand it, and thus to choose it, depends upon institutions and cultural understandings that transcend individual choice.

But what about Macedo's claim that when matrimonial law deviates from neutrality by embodying the moral judgment that marriage is inherently heterosexual it denies same-sex partners who wish to marry "fundamental aspects of equality?" Does a due regard for equality require moral neutrality? Well, I think that the appeal to neutrality actually does not work here. If the moral judgment that marriage is inherently heterosexual is false, then the reason for recognizing same-sex marriages is that such unions are as a matter of moral fact indistinguishable from marriages of the traditional type. If, however, the moral judgment that marriage is inherently heterosexual is true, then Macedo's claim that the recognition of this truth by government "denies fundamental aspects of equality" simply cannot be sustained. If, in other words, the marital acts of spouses consummate and actualize marriage as a one-flesh communion, and serve thereby as the biological matrix of the relationship of marriage at all its levels, then the embodiment in law and policy of an understanding of marriage as inherently heterosexual denies no one fundamental aspects of equality.

True, persons who are exclusively homosexually oriented lack a psychological prerequisite to enter into marital relationships. But this is no fault of the law. Indeed, the law would embody a lie (and a damaging one insofar as it truly would contribute to the undermining of the sound understanding and practice of marriage in a culture) if it were to pretend that a marital relationship could be formed on the basis of, and integrated around, sodomitical or other intrinsically non-marital (and, as such, self-alienating) sex acts.

It is certainly unjust arbitrarily to deny legal marriage to persons who are capable of performing marital acts and entering into the marital relationship. So, for example, laws forbidding interracial marriages truly were violations of equality. Contrary to the published claims of Andrew Sullivan, Andrew Koppelman, and others, however, laws which embody the judgment that marriage is intrinsically heterosexual are in no way analogous to laws against miscegenation. Laws forbidding whites to marry blacks were unjust, not because they embodied a particular moral view and thus violated the alleged requirement of moral neutrality; rather, they were unjust because they embodied an unsound (indeed a grotesquely false) moral view – one that was racist and, as such, immoral.

A sound law of marriage is not one that aspires to moral neutrality; it is one that is in line with moral truth.

Notes

1. An earlier version of this essay appeared as "Marriage and Moral Neutrality" in *Political Order and Culture: Towards the Renewal of Civilization,* eds. Bill Boxx and Gary Quinlivan (Ann Arbor, Michigan: Eerdmans, 1997).

2. Robert P. George is the Cyrus Hall McCormick Professor of Jurisprudence at Princeton University. He holds degrees from the Harvard Divinity School (M.Div.), the Harvard Law School (J.D.), and Oxford University (Ph.D.). He is the author, among other books and many articles, of the ground-breaking *Making Men Moral: Civil Liberties and Public Morality* (1993). He served as a Commissioner on the United States Commission on Civil Rights (1991–1997). He was the 1999 recipient of the Fellowship's Cardinal Wright Award.

3. The late John Boswell, for example, claimed that brother/sister-making rituals found in certain early medieval Christian manuscripts were meant to give ecclesiastical recognition and approval to homosexual relationships. See *Same-Sex Unions in Premodern Europe* (New York: Villard Books, 1994). However, as Robin Darling Young has observed, "the reviews [of Boswell's work] after the early burst of hopeful publicity, have been notably skeptical – even from sources one would expect to be favorable." "Gay Marriage: Reimagining Church History," *First Things,* 47 (November 1994), p. 48. Darling herself concludes that Boswell's "painfully strained effort to recruit Christian history in support of the homosexual cause that he favors is not only a failure, but an embarrassing one." (Ibid..)

4. Germain Grisez, "The Christian Family as Fulfillment of

Sacramental Marriage," paper delivered to the Society of Christian Ethics Annual Conference, September 9, 1995.

5. Adulterous acts, for example, may be reproductive in type (and even in effect) but are intrinsically non-marital.

6. Securely grasping this point, and noticing its significance, Hadley Arkes has remarked that "'sexuality' refers to that part of our nature that has as its end the purpose of begetting. In comparison, the other forms of 'sexuality' may be taken as minor burlesques or even mockeries of the true thing." Now, Professor Arkes is not here suggesting that sexual acts, in what he calls "the strict sense of 'sexuality,'" must be *motivated* by a desire to reproduce; rather, his point is that such acts, even where motivated by a desire for bodily union, must be reproductive in type if such union is to be achieved. This, I believe, makes sense of what Stephen Macedo and other liberal critics of Arkes's writings on marriage and sexual morality find to be the puzzling statement that "[e]very act of genital stimulation simply cannot count as a sexual act." See Hadley Arkes, "Questions of Principle, Not Predictions: A Reply to Stephen Macedo," *Georgetown Law Journal*, 84 (1995), pp. 321–27, at 323.

7. This is by no means to suggest that married couples cannot instrumentalize and thus degrade their sexual relationship. See Robert P. George and Gerard V. Bradley, "Marriage and the Liberal Imagination," *Georgetown Law Journal*, 84 (1995), pp. 301–20, esp. p. 303, n. 9.

8. On person-body dualism, its implications for ethics, and its philosophical untenability, see John Finnis, Joseph M. Boyle, Jr., and Germain Grisez, *Nuclear Deterrence, Morality and Realism* (Oxford: Oxford University Press, 1987), pp. 304–9; and Patrick Lee, "Human Beings Are Animals," in *Natural Law and Moral Inquiry: Ethics, Metaphysics, and Politics in the Work of Germain Grisez,* ed. Robert P. George (Washington, DC: Georgetown University Press, forthcoming).

9. John Finnis, "Law, Morality, and Sexual Orientation," in *Same Sex: Debating the Ethics, Science, and Culture of Homosexuality,* ed. John Corvino (Lanham, MD: Rowman and Littlefield, 1997), sec. III.

10. See George and Bradley, "Marriage and the Liberal Imagination," pp. 307–9.

11. See George and Bradley, "Marriage and the Liberal Imagination," p. 304.

12. I am not here suggesting that traditional ethics denies that it is legit-

imate for people to "desire" or "want" children. I am merely explicating the sense in which children may be desired or wanted by prospective parents under a description which, consistently with the norms of traditional ethics, does not reduce them to the status of "products" to be brought into existence at their parents' will and for their ends, but rather treats them as "persons" who are to be welcomed by them as perfective participants in the organic community established by their marriage. See George and Bradley, "Marriage and the Liberal Imagination," p. 306, n. 21. Also see Leon Kass, "The Wisdom of Repugnance: Why We Should Ban the Cloning of Humans," *The New Republic* (June 2, 1997), pp. 17–26, esp. pp. 23–24.

13. Stephen Macedo, "Homosexuality and the Conservative Mind," *Georgetown Law Journal*, 84 (1995), p. 278.

14. Richard Posner, *The Problematics of Moral and Legal Theory* (Cambridge, MA: Harvard University Press, 1999), p. 77. Apparently having in mind accusations that he had in an earlier publication unfairly quoted fragments of Finnis's argument without providing their context, Posner goes on to say: "It may seem unfair of me to quote Finnis out of context. But the context is dominated by even stranger sentences, which read as if they had been translated from medieval Latin and makes one wonder whether Finnis agrees with Aquinas that masturbation is a worse immorality than rape" (*Ibid*). A couple of points should be made about this unfortunate and, indeed, unworthy sentence of Posner's. First, it reads as if it had itself been extracted from the early mid-twentieth century writings of Paul Blanshard, and makes one wonder whether Posner agrees that "Catholic power" constitutes a threat to American freedom. Second, it responds to a charge of implicit unfairness (i.e., not providing the essential context of quoted material to which one directs criticism) by manifesting explicit, indeed blatant, unfairness – and doing so in a way that has no evident purpose other than to appeal to prejudices that many of Posner's readers can be counted upon to share. Having thus dealt with Finnis, Posner turns his attention to the present author: "Robert George makes the same point in a more modern idiom, but I still can't make any sense of it."

15. Ibid., n. 143.

16. Germain Grisez proposes a thought experiment. Imagine a type of bodily, rational being that reproduces, not by mating, but by some act performed by individuals. Imagine that for these same beings, however, locomotion or digestion is performed not by individuals, but only by

complementary pairs that unite for this purpose. Would anybody acquainted with such beings have difficulty understanding that in respect of reproduction the organism performing the function is the individual, while in respect of locomotion or digestion, the organism performing the function is the united pair? Would anybody deny that the union effected for purposes of locomotion is an organic unity?

17. See Robert P. George, "Can Sex Be Reasonable?" *Columbia Law Review*, 93 (1993).

18. Macedo, "Homosexuality and the Conservative Mind," p. 278.

19. Ibid., p. 280.

20. John Finnis, "Law, Morality, and 'Sexual Orientation,'" in *Same Sex*, Sec. V.

21. Ibid.

22. John Finnis has carefully explained the point:

> Sexual acts which are marital are "of the reproductive kind" because in willing such an act one wills sexual behavior which is (a) the very same as what causes generation (intended or unintended) in every case of human *sexual* reproduction; and (b) the very same as what one would will if one were intending precisely sexual reproduction as a goal of a particular marital sexual act. This kind of act is a "natural kind," in the morally relevant sense of "natural," not . . . if and only if one is intending or attempting to produce an *outcome*, viz. reproduction or procreation. Rather it is a distinct rational kind – and therefore in the morally relevant sense a natural kind – because (i) in engaging in it one is intending a *marital* act, (ii) its being of the reproductive kind is a necessary though not sufficient condition of its being marital, and (iii) marriage is a rational and natural kind of institution. One's reason for action – one's rational motive – is precisely the complex good of marriage. (Finnis, "Law, Morality, and 'Sexual Orientation,'" sec. V.)

23. Stephen Macedo, "Reply to Critics," *Georgetown Law Journal*, 84 (1995), p. 335.

24. Ibid.

25. Joseph Raz, *The Morality of Freedom* (Oxford: Clarendon Press, 1986), p. 162.

THE END OF MARRIAGE
A Response to Robert George
Prof. Gerard V. Bradley[1]

Professor George has made the best argument I have seen for the essential (i.e., necessary and categorical) exclusion of same-sex couples from marriage. Note well his precise claim: George does not, strictly speaking, argue that same-sex couples be prohibited from marrying, as if it were possible – but ill-advised or imprudent – for John to marry Joe. Professor George instead shows, on the basis of (if you will) entirely public reasons, that same-sex marriage is *impossible:* given what marriage is, Jack can no more marry Joe than either can marry an incompetent or a minor. Such couplings, whatever else they can be and do for the parties to them, simply cannot be marriages. Consent is essential to forming the marital bond, and so anyone incapable of consent – the very young, the unwitting – is incapable of marriage. I have nothing important of a critical nature to say about Professor George's superb paper. I should like therefore to briefly state why the question he addresses so masterfully is almost unsurpassably important.

Abortion is the greatest injustice in American society, but the late-century disintegration of marriage is more epoch-defining, and more hazardous to persons' moral health. The two phenomena – abortion and the end of marriage – are, of course, related. Marriage is, as Professor George reminds us, the principle of sexual morality. Immoral sexual acts are often wrong for other reasons, too, such as the injustice of imposing oneself sexually upon another without consent. But all immoral sexual activity is wrong because it is non-marital. It is the supreme value of Professor George's paper to explain, if in a confined space, how this is so.

That marriage was the unifying force of sexual morality was, until a generation ago, the common morality of Americans of diverse religious beliefs. And it was the central viewpoint of

American law. As Justice John Harlan wrote in 1961 (in an opinion favoring a constitutionally grounded legal immunity for contraceptive use by married couples): "The laws regarding marriage . . . provide both when the sexual powers may be used and the legal and societal context in which children are born and brought up . . . laws forbidding adultery, fornication and homosexual practice . . . express the negative of that proposition."

The important thing, beside the centrality of marriage to sexual ethics, is this: a social commitment to marriage entails a wide pattern of restraint upon all, married and unmarried alike. Simply put, marriage is not only a lot of work for married couples. It is a high maintenance deal for any society which recognizes it as the unique opportunity for human flourishing that it is.

What if a great many people come to believe that they are entitled to regular sexual satisfaction regardless of the willingness of their spouse, if indeed there is a spouse at all? It is not necessary to imagine this asserted right to sexual satisfaction would do to a society. We merely have to recall the sexual revolution of the Sixties, with its explosion in illegitimate births and divorce by the end of that decade – and the abortion right which came soon after! The same sexually autonomous self which unhinged marriage in order to sanction casual couplings dealt itself an abortion liberty to deal with the statistically predictable effects.

Abortion as a legal liberty and as a social practice may now have roots in the economic needs and aspirations of contemporary women, and it has always had a certain eugenic coloring. But *Roe v. Wade* was undoubtedly a decision midwifed by sexual freedom. Abortion was backup contraception. And, were it not the libido's bloody fixer, we would not have abortion as either a constitutional right, or as a widespread social practice, in our country today.

Thirty-five million legal abortions have not eroded the staunch pro-life commitments of more than half of this country's inhabitants. We may live in a culture of death, but many escape its corrupting influence. Indeed, the vast majority of Americans, whether avowedly pro-life or "pro-choice," know that abortion is wrong. If there is a classic case proving the Apostle's vision of a natural law written on the hearts of all, abortion is it. Many who support abortion rights obligingly cite their "personal" opposition, and even a pro-abortion President hoped to make it "rare." At a Congressional hearing in July 1999, a New York Representative, who would more fittingly be described as the Ayatollah of abortion rights, could not help speaking of "moms" and "expectant mothers" carrying "babies." Catching himself, he referred very deliberately, though unconvincingly, to "pregnant women." However, no one asks a pregnant woman how her "fetus" is doing. They ask how the baby is.

Why does abortion have so little traction upon our consciences? That abortions kill babies is undeniable; it is obvious; it is there for all to see. Every birth, every sonogram, puts the lie to "pro-choice" arguments. That the choice to abort is therefore a stark choice between life and killing is therefore also undeniable. We have endured now a whole generation of attempts to disguise abortion rhetorically, to redescribe it or to deflect attention from its baby victims to its adult "victims." Abortion on the ground is stubborn; it makes unshakable demands upon our consciences. Many run from the moral reality of abortion, but none can hide. The moral truth, at least in this case, is a tireless pursuer.

Abortions cast a thin shadow over the moral culture. They are performed in private, out of view and only here and there, behind bland facades, at the "Women's Health Center," in the unadorned building just off the strip mall. They are a one-off thing. Once done, they are not forgotten. But most women who have had abortions wish they could forget. For almost all of them, their abortions are a matter of regret, if not shame or self contempt.

And they are rarely discussed. Very few women are commonly known to have had abortions. There are few visible effects of abortions, save for the occasional ghastly discovery of "remains." (I leave aside the invisible mutilation of character, and the psychological harm to women, which may also be undetectable.)

Being "pro-life" may not win one friends in some quarters, especially in academe. But, at least generally, it is not considered a disqualification from politically correct company, or a reliable indicator of other "backwards" beliefs. Pro-life arguments are also generally considered to be available apart from religious authority or revelation. Reason is, at least by and large, believed to offer ample support, if not cogent or conclusive arguments, for the wrongness of abortion. One can be demonstrably pro-life with respectability.

Despite the salience of choice or autonomy as the foundation of ethical decision-making in other realms of life – especially with regard to sexual activity – few give choice a very wide berth in the ethics of life. That there is an inalienable right not to be killed for (regular, full-fledged) persons is hardly questioned. That persons at the edges of life are denied that right upon the basis of diminished capacity is a grave injustice. But each argument against their right not to be killed implicitly concedes the existence of that right for many, many others.

Choice *is*, however, very widely held to be the successor to marriage as the principle of morally permissible sexual activity. That choice is miscast in this role is surely true, but not obviously is it so. There is no sexual sonogram which demonstrates to all but the least sensitized the wrongness of mutually agreeable, emotionally intense, pleasurable non-marital sex. Many run from the moral truth about sex, and they seem able to hide from it, too.

Is it not because our moral compass is easily misled when it comes to sexual activity? There appears to be no victim. At least where unmarried adults consent, as in fornication or prostitution, and there is, in truth, no injustice. Fornication and prostitution are morally wrong, but they are not wrong by dint of applying the Golden Rule. There is, too, a limited sense in which the moral value of sexual acts depends upon subjective satisfaction. Not finally or decisively, of course. But even married couples with no other reason to abstain should abstain, where the prospect is simply disagreeable to one of the spouses.

That un-contracepted marital intercourse is the only morally upright genital sexual act is not obvious, though it is true. That marriage itself is indissoluble is not obvious, though it is also true. There are, moreover, divorced and remarried people in almost every family. They seem happy, even spiritually at peace. Is it obvious that, despite appearances, they are adulterers?

The temptation to rationalize sexual misbehavior is very great, because the emotions are so powerfully engaged in the acts themselves. Where the (emotionally appealing, physically exciting) act appears to have no victim, the elusiveness of the reasons for the act's immorality makes for a very faint pang of conscience, the light tug by one's better self. And where at the same time religious authorities speak diffidently and equivocally, for fear of giving offense, many people almost cannot be blamed for thinking it is all O.K.

This is true especially where the meaning of marriage has been transformed. What does it mean to say that marriage is the principle of upright sexual activity, where "marriage" includes same-sex couples? Then marriage *cannot* be understood to be essentially related to children and reproduction. No issue of the marriage is possible. Kids – not the fruit of the marriage in any case – are entirely optional. Thus, marriage cannot be a premise in the argument which shows the immorality of sodomy. For sodomy would be the seal of same-sex marriages. In that case marriage can hardly be understood as sexually exclusive; where sexual acts are not, morally speaking, necessarily reproductive in kind (as Professor George describes that type), then the ends of sex (friendship, pleasure, intimacy) simply do not imply or entail exclusivity.

How insidious same-sex marriage will be, then, and how difficult its mainstreaming will make living the upright life. For a same-sex couple is no private, shameful thing. The visible effects of same-sex marriage will be everywhere – at your PTA meeting, at Little League games, at Scout meetings, wherever "parents" or "couples" gather. You may hear that your new next door neighbors are an Episcopal priest and an Air Force pilot – and that both are women! Where such couples set up shop, they will become part of the neighborhood's furniture. You will be lucky to find a haven from them, and luckier still if you can somehow nevertheless convince your children of the truth about marriage.

Note

1. Professor Gerard V. Bradley is a Professor of Law at the University of Notre Dame Law School. He holds the J.D. from Cornell University, and was formerly an assistant district attorney in New York City. He is co-editor of the *American Journal of Jurisprudence*, and has authored many articles as well as the book, *Church-State Relationships in America* (1987). He currently serves as President of the Fellowship of Catholic Scholars.

SESSION IV
WOMEN'S ROLES AND FAMILY POLICY

FAMILIES AND CIVIC GOODS
Dr. Jean Bethke Elshtain[1]

The United States is not only the world's greatest superpower; it is also the world's oldest constitutional republic. Despite a strong overall sense of economic well-being and security, there is a gnawing sense among American citizens at present that all is not well with us. Over the past several years, I have chaired a council of distinguished citizens who have spent their time taking a good, hard look at the current state of American civil society. Two years ago, this group, the Council on Civil Society, issued a report to the American people. Our opening paragraphs help us to lay out a sense of trouble and what is difficult today. We said:

> What is the state of our union? Certainly there is much good news. . . . Across the planet, opponents of freedom are on the defensive, as the American idea increasingly becomes the world's idea. Today the United States is not only the world's outstanding superpower, but more importantly, the world's great exemplar of democratic civil society.
>
> But let us be honest. In what direction are we tending? In our present condition, are we likely to remain the best hope for a world in which so many human beings still endure neglect and injustice? Are we likely to sustain our commitment to freedom and justice for all, so that those in our midst who are suffering might yet be lifted up by our democratic faith and practice? No. Notwithstanding the achievements of which we are properly proud, our democracy is growing weaker because we are using up, but not replenishing, the civic and moral resources that make our democracy possible. This is why we come together. This is why we issue this call.

In addition, I served as a member of a group that deliberated for two years called the National Commission on Civic Renewal. We, too, issued a report and our findings were similarly mixed. Here is a flavor of that report:

> On the eve of the twenty-first century, the United States are prosperous, secure, and free. With lower levels of unemployment, opportunity is expanding. In recent decades, important social movements have helped protect individual rights and have brought long-suppressed voices into our public dialogue. While racial, ethnic, and class divisions persist, we are a more inclusive and tolerant nation than we were a generation ago.
>
> This should be a time of hope for Americans. And when we consider our economic circumstances, it is. But when we assess our country's civic and moral condition, we are deeply troubled.
>
> And with good reason.
>
> During the past generation, our families have come under intense pressure, and many have crumbled. Neighborhood and community ties have frayed. Many of our streets and public spaces have become unsafe. Our public schools are mediocre for most students, and catastrophic failures for many. Our character-forming institutions are enfeebled. Much of our popular culture is vulgar, violent, and mindless. Much of our public square is coarse and uncivil. Political participation is at depressed levels last seen in the 1920s. Public trust in our leaders and institutions has plunged.

On and on in this vein. Why are so many citizens, from diverse backgrounds and representing various religious, political, and civic commitments so worried? Because, they argue – and I am one of them and agree – that our civil society is in trouble. Indeed, civil society is on the tips of our tongues nowadays whenever the question is put of how well democratic societies, whether old or new, are faring. That this is so is perhaps unsurprising. For we have arrived at a point of recognition, namely, that neither markets nor states suffice to order a decent way of life in common.

Civil society speaks to this life in common, and to citizens with formed capacities for trust, responsibility, a sense of duty, and a concern for the other. Civil society refers to the many forms of social life that dot the landscape of well-functioning democratic cultures: from families to churches to neighborhood groups; to what we now call non-governmental organizations; to professional associations; to universities; to political parties; and on. Families and churches are surely the most important of all for these are our primary character-forming institutions. If families and churches falter, civil society falters.

Observers of democracy have long recognized the vital importance of civil society thus understood. Some have spoken of "mediating institutions" that lie between the person and the government or state. These institutions locate each of us in a number of little estates, so to speak, which are themselves (at least ideally) nested within wider, overlapping frameworks of sustaining and supporting institutions.

Perhaps one might think of all this as a densely textured *social ecology*. Civil society is a realm that is neither narrowly individualist nor strongly collectivist. It taps both the distinctiveness and autonomy of persons and helps to bind persons to associational networks that best reflect our intrinsic sociality and capacity for trust and responsibility. One aim of maintaining a robust civil society, beginning with families, is to forestall concentrations of power at the top. A second aim lies in the recognition that only many small-scale institutions enable citizens to cultivate democratic civic habits and to play an active role in civil life. Such participation turns on meaningful involvement in decent forms of community, by which I mean commitments and ties that locate us in bonds of trust, reciprocity, mutuality – and that build over-all civic competence.

Imbedded in this overall perspective is a recognition that our social and political worlds are enormously complex and that they emerge and take shape concretely over time. No social engineer could design a workable civil society from the top. No linear model can capture the complex interactions of families, churches, labor movements, professional associations, and NGOs in general. Civil society is a repository of generations of human actions and reactions to a material and moral environment. A sturdy yet supple civil society embodies the wisdom of the ages, yet remains open to new insights and challenges. If environmental thinkers have shown us how the cumulative effective of misuse of an environment can, at one point, be more than a natural ecology can bear, so civil society analysts argue along much the same lines. They call upon us to evaluate the ways in which depletion of civic resources can have debilitating, perhaps at some point even catastrophic, effects.

Thus, for example, the cumulative effect of thousands upon thousands of individual "choices" in a consumer culture may redound to the serious disadvantage of others. That is, if I live, as I do as an American, in a culture that encourages almost unlimited consumption, no single act of mine will be seen as harmful in a direct way to others. But hundreds of thousands of persons choosing in a way that encourages and even requires a culture of overconsumption promotes corrosive results over time. Even our great gift and responsibility of moral autonomy may grow distorted if freedom gets reduced to a selection from among a vast array of consumer choices in a world in which such individual goods triumph, but any notion of a common good is lost: a point that has been made repeatedly by Pope John Paul II in various of his great encyclicals, including *Sollicitudo Rei Socialis* and *Centesimus Annus*, among others.

The increasingly fragmented culture in which all of us in late modernity find ourselves pushes us in a highly individualistic direction and away from the saving grace and presence of our fellow human beings. Family disintegration is one powerful sign of this "de-socializing" of the human person. We may come to see ourselves as self-sufficient in all things rather than as existing in a world of complex interdependencies, modeled, in the first instance, by family life. Should this happen, our ability to recognize and to foster decent and life-affirming interdependencies more generally may slowly but surely be lost. We are called, by Christian Scripture and other great religious traditions, to serve our neighbor. But we cannot do this unless we have a neighborhood that calls us out to this service and helps us to understand what it means to love and to serve others. Without such concrete possibilities before us, it is much more difficult to think about the possible claims on us made by strangers, many thousands of miles away, who may also be crying for help. So we require institutions that are present and strong, beginning with families. Unless there are processes of moral formation through such institutions – institutions like the family that call us to moral autonomy as well as to responsibilities, and to recognition of limits as well as to action in freedom – civil society is in jeopardy.

Thinking about these matters reminds us that human beings are complex creatures who do not do good simply spontaneously. We must be taught to know and even to love the good and to strive toward it. Wanting to do good, we have turned, in different societies at different points, to government. Wanting to reap the rewards of self-discipline and hard work, we have turned to economies to generate jobs and hopefully, prosperity. In the minds of some, government became not only a line of defense against social distress, but the central site of civic life and concern. Too much power concentrated in government, however, had the effect, not of helping society to stay vital but of weakening it. Similarly, the market, in the minds of some, was turned into the source on nearly all social well-being in the conviction that individual opportunities and rewards would inevitably and invariably usher into a social benefit. But economies that function absent a moral sense also weaken civil society and strip persons of dignity.

What we have learned in this tormented century is that, even as families and churches and other associations of civil society have been buffeted about and undermined by external forces of many kinds, *there is no substitute for them*. Without strong, autonomous institutions, a political culture cannot sustain a decent moral and social ecology. The evidence is in and it tells us that government and markets may be harmful in direct ways. Rather than serving civil society, they may grow too powerful and come to dominate civil society, thereby eroding civic independence, social interdependence, and pluralism. So it is not surprising that a sense of disquiet pervades much of the moral landscape of developed and developing democracies as we near century's end.

At our best as social beings, we trust one another; we have some confidence in our ability to work together and to face our difficulties with hope; we try to act decently in our dealings and we expect the same from others; we understand the vital role of government but we know that we have direct responsibility for democratic civic life; we extol the workings of a free economy but we believe that economic forces must be shaped by a moral sense. The great moral teachers have long insisted that human beings are more likely to be stirred to action and compassion when they think concretely of fellow citizens and neighbors; when there are specific tasks they are called upon and able to do; when reciprocity is an ever present possibility and expectation. We need social institutions to channel, to shape, and to sustain our moral and civic dispositions.

Thinking about the autonomous yet overlapping institutions of civil society, beginning with families and churches, and their role in sustaining democratic life, represents a long tradition of thought. But one example must suffice – that famous Frenchman, Alexis de Tocqueville, whose *Democracy in America*, is a recognized classic. Tocqueville contrasted the rich world of associational self-help he found when he toured the fledgling United States in the Jacksonian era (c. 1830) with the Old World and, as well, with what might be called a "worst case scenario" of what he feared might be America's fate at some future point. According to Tocqueville, democracy requires laws, constitutions, and authoritative institutions – certainly. But it also depends on what he called the "habits of the heart" forged within the framework such institutions provide. He urged Americans to take to heart a possible corruption of their culture over time. For citizens of the American democracy might awaken one day and realize that something terrible had happened as individuals were increasingly separated from the overlapping associations of civil society and had grown more isolated and, therefore, more powerless. In such a situation, persons would be dominated by a lower and lower mean on the level of culture. They would be both conformist and isolated; both weak and "egoistic." Having grown apart from one another, we would have forgotten what it means to be a part of families, churches, unions, lodges, etc. – civil society itself, in short.

Let us zero in on one fault line currently running through such highly developed and technocratic consumer cultures as the United States. The number of Americans who hold two or more jobs is up 65 percent since 1980. The average American worker now spends 163 hours a year more working than he or she did in 1980: that's a whole month stolen from family, friends, church, and community. Fully 71 percent of school-age children have no parent at home full-time compared with 43 percent in 1970. Yet only 13 percent of mothers with preschool-age children say they want to work full time. They would rather have more time with their children.

The United States tax code has also been biased against two parent families with children, as witness the so-called "marriage penalty." All these pressures tilt against concrete, hands-on time with children. In fact, argues economist Alan Carlson, much of "what we measure as economic growth since 1960 has simply been the transfer of remaining household tasks uncounted in monetary terms – home cooking, child care, elder care – to external entities such as Burger King, corporate day-care centers, and state-funded nursing homes." A phenomenon called "quality time" is part of this "monetizing" of everyday life, as if time could or should be parceled out into measurable, efficient chunks, including "quality time" for one's children – in short, intense bursts.

If the available data afford an accurate representation of the present moment, it must be said that citizens of the United States are working longer and harder than they ever did to earn a living, to "get ahead," to save money, to buy things, to live out one version of the American dream. Of course, people believe that they are serving their families when they do this because they understandably want their children to live more prosperous, secure lives than their own. But the tragedy is that children are deprived of time and attention in the here and now, while they are before us; when we are living together in a home as we will not be in the future. Our churches and civic lives suffer as well. People are just too tired. There is nothing left to give.

At one point, as we all know, men worked hard to support families, although the hours most workers put in on the job were less twenty-five years ago in the United Sates, at least, than they are today. But the massive entry of women into the workforce, rather than spreading the burden of work between two people who might, then, have more time, each of them, for family, friends, church, and community, as well as work, has, instead, militated against any such possibility for the vast majority. Indeed, with women drawn away from families and communities and into the paid labor force, there are millions of fewer volunteers pitching in to do the work of community, again in the United States, than there was but three decades ago.

It is more difficult for those still engaged actively in their communities to sustain their efforts. Churches remain the most robust of our community institutions but they, too, have suffered. What we have learned in our work on both the Council on Civil Society and the Council on Families in America is that the *primary* concern of American parents is *time*. These parents believe that they are losing their children to a culture that is too materialistic, too individualistic, and too violent. But they do not see how they can do much about it. They are on the fast-track, and they cannot get off.

Part of what is happening, of course, is that our expectations about the roles men and women are to play in family life, church, community, and civil society have altered profoundly. We now hold that there are no legitimate and justifiable reasons writ in nature, so to speak, why a woman should devote herself *exclusively* to family and a man devote himself *exclusively* to work. The problem with the way this has worked itself out in practice, though, is that *no one is any longer charged with the singular task of devotion to family and community*. If men keep on working as before and women are now enjoined to work as men have always been required to, who tends to the smaller world, the hands-on tasks of love and service? To say that late-modern cultures have not sorted this out is to understate.

It is, admittedly, difficult to figure out what to do. Many men and women are trying to rearrange their priorities. But many others are in no position to step back from the economic treadmill: they are just barely keeping their heads above water. Besides that, the wider cultural surroundings spread the message of "more" without limit. Having lost an appropriate sense of limits, we have no criteria for determining any longer what counts as "enough." We just believe, and act on that belief, that you can never have "too much." We are trapped in patterns of habituation that preclude glimpsing some better or more decent way.

For all the salutary features in the direction of equal dignity imbedded in today's altered expectations about men and women, there is still what social scientists call the "unintended consequences." I have just been describing some of these; they must draw our critical attention. For we must find some way, as dignified human beings, men and women working together, to get back to certain basic truths. We must find new ways – perhaps rediscovering old ways – to support one another through good times and bad. For bad times always come sooner or later. At present, we are relying almost entirely on work as a frame of reference. But work increasingly fails to serve as such a stable frame of reference. Given de-skilling, out-sourcing, and down-sizing, workers in the United States face the prospect of changing jobs some eleven times over a lifetime, and that is an enormously unsettling prospect: it destabilizes families and communities.

Also, the enormously fast-paced technological changes that leave us gasping in their wake may well fuel a terrible sense of uselessness as the skills people have are no longer needed. At other points in our history, we had other sources of meaning and purpose – those institutions of family, church, and civil society. But with these primary institutions debilitated, one can see all too easily just how much human "lost-ness" may lie ahead. Perhaps we need to think about the difference between a cash economy and the very different economy imbedded in Christian resources, in the ideal of a gift economy and in the insistence that we are born to community and to solidarity.

We cannot offer the gift of self to one another if we ourselves are consumed by consumption, wholly given over to a relentless fast-paced life in which the more we earn, the more we spend, the more we need to earn – on and on without any apparent oasis in sight. But as we near century's end, it is time to take stock. Can we glimpse the alternatives that remain within our civic reach? Can we sustain ways of being that repudiate any and all invidious distinctions between men and women; and that, in so doing, free us for love and service and citizenship rather than for resentment and fear and anxiety? Free to be most fully human, to live life and to live it more abundantly?

Surely there is something profoundly distorted about a culture prepared to send nursing mothers of six-week old infants into a war zone (as did the United States during the Persian Gulf War); a culture that doesn't support parental leave in any generous way; a culture that cuts children and parents adrift from the moment of birth. Surely there is something distorted within a culture that makes men and women who want to stay home with their infants feel guilty because, especially in the case of women, they are living out some ideological ideal. I have argued in my own work that the historic devotion of women to families and communities was vital, dignifying, and important in ways we only now appreciate as women have more and more been drawn out of families and communities and into the paid labor force. The pity, surely, is not that women historically did so much of the work of sustaining the everyday world; rather, the pity is that this work was insufficiently honored and recognized. Now we expect that men and women should both be involved with families, children, and work. But we arrange economic and social life in such a way that families, consistently, get cheated.

This is a terrible problem, for the most fundamental form of civic association is marriage and the family. The massive loosening of family bonds fuels other troubles; and these troubles, in turn, further disentangle the family. Why should this surprise us? In the words of Ernesto Cortes, Jr.:

> Families teach the first lessons of relationships among persons, some of which are essential not only to private life but to public life as well. Within the family, one learns to act and to be acted upon. It is in the family that we learn to identify ourselves with others or fail to learn to love. It is in the family that we learn to give and take with others – or fail to learn to be reciprocal. It is in the family that we learn to trust others as we depend on them or learn to distrust them. We learn to form expectations of others and to hold them accountable. We also learn to hold ourselves accountable. These lessons of reciprocity, trust, discipline, and self-restraint are important to the forming of relationships in public life.

What happens when we don't learn these lessons? If we are lucky, other institutions and relationships are there to pick us up when we fall. But this we can no longer count on. We cannot assume an intact, robust, civil society. As a result, we are losing too many of our children. Protecting, preserving, and strengthening family autonomy, and the well-being of mothers and fathers, is a way of affirming our commitment to the person – and to that democratic society that best speaks to the aspirations of persons. The rights of persons are fundamentally social. What is at stake in family autonomy and our response to the terrible situations in which too many families around the globe find themselves today is nothing less than our capacity for human sociality – whether it will flourish or falter.

We need to take a long, hard look at the moral ecologies of all nations, developed and developing. We need to evaluate culture "on the ground," so to speak. In the words of President Vaclav Havel of the Czech Republic, in an address he delivered to the Parliament and Senate of the Czech Republic delivered on December 9, 1997, we learn the following:

> I have left culture to the end . . . I mean culture in the broadest sense of the word – that is, the culture of human relationships, of human existence, of human work, of human enterprise, of public and political life. I refer to the general level of our culture . . . you must know that I am talking about what is called a civil society. That means a society that makes room for the richest possible self-structuring and the richest possible participation in public life. In this sense, civil society is important for two reasons: in the first place it enables people to be themselves in all their dimensions, which include being social creatures who desire, in thousands of ways, to participate in the life of the community in which they live. In the second place, it functions as a genuine guarantee of political stability. The more developed all the organs, institutions, and instruments of civil society are, the more resistant that society will be to political upheavals or reversals.
>
> It was no accident that communism's most brutal attack was aimed precisely against this civil society. It knew very well that its greatest enemy was not an individual non-Communist politician, but a society that was open, structured independently from the bottom up, and therefore very difficult to manipulate.

Havel's words conjure up the concept of *subsidiarity*, the most powerful theoretical framework for explaining what a civil society is and what it does that cannot be done by other, more centralized and top-heavy institutions and forces. The family figures centrally in subsidiarity as the basic formative institution. Working from the principle of subsidiarity, pontiffs since Pope Leo XIII have argued that it violates a right order of things to assign to greater or higher associations what smaller associations can do. The purpose of larger associations, including the state, is to help members of a body politic and social rather than to erode or to absorb its many plural associations.

The life of a decent polity, after all, is not just about life but about the good life. The good life plays a formative and educative role. Families are central to this good life, as families help to induct each generation into a way of being in the world made possible only when people are taught how to live mutually and how to hold one another accountable. The stakes in the so-called "family debate" could not be higher. At the end of this troubled century, we find many of our fellow citizens perplexed and even in a state of something akin to moral exhaustion. A superabundance of material goods cannot make up for a deficit on the level of social and ethical life. We need hope and trust, but hope and trust must begin somewhere. They begin when each new child is greeted with love and tenderness and embraced as a gift within the framework of a strong, loving family.

Note

1. Dr. Jean Bethke Elshtain is the Laura Spelman Rockefeller Professor of Social and Political Ethics at the University of Chicago. Author of many books and articles, she is chairperson of the Council on Civil Society, a joint project of the Institute for American Values and the University of Chicago Divinity School. In 1998, the Council issued a report on the current state of civil society with "recommendations for renewal, focusing especially upon moral truth as the indispensable foundation upon which democracy rests."

THE EROSION OF CIVIL SOCIETY IN A CONSUMERIST CULTURE
Reflections on Consumption, Work, Women, and the Family
Dr. Patricia Donohue-White[1]

In her paper "Families and Civic Goods," Professor Elshtain forcefully argues that as a nation we are depleting the civic and moral resources that sustain our democratic way of life. Our families and communities are under intense pressures, our public spaces are shrinking and becoming inhospitable, our public schools violent, and our public discourse shrill, divisive, and seemingly disconnected from everyday realities. We are at a crossroads of sorts, since there is growing agreement on both left and right that neither the state alone nor the market – nor even the increasingly common combination of the two – can adequately address the deep societal ills which plague us.

It is widely recognized that any substantive social and cultural revitalization requires that we find ways to re-enliven the numerous small-scale associations and organizations identified with the term "civil society." For it is our engagement in these diverse groups that nourishes the "social ecology" needed for stable families and communities, and teaches us the "habits of the heart" which a flourishing democracy requires.

I am in profound agreement with Prof. Elshtain's analysis of our present situation and I am happy to take this opportunity to express my intellectual debt to her regarding these and many related issues.[2] As a response to her paper, I propose to push and probe some of the points she has raised, specifically regarding the interrelations between our consumerist culture and the unintended (as well as the intended) consequences of the large-scale entrance of women into the work place. In particular, I want to examine ways in which the interrelation of these two phenomena (a consumerist culture and women in the work force) affects the "smaller worlds" of family and community.

My pushing and probing on these issues is informed by the social thought of John Paul II as well as by the work of the social historian Christopher Lasch (whose analyses of these issues correspond in crucial respects with those of Prof. Elshtain). The juxtaposition of these two thinkers may seem unusual, but as I intend to indicate, there are provocative points of congruence in their ideas on consumerism, women and work, the family, and feminism which I hope can stimulate us to think creatively about where we are and where we are going as a nation.

The Logic of Consumerism

I want to begin by pushing the analysis of a consumerist culture and the "treadmill existence" it imposes. In consumerist cultures, persons are chiefly identified in terms of what they consume. We are not primarily citizens, parents, spouses, friends, members of communities, artists, farmers, professionals, or even workers. We are consumers. And in order to consume, we work. We thus find ourselves on a treadmill of work and consumption, trying to maintain our standard of living, weighed down by the strain and anxiety of what often appears to be running faster just to stay in place.

Because we are on the work-consumption treadmill, we have no time: for our children, our parents and extended families, our neighborhoods and Church communities, cultural life, political and social commitments, leisure and play, contemplation and prayer. Work and consumption absorb all our time.

We are absorbed in our work even as our work becomes less secure, satisfying or rewarding. Within the tradition of Catholic social thought, John Paul II makes strong claims about the importance of work for human persons: "Work belongs to the vocation of every person; indeed, [the person] expresses and fulfills himself by working."[3] But when work is not *meaningful* – when it produces nothing of value and reduces the worker to a replaceable, downsizeable, and outsizeable cog in the machinery of production and consumption, it demoralizes and alienates.[4]

In consumerist cultures, work tends to be demeaned in this way (because subordinated to consumption), and when it is, workers are demeaned as well; they are not *subjects* of social and economic life, as John Paul would say, but objects to be used, manipulated, and replaced.[5] Even in professions where work still entails intrinsic satisfactions, these satisfactions tend, in Lasch's words, to be "overshadowed by external rewards – high salaries, social status, the expectation of promotion, frequent changes of scene." Echoing John Paul, Lasch points out that what is generally missing "is the kind of work that might evoke a sense of calling."[6]

The treadmill analogy describes the perceptions of families at all levels of the economic spectrum: those well below the median income, those in the middle, as well as families in the upper strata whose conspicuous consumption often serves as the cultural paradigm of consumerism.

Descriptions of the median family perhaps better illustrate the acute difficulties imposed by a consumerist economy precisely because their consumption is not conspicuous. A recent *New York Times* story profiled families in the middle, i.e., families whose combined wages total between $46,000 and $50,000 a year. Statistically, they are middle class: they own their own homes, multiple cars (typically used) and what the *Times* calls "show case living rooms" – the one public room containing comfortable furnishings and expensive electronic equipment – which often contrast with small, cramped bedrooms and kitchens. Yet they do not *perceive* themselves as middle class; they are anxious and insecure about their social and financial status, worried about debt, and about keeping up with the seemingly steady upward pace of their neighbors; they are also worried about the future. Perhaps most strikingly, in contrast to their parents and grandparents, these families cannot maintain their middle income level on a single salary; on they average they are working at more than two full-time jobs and, in their own perception, this allows them to keep their heads just above the water line.[7]

The more familiar profile of the "quintessential consumer" is found in the young professionals who, as Lasch points out, now "dominate our airwaves and set the tone for American life." Lasch's description of this recognizable type is keen and incisive:

Addicted to work and consumption, their distinctive manner of life embodies the restless ambition, the nagging dissatisfaction with the way things are, that are fostered by a consumer economy. Their careers require them to spend much of their time on the road and to accept transfers as the price of advancement. Though they complain about having to move so often, their willingness to travel long distances even in pursuit of pleasure suggests that they would find a more settled life unendurable. Leisure for them closely resembles work, since much of it consists of strenuous and for the most part solitary exercise. Even shopping, their ruling passion, presents itself as a grueling ordeal: "shop till you drop." Like exercise, it often seems to present itself as a form of therapy, designed to restore a sense of wholeness and well-being after long hours of unrewarding work.[8]

John Paul II characterizes a consumerist culture as one that emphasizes "having over being."[9] It is a culture where achievement and worth are measured in terms of money and what money can buy, a culture in which everything is for sale, a culture in which we come to understand ourselves in terms of what we buy, own, and consume. When "having" is the measure rather than "being" (*who* we are as persons), we become blind to other values, values which fall outside the sphere of exchange or which lose their value once they are placed in the market: loyalty, courage, generosity, love, art, learning, personal achievement, meaningful work, health, children, life itself, holiness, salvation. When our experience is dominated by "having" rather than "being," we can only think of these precious goods as commodities to buy, to sell, or to consume – as commodities which we all can posses if only we work a little harder and longer. Strangely, they become goods *we have a right to* because we have the money to buy them, and so we have *earned* the right to them.

When goods such as children, life, health, and love are placed in the market to be bought and sold we fall prey to what John Paul calls the "idolatry of the market," or what also could be called the "hegemony of the market."[10] A recent story in *The New Yorker* chronicling the growth industry in young women's eggs provides a vivid illustration. Women at Ivy League schools are targeted by would-be parents who are willing to pay thousands and sometimes tens of thou-

sands of dollars for the eggs of the donor who most matches their
wish list: high IQ, light complexion, physical fitness, athletic and
musical ability. Young women are *selling* their eggs to finance
expensive educations, and professional class childless couples are
shopping for the closest thing to designer babies.[11] This is, of course,
only one example. We buy and sell body parts, children, sex, child
and elder care, and health. We try to buy and sell even happiness and
love.

In the process we are losing the *capacity* to think outside the
logic of consumption. When we can no longer think and speak about
goods in terms other than those of supply and demand and efficiency, when we can no longer speak the language of inherent value,
purposefulness, the common good, generosity, self-sacrifice, and
mutual obligation, we are trapped in the logic of consumerism.
When market principles trump all others in our discussions of health
care and child care, education and art, we have succumbed to the
idolatry of the market. And when we are unwilling or unable to place
certain goods firmly outside the market, we are in danger of losing
those goods *as goods* in the non-economic sense; and thus we are in
danger of losing our capacity to see and experience them as such.

John Paul II depicts consumerism as a sort of disease of the soul:
"A person who is concerned solely or primarily with possessing and
enjoying" is a person "who is no longer able to control his instincts
and passions, or to subordinate them by obedience to the truth."
Such a person, John Paul II says, "cannot be free."[12] This individual
disease becomes "social" – an example of what John Paul calls a
"structure of sin" – when it informs the basic praxis of a society, a
praxis which ensnares people in "a web of false and superficial grat-
ifications" rather than helping people "experience their personhood
in an authentic and concrete way."[13]

Lasch describes consumerism in the language of addiction.
Advertising and the logic of consumerism transform consumers into
addicts "unable to live without increasingly sizable doses of exter-
nally provided stimulation."[14] The debilitating vices are familiar: the
inability to delay gratification, the boredom, restlessness and nagging dissatisfaction with the way things are, the anxiety and fear that
somehow "one is missing out" or "falling behind"; the compulsion
to make more, buy more, consume more; the growing loss of the

power to act from genuine self-interest, let alone from generosity or justice.

This analysis of consumerism prompts questioning on a fundamental level: is consumerism built in to the very structure of our economic practice? In other words, is unlimited consumption the very engine of our economic growth? Lasch certainly thinks so. On Lasch's reading of the rise of capitalism, Adam Smith's great discovery was that economic growth could be tied to desire; and if desires could be made "insatiable," than economic growth could be unlimited. What Lasch calls the "rehabilitation of desire" requires that desires be incessantly stimulated and new "needs" constantly created. Goods must be not only possessed but consumed, and when not literally consumed, made obsolete by newer and improved versions of what went before. Such an economy can grow without limits since it thrives on continual consumption. But this means that economic growth depends upon feeding the "desire to consume" itself, in other words, it depends upon addiction.[15]

If this sort of analysis has validity, we must ask ourselves some hard and troubling questions: if consumption is the engine of our economic growth, can we slow consumption and continue to maintain our economic prosperity? And if not, are we willing to take the risks (for ourselves and others) which transforming ourselves and our economic practice may well entail? On the other hand, if John Paul II is right that consumerism is a disease of the soul and a structure of sin, can we really "afford" in the ultimate sense of the term, to continue in this way? Shouldn't we at least begin to try to talk honestly about the effects of consumerism on our culture and society? Can't we at least begin to creatively envision ways to alter our fundamental evaluations and reject the implicit determinism which assumes the inevitability of consumerism and its globalization?

Even if one is unable to follow either John Paul II or Christopher Lasch in all dimensions of their respective critiques of consumerism, I submit that we must at least acknowledge the erosive effects which consumerism and the hegemony of the market continue to have on the stability and moral resources of "the smaller world" of family and community. And as part of our commitment to reinvigorating civil society, we must work to protect and promote public social spaces and spheres of activity (as well as spheres of public discourse) which are independent of consumerist and market logic.

Feminism, Women, Civil Society and the World of Work

This brief and admittedly stark analysis of consumerism leads me to the second cluster of issues I want to probe: the changing roles of women, particularly our large scale entrance into the work force, and the consequences – both intended an unintended – of these changes on the smaller world of family and community.

The popular reading of the history of women in America neatly divides the status of women at the sexual revolution of the 60s and 70s. It characterizes the "pre-evolutionary" period primarily in terms of the sexual division of labor whereby women were confined to the unpaid domestic sphere and only men occupied the larger public world of careers, salaried work, and power. Historians, Lasch among them, challenge this perhaps comforting but simplistic view. In his essay, "The Sexual Division of Labor, the Decline of Civic Culture, and the Rise of the Suburbs," Lasch focuses on the progressivist era (1890–1920) and describes the very public involvement of women in the great movements to improve civic life, to form public culture, and to inculcate the virtues of democracy.

Millions of women involved themselves in movements for social reform: to abolish child labor, establish juvenile courts, build housing for the poor, require factory inspection, strengthen food and drug laws, and abolish prostitution. Women were engaged in the temperance movement, in peace movements, and earlier, in the abolitionist movement. They were volunteers at hospitals, museums, libraries, social settlements, playgrounds, parks, and elementary schools. In other words, women were deeply engaged in building and sustaining civil society in what could be called the golden age of its flourishing. Lasch goes so far as to say that the achievements of the progressive era were "largely sustained . . . by the unpaid labor of women, who raised the money, performed the daily drudgery, and furnished much of the moral vision behind the civic renewal of the early twentieth century," keeping alive a "vision of a civic culture open to all."[16]

The high point of the early feminist movement coincides with this period. What is interesting to note for our purposes is that these women did not simply identify the emancipation of women with entrance into the work force (though there was a keen sense of the importance of economic independence). They did not make this simple identification *because they did not identify public life with the marketplace and the world of wage labor.* What they were after was the right to participate in the *common life,* understood as a life beyond the confines of the intimacy of family and yet also distinct from the world of the market. Lasch observes that, in the common perception of these women, involvement in civil society was, in their words, *participation in the "world's work."* Thus they did not share the later prejudice which assumes that any work worthy of the name is "dignified by a salary or wage."[17]

Lasch's point here goes beyond considerations of the effects of women's involvement in civic life in the earlier part of this century. What it indicates is the subsequent loss not only of a vibrant civil society, but of our ability to value and even conceptualize spheres of meaningful activity beyond both the responsibilities and pleasures of family life and the demands and rewards of paid work. But let's continue with the story.

While the first wave of feminism peaked with the progressivist era, the second wave began as a reaction to what Lasch calls the "suburbanization of the American soul." The massive post-World-War-II exodus to the suburbs coincided with and in many ways contributed to the gradual collapse of the civil society which had flourished in city neighborhoods and small towns. It also coincided with an extraordinary acceleration of the move towards a consumerist economy. Suburbanization constitutes a fundamental reorganization of social and economic life premised on the sharp separation of family life from the world of work, commerce, culture and education. In order to transform the modern American home into a "haven in a heartless world,"[18] the home had to be disconnected from any link to productive work and removed – both physically and psychologically – from the complex bonds and demands which life in a city neighborhood or small town imposed. In a kind of extension of individualism from the individual to the nuclear family, the home became privatized, isolated, and freed from external demands and obligations.

Suburbanization gave rise to the stark sexual division of labor whereby men went off to the public world of work and presumably power, while women were left in the isolation of the suburban home to find fulfillment as full time "homemakers." Thus woman's place, radically cut off from the world of production, civic engagement and politics, became defined in such a way as to "exclude her from participation in the common life beyond the household."[19]

Lasch reads Betty Friedan's *The Feminine Mystique* as a perceptive critique of the suburbanization of the American soul – particularly in its upper middle class feminine instantiation. What Friedan and the feminists who followed her failed to see, however, was that the "man's world" of paid labor could hardly be an antidote to the privatized world of women since it was governed by the same basic social and economic forces: the re-configuration of the public and private imposed by a consumerist culture.

Thus, instead of challenging the fundamental assumptions of suburbanization and consumerism by attempting to re-envision the organization of social and economic life, post-1960s feminism embraced its logic and sought to "integrate women into the existing structures" of consumerist culture. Feminism thus effectively reduced women's choices to two: the privatized, isolated world of the full-time homemaker, or paid labor in the market. No other options seemed available or even imaginable. Thus women in large numbers opted to leave the dreary boredom of *home and consumption* in the suburbs for the rat race and the treadmill of *work and consumption* in the marketplace.

The upshot of Lasch's analysis is not to propose that women leave the paid labor force *en masse* to take on the responsibility of renewing civil society. Like John Paul II, Lasch insists on the importance of meaningful work and recognizes the necessity of economic independence for both women and men.[20] Lasch's criticisms are deeper and more structural and so are his proposals.

Proposals for a "New Feminism"?

In closing his essay, Lasch proposes a sort of reinvigoration of feminism as a social movement, a reinvigoration which, in his view, would be more consistent with feminism's historical origins. Such a movement would respect the achievements of women in the past and thus "not disparage housework, motherhood, or unpaid civic and

neighborly services." More importantly, it would explicitly challenge the existing assumptions regarding the organization and evaluation of our social and economic practice. Instead of seeking to
integrate women into the existing structures of the consumerist
economy, "it would appeal to women's issues in order to make the
case for a complete transformation of those structures." It would
challenge "the ideology of economic growth and productivity,
together with the careerism it fosters" and the "prevailing definition
of success" that insists a paycheck is the only symbol of accomplishment. "Instead of acquiescing in the family's subordination to
the work place, it would seek to remodel the work place around the
needs of the family." It would reject "not only the 'feminine mystique' but the mystique of technological progress and economic
development."[21]

In summary, such a movement would challenge the assumptions
of a consumerist culture and engage in the creative work of rethink-
ing the ways in which we balance the private and the public, the personal and the political, the demands of participation in a common
life with the claims and needs of families. Were the feminist movement to adopt such a stance, Lasch muses, it would no doubt "put
itself beyond the pale of respectable opinion – which is to say, it
would become radical as it now merely claims to be."[22]

In terms of both his social critique and his feminist proposals,
Lasch's ideas have strong parallels with those of John Paul II.
Having already indicated points of contact in their respective criticisms of consumerism, I will now briefly highlight congruences in
their feminist proposals.[23]

In his call for a "new feminism," John Paul II shows himself an
astute student of the history of the women's movement.[24] While
granting the feminist movement's excesses, he clearly endorses its
achievements, insisting that the "unfinished journey" of "the great
process of women's liberation" must go on.[25] A great defender of the
dignity and rights of the person, John Paul II explicitly and rigor-
ously extends the language of rights to women, calling for "a culture
of equality" in which real equality of participation is achieved in all
areas – familial, economic, social, political, and cultural.[26] Rather
than confirming a stark sexual division of labor and the privatization

of women that this typically entails, John Paul strongly and repeatedly advocates the full participation of women in all spheres of public life (and in Church life as well, excluding the office of the priesthood).[27]

However, in ways similar to Lasch, John Paul II's proposals for a "new feminism" envision a social movement which challenges the basic assumptions of a consumerist culture as well as the organization of social and economic practice which it entails. Thus, in order to understand John Paul II's feminist proposals (and, I would submit, their radicality), they must be situated within his social thought as a whole and particularly within the context of his critique of consumerist culture.

In language similar to Lasch's, John Paul II encourages women to challenge "the contradictions present when a society is organized solely according to the criteria of efficiency and productivity."[28] He insists that the needs of persons and families be given priority over the demands of the market, and that the organization of work be modified in ways more conducive to the requirements of families. While demanding that women be treated with full equality in the work place, John Paul also maintains that mothers be given the freedom and the security they need to care for the needs of their young children. To meet these needs he has proposed, among other things, a family wage, family allowances, the remuneration of parents who forgo paid work in order to care for their children, and greater flexibility in the organization of work generally.[29]

Again in a way reminiscent of Lasch, John Paul II underscores women's achievements and contributions to civil society in the past and contends that women continue to make irreplaceable contributions in these spheres. In some of his most powerful language, John Paul calls on women to counter all forms of violence and the erosive effects of consumerism by being agents of peace and defenders of life in their families, local communities, nations, and in the international community.[30]

For John Paul II, these proposals are not calls for change on a purely personal level (though they entail such transformation); nor are they meant to simply promote the insertion of women into existing structures. In his own words, the pope says that:

> *Profound changes are needed in attitudes and [the] organiza-*
> *tion of society* in order to facilitate the participation of women
> in public life, while at the same time providing for the special
> obligations of women and men with regard to their families
> (italics added).[31]

These profound changes are not only meant to benefit women.
The pope's advocacy of a new feminism is a key component of his
general call to social renewal and his specific critique of consumerist
culture:

> A greater presence of women in society will prove must valu-
> able, for it will help to manifest the contradictions present
> when society is organized solely according to the criteria of
> efficiency and productivity, and *it will force systems to be*
> *redesigned* in a way which favors the processes of humaniza-
> tion which mark the civilization of love (italics added).[32]

Advocating a "civilization of love" is a radical proposal indeed!

Notes

1. Dr. Patricia Donohue-White is an assistant professor of theology at
the Franciscan University of Steubenville in Ohio. She holds the S.T.L.
from the John Paul II Institute in Rome and is ABD in philosophy from
the International Academy of Philosophy.

2. In particular, see Prof. Elshtain's *Public Man, Private Woman:*
Women in Social and Political Thought (Princeton: Princeton
University Press, 1981); idem, *Women and War* (Chicago/London:
University of Chicago Press, 1987); and also her numerous articles on
family issues.

3. *Centesimus Annus,* 6; see also *Laborem Exercens,* 9.

4. See the analysis of alienation in John Paul II's *Centesimus Annus,*
41–42.

5. See *Laborem Exercens,* 5–6.

6. C. Lasch, *The True and Only Heaven: Progress and its Critics* (New
York/London: W. W. Norton, 1991), p. 522.

7. L. Uchitelle, "The American Middle; Just Getting By," *The New York*

Times (Sunday, August 1, 1999).

8. Lasch, *The True and Only Heaven*, p. 521.

9. *Centesimus Annus*, 36.

10. *Centesimus Annus*, 40.

11. R. Mead, "Eggs for Sale: the Fertility Industry's Motherhood Auction," *The New Yorker* (August 9, 1999).

12. *Centesimus Annus*, 41.

13. Ibid.

14. Lasch, *True and Only Heaven*, p. 519.

15. Ibid., pp. 52–55.

16. C. Lasch, "The Sexual Division of Labor, the Decline of Civic Culture, and the Rise of the Suburbs," in *Women and the Common Life: Love, Marriage and Feminism*, ed. E. Lasch-Quinn (New York/London: W.W. Norton 1997), p. 98. Lasch is by no means uncritical of the progressive era. See his *True and Only Heaven*, ch. 8.

17. Lasch, "The Sexual Division of Labor," p. 96.

18. Lasch's *Haven in a Heartless World: The Family Besieged* (1977) deals primarily with the effects of the "therapeutic culture," a significant and essential component of Lasch's criticism which I cannot go into here.

19. Lasch, "The Sexual Division of Labor," p. 94.

20. See especially his remarks in "Gilligan's Island" in *Women and the Common Life*.

21. Lasch, "The Sexual Division of Labor," pp. 119–20.

22. Ibid.

23. On John Paul II's call for a "a new feminism," see *Evangelium Vitae*, 99, and also his various writings on women's issues released at the time of the Fourth World Conference on Women in Beijing. These have been collected in *The Genius of Women* (NCCB No. 5–113: 1977).

24. On situating John Paul's writings on women within the history of feminism, see my "A Feminist Pope? Women and the Family in the Social Thought of John Paul II," *Catholic Social Science Review* (forthcoming).

25. John Paul II, "Letter to Women," in *The Genius of Women*, 4.

26. See "Letter to Women" and "Welcome to Gertrude Mongella" in

The Genius of Women.

27. See the various "Angelus Reflections" in *The Genius of Women*; particularly "Closing the Gap between Cultural Opportunities for Men and Women" (August 6, 1995); "Equal Opportunity in the World of Work" (August 20, 1995); "Women in Political Life" (August 27, 1995); and "Women's Role in the Church" (September 3, 1995).

28. John Paul II, "Letter to Women," 4.

29. See John Paul II, "Letter to Women," 4; "Welcome to Gertrude Mongella," 5 and 8; and "Equal Opportunity in the World of Work" all in *The Genius of Women*; also *Familiaris Consortio*, 23; and *Laborem Exercens*, 19.

30. John Paul II, "Letter to Women," *passim.;* also "World Day of Peace Message" (1995) in *The Genius of Women*.

31. John Paul II, "Welcome to Gertrude Mongella," 5.

32. John Paul II, "Letter to Women," 4.

SESSION V
ECONOMICS AND MARRIAGE

THE FAMILY AND THE AGING OF THE POPULATION
Amb. Alberto M. Piedra[1]

Introduction

Very few people would deny that at the dawn of the new millennium the basic principles of our Judeo-Christian heritage are not only being questioned; they are being challenged by powerful forces which either openly or surreptitiously deny the very existence of the transcendental and reduce man to the purely immanent. From the deistic and utilitarian interpretation of life, an assessment endorsed by most of the philosophers of the Enlightenment, man has gradually slipped into other types of "isms" such as positivism, relativism, and, in many instances, outright atheism. To reject past values and institutions in the name of progress is one of the major characteristics of our contemporary society. Not to do so seems to imply a repudiation of modernity and a return to the "oppression" and "tyranny" of the Dark Ages.

The tremendous achievements in science and technology that took place in the Western world during the Industrial Revolution and its aftermath gave added credence to the belief that progress was the result of man's power to control the laws of nature; it was a power that acquired special significance in the area of economics, where man's innovative spirit gave rise to tremendous improvements in his standard of living. An ever increasing number of goods and services invaded the marketplace, giving rise to a wave of almost unlimited optimism in the future well-being of mankind.

New values, more in accordance with "the spirit of the times," began to permeate large sectors of society. An ethos based primarily on the love of wealth and material well-being became a natural substitute for the old-fashioned spiritual and cultural values of the past. A new type of consumer society, imbued with a high dose of hedonism, was in the making, to the detriment of many of the most basic traditional values which for centuries had characterized Western societies. In particular, man's spiritual dimension apparently had drowned under a sea of material well-being.

The family, the fundamental pillar of a healthy society, is not immune from the buffeting winds of the so-called "new" and "progressive" ideas that oftentimes threaten its very existence. The traditional Christian concept of the family is gradually being undermined under the pretext that it requires certain fundamental changes if it is to keep up with the modern trends of our contemporary society.

Given the complexity of the many problems involved in this phenomenon, we will limit ourselves in this paper to only one important aspect of this threat to the security of the family which, in our opinion, can jeopardize the future well-being of society. I am referring to the influence that changing population trends will have on the structure and future stability of the family, in particular, to the decline in fertility rates and the rapid aging of the population.

Under the banners of postmodernism and deconstructionism, the new generations were made to believe that the family had lost its significance as a major player in the moral, cultural, and economic life of nation. The very concept of the family was challenged, and its role limited to a transitory arrangement between two persons who were free to terminate it whenever it suited their purpose. The traditional family was no longer considered the pivotal factor of a healthy society. The state, the community, and other collective agencies would replace the major functions that previously had been performed by the family. The elderly parents no longer had to worry about their economic and social needs once they reached the age of retirement and were unable to earn a living because the state would provide for their well-being. Government authorities would always be there to protect their interests through extensive social and medical security plans.

The same philosophy applied to the education and health care of children. State-run day-care centers for young children would permit mothers to join the work force. This way they could earn an income which would give them a certain degree of independence. The children, meanwhile, would be under the tutelage of specialized government personnel who would take care of them physically whilst at the same time providing them with the most elementary standards of education. The state with its numerous bureaucratic institutions for the aged and the very young would see to it that all their basic needs would be taken care of.

Leaving aside a debate on the possible merits or serious flaws of such a philosophy which, we personally believe, has many dangerous ramifications to it in terms of the future moral well-being of the family, the fact still remains that, economically speaking, such extensive social government programs are running into serious financial problems. It is ironic that the state, the modern *deus ex machina*, which supposedly was going to supplant the family as the purveyor to the needs of the old, the infirm, and children, now finds itself in a situation where very soon it will lack the necessary funds to carry out such an altruistic mission. The social security systems and other state-run medical plans are on the verge of bankruptcy and, if this occurs, the state will then have to rely once again on the family, and on private religious organizations, to take care of the pressing and increasing needs of the young and the old. This is especially true of the old who, in relative numbers, are increasing at an unprecedented rate. This can be easily verified by looking at the latest figures on population trends of the United Nations. How ironic will it be if, in the new millennium, the traditional family so belittled by certain sectors of society turns out to be the main reliable supporter of the old and the young.

The latest data on population clearly show that in Europe and the United States the ratio of the elderly with respect to the total population has increased significantly during the last few years whilst, on the other hand, the proportion of the young has decreased.[2] This trend, if it continues, will have serious negative consequences for the future well-being of our societies, not to mention its depressive economic impact.

In this paper, we will discuss the phenomenon of the aging of the population and how it will affect the role of the family in our contemporary society. For this purpose, we will have to analyze certain population trends that will help us understand the gravity of the present situation. Without being alarmist, it cannot be denied that the aging of the population, together with the fall in the ration of young people within the total population, gives ground for serious concern. Hopefully, Professor Pierre Chaunu's predictions concerning the future of Europe will not materialize. In his book *La Peste Blanche,* he stated in no uncertain terms that, just as the plagues of medieval times decimated the population of Europe, so in our own time the "white plague," caused by persistent radically low fertility rates, is performing the same destructive role on the European continent.[3] The delusion of overpopulation led governments to sponsor policies geared toward population control, which then led to low fertility rates and contributed to the present population problems.[4] Such policies became an infatuation for demographers and for many western governments.

For many years the major concern of the majority of demographers was the specter of overpopulation and its negative political, economic, and social implications for society as a whole. The United Nations and other international organizations joined the chorus of dire warnings concerning the future of mankind resulting from a global population explosion that was not far from occurring. The Malthusian theories of the dangers of an overpopulated world incapable of freeing itself gained renewed impetus in the most influential circles of contemporary society. But was this threat a myth or a reality? The most recent data available on population trends will help us verify the accuracy of these predictions.

Population Trends

During the 1960s official publications on population trends predicted that by the year 2000 the world population would reach 7.5 billion people and would continue growing in the future.[5] Predictions such as these proved to be incorrect, giving ample ground to doubt the soundness of certain population policies which were based on unfounded fears.[6] By the 1970s, some forecasters were already predicting the opposite, a decline in population by the year 2000, a prediction which also proved to be wrong. These flip-flops in population forecasts prove that forecasting is a dangerous subject that must be taken with a grain of salt.

In spite of the uncertain results of forecasting, data provided by some of the best demographers of our century have kept warning us once again about the dangers of overpopulation. They have insistently claimed that the world's population has been increasing at such high rates that a future food crisis and the total breakdown of our civilization is close at hand. The 1966 Club of Rome's famous report with its estimates on the rapidly declining resources of our planet had a tremendous impact on world opinion and seemed to corroborate the dire predictions of the prophets of gloom and doom.[7]

More recent statistics provided by well-known demographers and international organizations have tended to minimize those scary forecasts; and have seriously predicted that the world population is not only showing signs that it will soon reach its peak, but that there are already indications of a future steady decline in its absolute rate of growth. They clearly indicate that in the more developed countries negative rates of natural increase will occur after the year 2000. In other words, the death rate will be higher than the birth rate. This decline in natural population growth rates will be partially compensated for by net immigration, but only until the year 2005. Given the present political trends in Western Europe and the other more developed nations of the world, net migration flowing into most of them will tend to taper off from the observed levels of the early 1990s. In the less developed countries, the negative natural rate increase will only appear after the year 2045.

The latest data provided by the United Nations seem to provide ample proof of this trend.[8] The "low/medium variant" (low/medium fertility scenario) projections of the likely future demographic trends indicate that by the year 2150 the world population will have increased by only 713 million people. On the contrary, if the "low variant" is applied total world population will fall to 3550 million in 2150.[9] According to these projections, and using the same "low/medium" variant, the world population would increase form 5687 million in 1995 to 6400 million in the year 2150. In the case of Europe, the decrease in population would be even more significant, from 728 million in 1995 to 368 million in 2150. Applying the "low/medium," variant which would be more appropriate for Europe given its low fertility rates, the continent's total population would fall to 137 million in 2150.

Assuming the trend toward continued low or even lower fertility rates in most areas of the world, the human population will crest around the year 2050 at about 7.7 billion people, and then begin to fall dramatically. This phenomenon will be accompanied by a substantial geographical shift in the world population from the more developed regions to the countries in the process of development. The share of the world population living in the currently more developed countries will shrink from 19 to 10 percent between the years 1995 and 2150.

These projections of the United Nations do not assume the possibility of future catastrophes, as Malthus had assumed in his famous book on population published in the nineteenth century.[10] The projected global depopulation of the second century of the second millennium has not been calculated on the basis of possible famines, wars, or plagues, as Malthus had envisioned. If these calamitous events were to take place, the projected depopulation would be much greater. But, even leaving aside these catastrophic factors, projections of future demographic trends in the more developed countries do reflect persistent low fertility rates combined with higher life expectancy ratios and continued immigration flows. These projections may differ significantly depending on the database used.

Declining Fertility Rates and the Rise in Life Expectancy

According to the United Nations, the world's average fertility level in 1990–1995 was 3.0 births per woman of childbearing age. However, this average figure does not show the disparity in rates between different areas of the world. Fertility rates for major areas and regions of the world (1990-1995) varied from a low of 1.6 in Europe to a high of 5.8 in Africa. In the other major regions of the world, fertility rates were as follows: Asia 3.0, Latin America and the Caribbean 3.1, North America 2.1 and Oceania (Australia and New Zealand) 2.5.[11]

Average fertility rates in the more developed countries fell to a low of 1.69 for the period 1990–1995. This rate is well below the 2.1 required for long term replacement of generations. In Western Europe the following nine countries had fertility rates of 1.5 or less: Italy (1.2), Spain (1.3), Germany (1.3), Austria (1.5), Greece (1.5) and Portugal (1.5). Another six countries had fertility rates of 2 or less than 2. They were, Belgium, Denmark, France, Netherlands, Norway, and Switzerland.[12]

In Eastern Europe, fertility rates declined precipitously from 1980–1985 to 1990–1995. They fell in every single country, including the Baltic States, from 2.1 to 1.6. The decline was especially acute in the Russian Federation, from 2.1 to 1.5. These low fertility rates in Western and Eastern Europe contrast sharply with the much higher fertility rates in Asia (3.0), Latin America and the Caribbean (3.1), not to mention its neighbors to the south in Africa (5.8).

On the other hand, during the period 1990–1995, Western Europe had an average life expectancy of 76.7 years. In Eastern Europe and the Baltic countries the average life expectancy was 72 years. The Russian Federation experienced the lowest life expectancy (66.5) and recent data tend to indicate that there has been no improvement during the last two years. The low life expectancy rate in Eastern Europe and the Baltic States was mainly the result of an extremely poor health situation which was responsible for the region's high mortality rates. However, the drastic decline in population that occurred in Eastern Europe and the Baltic States was due, in large part, to international migration which was to be 1.4 million during the same period 1990–1995.

Radical Changes in the Age Structure of the World's Population

The declining birth rates, resulting from the low fertility rates, together with the assumption that life expectancy at birth will rise significantly, will affect drastically the age structure of the world's population. All demographers agree that the world's population is getting older whilst the young are diminishing both in absolute and relative numbers, a trend that can have serious consequences for the planet's future economic growth. The major impact of these changes will be felt in the more developed countries, in particular Western Europe, where the declining birth rates have reached critical proportions.

For many years the world has been hearing about the threat posed on society by a dangerously high total dependency ratio which is defined as the population 0 to 14 and 65 and over to the population aged 15 to 64 (the economically active population). However, the dependency ratio was often understood as the ratio between the number of children aged from birth to 14 years of age and the total active population. Emphasis was always placed on the theory that the greater the number of children in relation to the economically active population, the larger would be the dependency ration and, consequently, it was concluded that the standard of living would be higher if the birth rates were lower. There would be fewer children of an unproductive age to be taken care of by the economically active population who, as a result, would be able to enjoy a greater share of the nation's output. The argument was used to justify population control policies that would reduce the birth rate and lower the child dependency ratio. Very little, if anything, was said about the aging of the population and the elderly dependency ratio which relates the older and retired persons with the economically active population.[13]

Nevertheless, counter to the expectations of the prophets of doom and gloom, fertility rates are declining and the population is rapidly aging both in absolute and in relative numbers.[14] It is ironic that it now turns out that one of the greatest dangers to the economic and social stability of the industrialized countries is not the persistence of high fertility rates but the aging of the population and the critically high elderly dependency ratios.[15] Although it may be true that simple arithmetic would give credence to the fact that, in the short run, each additional baby means less goods to go around, it is also true that as the population grows older each person in the labor force has a larger number of elderly people to support and the cost of supporting a retired person is much greater than supporting a child.

The drop in the child dependency ratio due to the fertility decline will not necessarily free resources to meet the needs of the growing older population. It has been shown that reallocating resources from children to old people is an arduous and difficult task. Serious studies have demonstrated that in the Organization for Economic Cooperation and Development (OECD) countries public spending per old person on social services and transfers have been 2–3 times larger than public spending per child.[16] Public and private resources freed up will be significantly less than those needed by the aging population. Furthermore, the fewer the number of children per family, the greater will be the tendency to invest in each child and as a result fewer resources will be available at the margin. Thus, both the young and the old will need increasing costly social services and financial support. To meet these needs will require a thorough reevaluation of existing social security systems.

The High Cost of Old Age Social Security Systems and the Increasing Dependency Ratios

Old age social security systems are in trouble worldwide. As community and government based arrangements are beset by escalating costs which require high tax rates, the burden of responsibility for maintaining the aging population will fall more and more into the hands of private individuals and families.

Furthermore, the changing values on the role of women in society has created conditions which tend to favor the gradual movement of women from the home to the work-place. Economic reasons have also forced many families to rely on both parents joining the work force. Otherwise, they would not be able to maintain a reasonable standard of living that would permit them to educate their children in a satisfactory manner. Expenditures in our contemporary consumer society have become so weighty that the average working family cannot prosper without the additional income provided by the working mother. These trends do not seem to be propitious for a reversal of the declining fertility rates in Western Europe, at least in the short run.

There is also the added problem that by the year 2050 more than 55 percent of the world's women will be outside childbearing age. The situation will be even worse in the industrialized nations where it is estimated that over 65 percent of all women would not fall within the reproductive range. This is in sharp contrast with the approximately 50 percent figure which demographers believe was the percentage of women of childbearing age in the past.

The real tragedy of this hazardous trend is the fact that the number of young people, the cream and future of any healthy society, will decline within the total population in both absolute and relative terms. By the year 2050, it is estimated that adolescents and young adults will represent less than 12 percent of the world population. This constitutes a significant fall when compared with the 18 percent of 1995. The decline in the industrialized nations will be even worse, less than 9 percent.

The full realization of the economic and social consequences of the rapid aging process has not dawned yet on large sectors of the population. They are still not fully aware that the present demographic trends of longer lives and falling fertility rates has brought about a radical aging of the human population, a phenomenon never before experienced in the history of mankind. Europe, in particular, is exposed to the dangers of an aging population that will require ever increasing security assistance when the old are no longer able to maintain themselves. The consumer oriented societies of our postmodern age, with their tendency to have low savings rates, do not seem to provide adequate mechanisms for a viable and satisfactory solution of this very real and threatening problem.

The gravity of the situation should not be underestimated. The figures speak for themselves. The short-term demographic outlook leaves no doubt that by the year 2030 the elderly dependency ratios will have reached 49.2 percent in Germany, 48.3 percent in Italy and almost 40 percent in France and the United Kingdom, more than double what they are today. Population aging is less pronounced in the United States and in Canada. Nevertheless, the elderly dependency ratios will reach almost 40 percent by the year 2030. After the year 2030, elderly dependency ratios are expected to stabilize in most countries except Japan and Italy where they will experience a further increase of ten percentage points.

By the year 2030, the projected long-term increase in the very elderly dependency ratio will reach slightly over 48 percent in France and Italy.[17] In Sweden the rate is expected to attain 52.2 percent and approximately 45 percent in Germany, the United States, the U.K. and Canada. Japan will have the highest rate (56.3 percent) followed closely by Sweden (52.2 percent).[18]

The significant rise in the projected elderly dependency ratios of most countries is, to a large extent, due to the passage of the post-war baby-boom generation into retirement.[19] However, independently of the reasons for the rise in the projected elderly dependency ratios, the fact still remains that the world's population is aging rapidly.

In 1990 slightly more than 9 percent of the world's population (almost half a billion people) was 60 years or older. By the year 2030 the number will triple to 1.4 billion. In the OECD countries, the average percentage of the population over 60 years old will climb from 18.2 percent in 1990 to 30.8 percent in 2030. In Eastern Europe and the former Soviet Union the percentage rise will only be from 13.8 percent to 22.2 percent. The expected increase in North Africa and the Middle East will be from 6.2 percent in 1990 to 13.1 percent in the year 2030 whilst in Sub-Saharan Africa the rise will be much smaller, from 5.2 percent to 6.8 percent in 2030. Asia and Latin America will also sustain increases, from 6.3 percent to 11.6 percent in the former and from 8.2 percent to 16.4 percent in the latter.

The need for new arrangements for old age security becomes more critical as the percentage of the population over 60 increases and that of the young decreases. By the year 2030, when the very elderly dependency ratios will have reached an average of approximately 50 percent in Western Europe, the Old Continent will face a critical stage.[20] The traditional old age security arrangements will have to be reformed and made more viable if social upheavals are to be avoided. Public and private institutions have no choice but to take the necessary measures that will help solve a rapidly deteriorating situation. A just and satisfactory solution must be found, keeping in mind the well-being of the old and the young who, at the same time, cannot disavow the serious responsibility that they have towards their elders.

As most countries can no longer afford the formal programs of old age security that, in many cases, are on the verge of bankruptcy, the need for a thorough reevaluation of existing policies is no longer a question of debate. It is an accepted fact that liberal early retirement schemes and generous benefits can no longer be maintained. The fabulous and idealistic goals of the Welfare State have proved to be unattainable. The state itself also has its limitations, as recent events have demonstrated. Can the Welfare State survive the challenges of the twenty-first century? At present it seems doubtful unless it experiences fundamental changes more in accordance with the needs of our times and the resources available.

The Crisis of the Welfare State

During the years following the Second World War, the trend toward the Welfare State seemed irreversible. "Freedom from Want" and the guarantee of security for everybody, together with drastic income redistribution policies, became the main objectives of the numerous Economic Plans introduced by many European socialist governments. The utopian promises of "Freedom from Want" and general welfare became well-know slogans in the European political scene of the sixties and seventies. It was believed by many a prominent economist and social scientist, not to mention politicians, that the Welfare State was capable of solving the most pressing problems of postmodern society. The state, with its generous distributive plans and social security schemes, was to become the *deus ex machina* that would eliminate poverty whilst, at the same time, posing no overwhelming macroeconomic threat to future generations. The state was to become a sort of Father Christmas in charge of the distribution of "goodies" – as if that were the normal and only way of satisfying the needs of large sectors of the population. The goal of "Freedom from Want" would finally be attained through the generosity and patronage of government authorities.

The optimism and faith in the bounties of the Welfare State that characterized the sixties and seventies gradually turned to skepticism, even among those who had most strongly espoused its interventionist policies. After years of Welfare State initiatives, many countries are beginning to realize that the utopian ideals of its sponsors – among them Freedom from Want – have not materialized. On the contrary, there are already signs of possible economic and social upheavals in the near future if present trends continue. As we mentioned in a paper on the Welfare State and its ethical implications: "The costs of the Welfare State have become too high even for the industrialized countries to afford. Governments no longer have the financial means to maintain the same level of public expenditures without running into serious economic difficulties."[21]

It is a well-known fact that the budget deficits of many European countries are at an all-time high.[22] The rise in unemployment rates complicates even more an already deteriorating budget deficit situation, threatening the political and social stability of the continent and casting a shadow on the future of the Euro. Drastic austerity measures, although unpopular, will have to be taken in order to reduce government expenditures and alleviate an already overburdened deficit. The European governments are well aware of the great need to reevaluate their social security systems and their often abusive redistribution policies. If they are not able to cut their deficits to 3 percent of gross domestic product (GDP), the European Union may become another utopia for future historians to discuss.

France, for example, with its over-extended Welfare System, has no choice but to re-evaluate its entire social security system. The French fully realize that the time has arrived for the government to take action and inform the public about the seriousness of the problem: the near-bankruptcy of the Welfare State. The government realizes that if it does not take strong measures in the areas of social security, pension plans, etc., France faces, at a not too distant future, a rude awakening, the consequences of which can be disastrous for the French nation. The numerous strikes that took place in November-December 1995, were already scary warnings of what might come later.[23]

It seems that for many European countries the moment of truth has finally arrived. The great Welfare State ideal of the famous Lord Beveridge has run afoul of its own grandiose expectations.[24] The Beveridge Report in England promoted a much larger role for the government in old-age security. Under the assumption that the government was able to compensate for private market failures, he saw publicly financed pensions as a way for the state to guarantee a minimum income to all older persons. The pension was clearly meant to provide a very generous pension to the old.[25] However, his belief that no power less than the state "can ensure adequate total outlays at all times" has not materialized. It is time that the Europeans become aware that the state is not omnipotent and cannot solve all problems. With the below-replacement fertility rates and increasing longevity, the elderly dependency ratio has increased to such a level that the usual pay-as-you-go retirement system can no longer be sustained. The entire system is on the verge of bankruptcy. To avoid such an outcome the only viable alternatives are to increase taxes, reduce pensions benefits, or increase significantly the retirement age. But these are alternatives which are difficult to enforce in democratic states where the retirees and older generations constitute such a large proportion of the total population.

Governments that find themselves with serious budget problems, as is the case in many European countries, will no longer be able to finance the overgenerous social security plans that were promised by the Welfare State. It is obvious that the State will no longer be able to maintain the level of expenditures that it had in the past, especially when government spending represents one-half of the GDP. The tax load is already so heavy that in certain countries tax revenues represent almost 50 percent of GDP. Thus, the need for cuts in social programs which are no longer indispensable becomes imperative.

When people of working age outnumber the retirement age group (five to one), the danger of the social security system going into bankruptcy is less imminent and the much needed revisions can be postponed, at least in the short run. However, once the ratio of the economically active population to the retirees falls and becomes two to one, as it is expected to be in the year 2050, the situation becomes really critical. Therefore, drastic revisions of the social security system must start taking place much before that date if total bankruptcy is to be avoided with its concomitant disastrous effects for the economy.

Time does not permit us to go into the various restructuring plans that have been suggested. Perhaps, in order to avoid further encroachments on the private lives of the population and reduce the size of an overburdened State, the solution may lie in the privatization of social insurance.[26] The challenge consists in devising new old age security systems that are acceptable to the old but that do not hamper sustainable economic growth and the proper development of the young. The family may have to be called to play a new and more significant role in this important area of social security for the elderly as the world approaches the dawn of the new millennium.

The Benefits Derived from the Traditional Large Families

The sharp decline in fertility rates will unavoidably affect the composition of the family. If the present sub-replacement fertility rates continue, as they are expected to do according to United Nations estimates, the family will undoubtedly experience substantial changes. With fertility rates in many European countries below 1.5 percent, the former family units composed of grandparents, aunts and uncles, not to mention cousins, etc. will be a thing of the past. The cohesiveness and unity of the traditional large family will be replaced by a family composed of a single son or daughter, his parents, and grandparents. The only child of the future "progressive" family will no longer have the benefit of enjoying the assistance and advice of relatives who in the past had often served as a fallback when the family was experiencing difficulties and had to rely on them for assistance.

On the basis of the existing estimates on population trends that we have discussed above, it is not too difficult to visualize the new typology of the family in the years to come. It is still too early to determine with certainty the economic and social consequences of such a change in the family structure. However, Nicholas Eberstadt does give us a good idea as to how family and social life will change under these new parameters. He says the following: "Throughout the remembered human experience, the family has been the primary and indispensable instrument for socializing a people. In the family, the individual found extended bonds of obligation and reciprocal resources – including emotional resources – upon which he could draw." Under the demographic projections generally accepted, he continues, "all that would change momentously. For many people, 'family' would be understood as a unit that does not include any biological contemporaries or peers."[27]

The aging of the population will only aggravate an already precarious situation. As the population grows older, there is a greater need for a secure source of income for old age. Governments have mechanisms to provide income security for the elderly as part of the social safety net to reduce inequalities and other economic needs of the poor and unemployed. But as formal programs are beset by increasing costs that require high tax rates and deter private sector growth, a viable alternative may lie in informal arrangements, especially those that are family based.

It was common in the past, and even today in large areas of the world, for informal and traditional arrangements to take care of the old, providing them with some type of income security. The elderly would receive from close relatives or extended family the necessary requirements of food and shelter. But, as the size of the families becomes smaller and smaller the burden of assistance increasingly falls on a smaller number of family members. In some cases, an only grandson or granddaughter. In addition, as employment opportunities for the younger generation increase, the opportunity cost of taking care of the old increases and the young are less willing to dedicate time and effort to satisfy the needs of their progenitors. The same occurs with those women who, in order to supplement their household income, have found it necessary to find outside jobs away from the family rather than to remain at home and take care of the young and the old that need assistance. This trend has become more acute as the number of women in the labor market has increased significantly. These changing family patterns have weakened traditional arrangements for income security for the old as in the case of the extended family.

The family has always been considered the foundation on which is based the broader communion of parents and children, of brothers and sisters, and of relatives and other members of the household. The union that characterizes the interpersonal relationships of the family has constituted the inner strength that animates the family and the community. All members of the family share in the responsibility for the care of small children, the sick, and the aged. But, this family communion will occur only when parents educate their children in an environment of responsible freedom and a spirit of self-giving.

To avoid the many and varied forms of tension and discord that frequently appear in families, parents have the responsibility to prepare their children form early childhood for the day when they become adults and claim their rightful independence to be free from parental authority. At the same time, they must be taught to avoid selfishness and develop a spirit of sacrifice and self-giving, a difficult task in our contemporary materialistic society. This is the only way to achieve the fullness of community life within the family and its broader ramifications in society. Otherwise, societies will continue to be torn and split by tensions caused by a false understanding of freedom and unrestrained individual and group interests; this is especially true of societies that lack the necessary moral principles that will help curb the excesses of man's selfishness.

With the arrival of the industrial revolution and in the wake of disordered industrial and urban development, family bonds have been weakened and the spirit of sacrifice and service has been evaporating gradually. It is precisely the weakening of these family bonds and spirit of sacrifice, together with a decline in moral principles, that may limit the effectiveness of the role of the family as a partial substitute for the existing and nearly bankrupt public security arrangements. The family, undermined by a spirit of selfishness, and guided by utilitarian principles that do not recognize the virtues of sacrifice and self-giving, will be deprived of playing the role for which it is naturally fitted: the protection and assistance of the elderly, especially those within its own extended family. What a lost opportunity this would be!

Conclusions

If by modernity is meant the gradual breakdown of many of the principles and values which, through the ages, constituted the foundation of our civilization, then modernity means that the world is on the path to self-destruction. Selfishness grounded on a utilitarian philosophy that stresses the importance of the "ego" and considers all past values as "*demode*" cannot but lead in the end to a society that rests on the Darwinian principle "the survival of the fittest." Such a philosophy carried *à outrance* leaves no place for love and understanding and much less for the non-productive infirm and the old.

In a depopulated world, the family, or better still, the family of the future, will be reduced to a minimum expression in which the very concept of close relatives will be a thing of the past. Based on purely utilitarian principles and under the influence of "modernity" with its new set of "morals," the value of a person will be measured almost exclusively in terms of his material contribution to society. Under those circumstances, it would not seem very probable that the younger generation, educated and formed under those set of principles, would be inclined to finance the security of its elders. The opportunity cost, measured in dollars and cents, would be too high.

In spite of the failure of the Welfare State, there would still be people who would place on the public sector the responsibility for the care of the sick and elderly. The claim would persist that, given the fact that the elderly did not take the necessary provisions for the future during their productive years, the young should not be held responsible for their needs. However, the problem remains as to how the state with a bankrupt public social security system will be able to assist in the near future the increasing number of elderly people.

A philosophy based on the principle that "in the end we will all be dead" tends to lead to a society that scorns savings and is geared toward consumption. The enjoyment of life in the present takes precedence over the virtue of saving for the future. The future will take care of itself! A rude awakening may be in store for those who still believe that there is always the state to rely on in time of need. If the young follow this philosophy, they will have to confront problems similar to the ones facing their parents and grandparents.

A society ruled by such norms, where selfishness and pure egotism prevail, has no time for unremunerated sacrifice and self-giving. To expect that the family will play a significant role among the informal security arrangements that are under discussion is extremely doubtful unless there is a renewal in family values and a deeper understanding of the positive effects of human virtues.

Unfortunately, a so-called "progressive" society guided primarily by utilitarian principles will most certainly not nurture among the young the development of a virtuous life. Consequently, individuals and families, carried away by their materialistic and selfish interests, will not be inclined to accept generously the responsibility and burden of assisting the elderly, the sick, and the infirm. On the contrary, they would still claim that the responsibility for their care, rests on a vague term called "society," whatever that may mean. As a result, the elderly will be neglected in ways that are totally unacceptable, not only because of the suffering it causes them, but also because of the spiritual impoverishment of many families that no longer would enjoy the love and understanding of the elderly.

Among the victims of this late twentieth century phenomenon which is characterized by declining birth rates and the aging of the population, the elderly have been especially affected. As the productive years of the old tend to be a thing of the past, they are considered no longer a useful asset for society and are liable to be easily ignored or even discarded. This danger is not to be taken lightly.

The increasing demand for what is now called mercy killings or assisted suicide cannot be ignored in a society that is gradually running the risk of becoming more depersonalized and inhuman.

However, the family still possesses sufficient energies capable of rescuing man from his dehumanizing selfishness. It has the potential of making its members aware of their personal dignity, whether young or old, and by so doing contribute also to the improvement and stability of society. Inspired and guided by the principle of self-giving, the family can serve as the perfect catalyst for performing acts of service and solidarity. There is no better way to demonstrate this spirit of self-giving than by assisting those family members who, because of illness or old age, can no longer help themselves, and to whom the young generations owe an eternal debt of gratitude. The new generations of the young should always remember the contribution made by their parents and grandparents to their lives. They should not hesitate to give them the much needed security and love that they need and long for during the declining years of their lives.

Over two thousand years ago Aesop, the great Greek writer of fables, wrote in "The Frog and the Ox": "Gratitude is the sign of noble souls." Let us hope that the new millennium will bring to our disturbed world many noble souls that will not hesitate to meet their family obligations in a spirit of true self-giving and love. The economic needs of the population will best be served in an environment of love and mutual solidarity and this has to start within the family where parents and children learn to live in harmony and mutual assistance.

Notes

1. Ambassador Alberto M. Piedra is Professor Economics at the Catholic University of America. He has published widely on economics and ethical issues. From 1984 to 1987 he served as U.S. Ambassador to Guatemala. He holds earned doctoral degrees in law (University of Havana), political economy (University of Madrid), and economics (Georgetown University).

2. The well know French demographer Alfred Sauvy for many years has been warning his countrymen of the dangers posed by declining fertili-

ty rates. He unequivocally mentions that governments have tended to ignore the negative consequences of such a trend, in particular with respect to the aging of the population and the continuous decline in the relative number of young people. As far back as 1987 he went as far as to say that the aging of the population can be just as dangerous for France as the spread of AIDS. He claimed: *"Bien moins connu, bien moins redoute que le SIDA, le vieillissement de la population. Il reste a savoir lequel est le plus dangereux pour la nation. Edifiant serait un sondage sur cette question, suivi d'une etude serieuse."* See: Alfred Sauvy, *L'Europe Submergee* (Paris: Dunod, 1987), p. 128.

3. When asked how he would define the "white plague," Chaunu answered: *"Qu'est-ce que la peste blanche? La desesperance generalisee. L'indifference a la vie, le refus de tout systeme de valeurs, l'egoisme presente comme le plus raffine des beaux-arts."* See Pierre Chaunu and Georges Suffert, *La Peste Blanche, Comment eviter le suicide de l'Occident* (Paris: Editions Gallimard, 1976), p. 8.

4. See Paul R. Ehrlich, *The Population Bomb* (New York: A Sierra Club Ballantine Book, Ballantine Books, 1971), chs. 1 and 5. See also Donella H. Meadows, Dennis L. Meadows, Jorgen Randers, and William W. Behrens, III, *The Limits of Growth* (New York: Universe Books, 1972).

5. See United Nations, *World Population Prospects, as Assessed in 1963* (New York: United Nations, 1966). See also U.S. Department of State Bulletin, Washington, DC, 1969. Data taken from Julian L. Simon, *The Ultimate Resource* (Princeton, NJ: Princeton University Press, 1981), p.169.

6. In the 1930s the fear was exactly the opposite. A large number of countries were concerned with the expected decline in population growth. This was particularly true in the case of France. Many prominent economists were predicting stagnation as one of the most important dynamic variables of growth; and population was expected to decline. See among others, Alvin Hansen, *Business Cycle Theory* (Boston: Ginn & Company, 1927); *Full Recovery or Stagnation?* (New York: McGraw-Hill Book Company, 1938); and *Fiscal Policy and Business Cycle* (New York: W. W. Norton & Company, 1941).

7. Among the better known prophets of gloom and doom during the 1960s and 70s the following can be mentioned: Donella H. Meadows,

Dennis L. Meadows, Jorgen Randers, and William W. Behrens, III, *The Limits to Growth*, A Report by the *Club of Rome's* Project on the Predicament of Mankind (New York: Universe Books, 1972). See also Paul R. Ehrlich, *The Population Bomb* (New York: A Sierra Club/Ballantine Book, 1968); Rene Dumont & Bernard Rosier, *The Hungry Future* (New York, Praeger Publishers, 1969); and William & Paul Paddock, *Famine 1975! America's Decision: Who Will Survive?* (Boston: Little, Brown & Company, 1967). On the other hand, there were prominent economists during that same period who challenged their pessimistic views on the future of the world. See Colin Clark, "World Population (1958)," in *Population,* ed. Edward Pohlman (New York: A Mentor Book from the New American Library, 1973); Julian Simon, "Science Does Not Show that There Is Overpopulation in the U.S. – or Elsewhere," in *Population*, ed. Pohlman; and, finally, Simon Kuznets, *Population, Capital and Growth* (New York: W. W. Norton Inc., 1973).

8. See Department of Economic and Social Affairs, Population Division, United Nations Secretariat, *World Population Projections to 2150* (New York, NY: February 1998).

9. The United Nations data on fertility rates present six possible fertility scenarios, ranging from high fertility to low fertility. Medium fertility rates which lie at the center of the projection scenario imply that each woman of child bearing age will have 2.2 children. The fertility gap between the high (more than two) and the low fertility (less than two) scenarios is about one child. The average fertility rate in Europe was approximately 1.4 in 1997 whilst in Africa it was above 2.5. As the world fertility trends seem to fluctuate between 2 and 1.5, we will use the low/medium scenario for the purpose of this paper. See: United Nations Secretariat, Population Division, New York, February 1998.

10. Thomas Malthus, *On Population* (New York: Random House, 1960).

11. See United Nations, Population Division, Department of Economic and Social Information and Policy Analysis, World Population Prospects, 1995.

12. The contrast between the large and increasing population of the impoverished nations of the world and the rapidly declining population of the rich countries, especially in Europe, is so great that even novel-

ists have written about the threat such a gap poses for Western civilization. See Jean Raspail, *Le Camp des Saints*. (Paris: Editions Robert
Laffont, 1985).

13. See Alberto Martinez Piedra, "The Welfare State and its Ethical
Implications: A Viable Alternative for Post-Castro Cuba?" *Cuba in
Transition*, vol. 6 (Springfield, MD: ASCE Books, 1997), pp. 352–72.

14. Conscious of the fact that the aging of the world's population represents an unparalleled, but urgent, challenge to governments, non-governmental organizations and private groups, the United Nations General
Assembly (resolution 47/5) decided that the year 1999 be observed as
the "International Year of Older Person." See "The Aging of the
World's Population," United Nations, Department of Public
Information, DPI/1858/AGE, October 1996.

15. Elderly dependency ratios are defined as "the ratio of the population
aged 65 and over to the population aged 15 to 64." International
Monetary Fund, *Aging Population and Public Pension Schemes*
(Washington, DC, 1996), p. 4.

16. OECD (1998) (cited in Palmer, Smeeding, and Torrey, 1998).

17. The very elderly ratio is defined as the population aged 75 and over
as a percent of the population aged 65 and over. International Monetary
Fund, *op. cit.*, p. 4.

18. Ibid., p. 4.

19. Ibid., p. 3.

20. Ibid., p. 4.

21. A. M. Piedra, "The Welfare State," p. 157.

22. For a very good analysis of the implications of the prospective aging
of the U.S. population for the security system see: Liam P. Ebrill, *Social
Security, Demographic Trends, and the Federal Budget*. Unpublished
manuscript, The International Monetary Fund, Washington, DC, March
1990.

23. For an excellent summary of the many problems facing the Welfare
State in France, see: Patrice Bourdelais, Xavier Gaullier, Marie Jose
Imbault-Huart, Denis Olivennes, Jean-Marie Poursin, Francois Stasse,
Etat-providence, Arguments pour une reforme. (Paris: Editions
Gallimard, 1996). It is in this book that the authors ask the pertinent
question: *"Qui l'ignore? La reforme de l'Etat-providence constitue
l'horizon indepassable de nos prochaines annees. Probablement les*

greves de novembre-decembre, 1995, ont-elles marque un tourant a cet egard, l'entree dans une phase de turbulances durables."

24. William H. Beveridge, *Full Employment in a Free Society* (New York: W. W. Norton & Company, 1945), p. 36.

25. A. Atkinson, *State Pensions, Taxation and Retirement Income: 1981–2031* (London: Simon and Schuster International, 1989).

26. For an excellent study of the Chilean alternative to the public pension and health insurance system and its intention to replace the old system with a private sector security system see: G. A. Mackenzie, *Social Security Issues in Developing Countries: The Latin American Experience.* Unpublished document issued by the International Monetary Fund, Washington, DC, February 22, 1988.

27. Nicholas Eberstadt, "World Population Implosion?" The Public Interest, Number 129, Fall 1997.

ESTIMATING THE CONTRIBUTION TO THE NATIONAL ECONOMY OF DIRECT PARENTAL CHILD CARE SERVICES

Dr. Guillermo Montes[1]

Introduction

Ambassador Piedra has mentioned that as the population ages there will be, among other consequences, important ramifications for child care services. I could not agree more. In her book *Who Needs Parents?* Patricia Morgan[2] describes how out-of-the-home child care is viewed in Britain as a demographic necessity. Mothers of young children are being pressured to join the labor force as a way to increase the labor supply of the country.

An increase in the female labor participation rate is good news for business. As women join the labor force they compete with each other and with men and keep wages low, which in turn helps keep inflation in check and contributes to a moderate interest rate policy. All of these likely consequences are favorable to business interests.

Yet, business interests are not necessarily national interests. Providing incentives for women to change occupation from full-time mothering to becoming full-time workers may or may not be an efficient proposition for the national economy. We often think that it is, but that is because we tacitly assume that women caring for their children at home are not engaged in any meaningful economic activity. Reinforcing this unstated assumption, that mothering does not count as work, is a complete blackout of the productivity of these women and their contribution to the national economy in the national economic statistics and accounts. Open the *Statistical Abstract of the United States*, and you will not find any direct information on what the contribution of these women to the national economy is. In fact, the national accounts simply omit the contribution to the national economy of the family-provided social service sector entirely.

Consequently, social services are counted as economic activity only when someone other than the family, typically government agencies, is paid for delivering them[3]. At the root of the whole issue lies the difficulty in solving the tough methodological and implementation issues needed to obtain a direct measure of the family contribution.

I have set for myself a limited task: to calculate a lower bound estimate of the contribution to the national economy of full-time direct parental child care services. I propose a thought experiment to by-pass the problems blocking any direct approach. Consider the following:

> *You wake up tomorrow to a different world. In this world, every parent who cares full-time for one or several children goes to the house of another such parent; they care for each other's children, and then they swap checks for the same amount.*

If we assume that a stranger is as well suited as a parent to care for a child,[4] then this experiment should result in no substantial change in the national economy. Someone else provides the service individually, but collectively, the same services are provided to the same children by the same providers. Yet, because now we have an exchange of checks, such services would qualify as economic activity, and hence are susceptible to measurement using standard approaches.

They are two ways to calculate the collective volume of these checks: child care worker's wages and going market price.

Approach 1: Each parent would provide a check for the typical child care worker wage to the other provider. Essentially, the parents estimate the payment by what people in a similar occupation are paid. It is an application of the equal pay for equal work principle.

Approach 2: Each parent would provide a check for the going rate for child care services times the number of children. This approach is an application of "the market price as value of service" rule.

Using readily available data from the *Statistical Abstract of the United States*,[5] the *Occupational Outlook Handbook*[6] and Casper's (1995)[7] report on the cost of caring for preschoolers, I will calculate an under-estimate (a lowest bound) of the full-time direct parental child care contribution to the economy. There are several reasons why my estimates are under-estimates:

> – First, I do not have data on all parents but only mothers. I under-estimate by ignoring the contribution of stay-at-home dads.
> – Second, I will concentrate exclusively on married mothers of children under 6 who are not in the labor force. I under-estimate because some non-married mothers are providing direct child care services; and because many part-time workers (who are thus in the labor force) are providing full-time direct parental child care as well. They are simply holding two jobs: one paid and the other unpaid.
> – Third, many parents provide direct parental care after-hours. If they were compensated for these activities we would classify them as weekend or after-school programs and consider them economically active. In this brief article, I am ignoring this after-school aspect, although it is potentially a very large contribution because it involves almost all parents of young children regardless of their working status.

Therefore, the numbers calculated here are *the lowest bound* of what the real economic contribution of parents providing direct parent care truly is.

Preliminary Calculations

Since some of the data I have is only available for or about 1994, I will provide calculations for 1994. For the purposes of this article, full time work is 2080 hours per year (40 hours a week for 52 weeks).

The number of married women with children under six out of the labor force in 1994 was 4,779,741.[8]

Solution 1: Paying These Women a Fair Wage

The approach of Solution 1 is very simple. How much should a mother be paid for caring full-time for her children? This is not an idle question, by the way. In Europe, countries like Spain are seriously considering paying women who choose their traditional occupation. I will provide two estimates: a rock-bottom estimate utilizing the minimum wage, and a more reasonable estimate using the median child care worker wage.

Rock-bottom Estimate

Regardless of the quality of these mothers' service provision, if they had done it for pay they would be compensated at least with the minimum wage. A full-time mother in 1994, receiving the minimum wage, would have an annual wage income of $5,921.76. The collective earnings of this sector would thus be *$48.03 billion.*[9]

Since the minimum wage has increased considerably since 1994, in 1997 full-time married mothers of children six or under would collectively receive some $46.59 billion.

A More Reasonable Answer

A more reasonable answer would be to pay these mothers what we pay other people (mostly women) who work in the child-care field. The 1996 *Occupational Outlook Handbook* reports that in 1994 the median wage income of child-care workers was $260 per week.[10] Therefore, each mom would be paid an annual income of $13,520. Collectively, this sector would receive wages totaling $64.62 billion dollars.

Approach 2: Paying the Going Market Rate

The second approach has each parent writing the check for the going market care for child-care services times the number of children. Therefore, I first need an estimate of number of children under six in the households of married mothers with children in that age range. Table 77 from the *Statistical Abstract of the United States* shows that 15 percent of all families had 1 child and 7 percent had two or more children under age six. Since, by definition, all the families in the analysis have one or more children under six, the resulting average is 1.32 children per family for the mothers we are studying.

This is a *conservative estimate* for two reasons. First, we counted every family with more than 2 children as having *only* two children under age six. Second, women who choose not to work in the labor force are more likely to have more children than their counterparts in the labor force because child care costs increase with the number of children.

Again, I will provide a rock-bottom estimate using data from the Survey of Income and Program Participation, and a more reasonable estimate using per-pupil expenditures form the public school elementary instruction.

Rock-Bottom Estimate (SIPP-Data)

Casper (1995),[11] using data from the Survey of Income and Program Participation, reported that in 1993 the hourly price of day care for working for pay mothers was $1.85. I will assume this price was stable until the end of 1994. This number is low because child care is more expensive for infants than for preschoolers, among other reasons because the adult to child ratio is smaller. Therefore, this figure will be used as our rock-bottom estimate using payment data.

At $1.85 per hour, full-time child-care for one child will have an annual price tag of $3,848. Collectively, this sector would pay that amount per mother for 1.32 children resulting in $24.24 billion.

Reasonable Estimate

A more reasonable estimate would use the per-pupil cost of elementary school, which was $5,333 in 1994.[12] This estimate is reasonable because New York and Georgia have instituted universal pre-kindergarten services, with an on-going national debate on the issue; and also because the adult to child ratios are larger for elementary school instruction than for pre-kindergarten services. In addition, in its "Principles for Financing Reform" regarding child-care by Gomby et al. (1996),[13] it is stated that the financing system should eliminate inconsistencies between child care and early education policies. This is a movement to eradicate the lines between child care and early education.

As a form of corroboration, data from Rochester's child care council on actual full-time child care prices (including both center and family day care) averaged $115.02 per week (more expensive for center care and for younger children), which is the equivalent of $5,521.20 annually per child.

At a cost of $5,333 per child, this sector would collectively pay $33.60 billion.

In summary, the contribution of married mothers providing direct child-care services to their children under six ranges from $24 billion to $60 billion. The $24 billion estimate pays the mothers less than what we pay any other worker in America, the minimum wage. All estimates paid equal or less than the median child-care worker wage. (A Table at the end summarizes all these calculations.)

Size of Sector

As related to government expenditures: The sector of married women with children under six engaged in full-time child care is equivalent to anywhere form 9 percent to 23 percent of the Federal government 1994 expenditures to support national defense or the department of Health and Human services. It is about the same size (0.7 to 1.9 times) of the Department of Defense budget for research, development, evaluation, and testing. It is 9 to 24 times *larger* than what Americans spend to maintain the Federal Judiciary. It is 3 to 9 times *larger* that what Americans spent in international development and humanitarian assistance in 1994.[14]

As related to private industry: The sector of married women with children under six engaged in full-time child care is slightly larger (1 to 3 times) than the furniture and fixtures manufacturing industry, and the railroad transportation industry (1 to 2.6 times). It is about the same size as the motion picture industry (0.98 to 2.6 times), and the radio and television broadcasting industry (0.6 to 1.6 times).[15]

Remember that these are extremely conservative estimates. Nevertheless, we still find that the sector is an important portion of the American economy. Since this sector is only a slice of families' provisions of different social services (homeschooling, part-time child care, after-school programmed activities, transportation of children to activities, elder care, care for the disabled, job counseling, personal counseling, educational remedial services, etc.) I am quite certain that the family's contribution to the national economy via its provision of social services is very large indeed.

Since women have been the principal architects of the family social care system throughout history, undervaluing or completely ignoring the contribution of such services to the national economy and the development of nations is, plainly, an insidious form of sex discrimination.

Efficiency Issues

I would like to draw attention to a double standard present in much of society today, and to the implications this has for the relative efficiency of the domestic provision versus the government provision of child-care services.

When a mother has four children under six, the typical response from society is that it is almost an overwhelming mothering task. How can a mother provide a quality environment for her children when she must care for four young children simultaneously? And if caring for four children under six is tough, then what should we say about four infants? Perhaps it is an impossible task. Yet, if the mother goes to work as a child-care provider assigned to four infants, not only does she meet New York State regulations specifying the infant adult to child ratio as 1 to 4, but she would probably be regarded as having a good job, at a good quality center, performing a needed social service. This is clearly a hypocritical double standard.

Yet, this form of hypocrisy reveals that the mothers are more efficient and cost-effective because we have calculated their contribution at a low price for a service that not only meets, but it is vastly superior to, the regulations regarding adult to child ratios.

All of our estimates pay the mothers less than or equal to what we pay an average child-care worker. Yet, the adult to child ratio used to make the calculations was only 1.32, which is almost individualized care. Individualized care, if provided by government or market, would be much more expensive than what we pay now. In other words, by estimating the direct parental child care contribution using current numbers applicable for larger adult to child ratios, I am implicitly stating that the direct parental child care service is necessarily more cost-effective than its competitors.

This is not surprising. Mothers run a more efficient operation. They have lower transaction costs, no communication costs, no transportation costs, no hiring and promotion costs, no staff turnover costs, no background checks are needed, no costs derived from heterogeneity of parental values or between parental and center values, no security equipment to prevent strangers form kidnapping the child, and no cost from expensive state and federal regulations that have no practical application to their situation (like ADA compliance, etc.).

The child-care professional industry (particularly the government subsided and operated portion of it) cannot have better outcomes at a lower cost for the general population. To get comparable outcomes, quality is required. Quality, in turn, means professional staff, and that implies professional salaries. Those salaries are inevitably higher than the median salary of women working out of the home. The reasons why the child-care professional sector is asking for subsidies is because they cannot compete without them.

This is not to say, that interventions cannot show effects for families who have serious deprivation or neglect or some other condition that interferes with delivering child-care services properly speaking.[16]

In terms of public funds, the issue could not be easier. Since mothers who choose to care for their children full-time get no public funds of any kind (not even a tax credit for preschool equipment and materials!), there is absolutely no doubt that these women provide the service in a vastly more cost-effective manner to the taxpayer than equivalent care provided by subsidized public or private providers.

Policy Implications

There may very good economic reasons to help *particular* populations to afford child care. After all, two parents with full-time incomes at the minimum wage ($21,424 annually) would have to dedicate 42 percent of their pre-tax wage earnings to pay for good quality out of the home child care for two children (at a conservative $4,500 per child). However, the same argument can be made for helping families afford staying home to care for their children, if that is what they want. After all, one parent maintaining a family of four on the minimum wage ($10,712) cannot afford to have the other parent stay home.

The government's traditional concern with protecting women's occupational freedom, particularly in light of historic discrimination, is warranted; but it must be applied to protecting women's freedom to choose the traditional occupation as well. Increasingly, it is the traditional occupation women want to access but cannot. To ignore this issue is equivalent to stating officially that the mother who cares for her children at home does not work, that she only works if she cares for other's people children for pay. That is blatant occupational discrimination.

For the general population, however, there are few economic grounds on which to advocate financial incentives for families to choose home care over direct provision of care. Double-income families earn about $20,000 per year[17] more than single-income families. Is it fair to tax direct parental providers of child care to provide funds for families who contract out, are richer, and use a less cost-effective service? Would you tax a family who lives in the city, cannot save for college, and is providing child care in a cost-effective manner so that a suburban family with a nice college savings account can afford a less efficient child care arrangement?

From an economic point of view, the government should realize that the professional social service sector is an industry trying to obtain subsidies from the government to acquire unfairly a greater market share at the expense of America's cost-effective domestic sector. To help us obtain a more balanced perspective, let's consider how the current tax structure would look in a different industry.

The current situation would be similar to getting a credit on your taxes for buying GM cars but not any other firm's. The rationale would be that, according to GM, they make better cars! To boot, you would tax the people who cannot afford a car to pay for the subsidy. This is a form of protectionism, and it leads to services that are either of low quality and moderate cost, or of high quality and exorbitant cost. It simply makes no sense to tax poorer single-income families, so that a particular child care choice of richer families can deliver quality only at a cost that even the advocates themselves admit is so expensive America's families cannot afford it. *The government should abandon its protectionist policy.*

I propose that the government should be strictly neutral with respect to maternal occupational choice. Let these two sectors compete on equal terms. If the professional child care sector wants to have a bigger market share, let them earn it the old fashion way: *by providing better quality at lower cost.*

TABLE: SUMMARY OF CALCULATIONS[18]

The Check Is a Wage		The Check Is a Price	
Minimum wage[19] (Rock-bottom estimate)	Median child-care worker wage	SIPP data (Rock-bottom estimate)	Elementary school per pupil expenditures
$5,921.76	$13,520	$3,848	$5,333[20]
Annual Wage Inc.		Annual Price/Child	
$48.03 billion	$64.62 billion	$24.24 billion	$33.60 billion
Overall Contributions			

Notes

1. Dr. Guillermo Montes holds a Ph.D. in economics, and specializes in the economics of education, labor, and industrial organization. He is affiliated with the Center for Community Study at the University of Rochester, and is currently an adjunct professor there and research associate in the university's Primary Mental Health Project.

2. Morgan, Patricia, *Who Needs Parents? The Effects of Childcare and Early Education on Children in Britain and the USA* (London, U.K.: IEA Health and Welfare Unit, 1996).

3. The only exception to this occurs when a family member contracts with another family member to care for the child.

4. If one assumes that parents are better matched to care for their own

children, then this swap of payments and kids would result in a reduction of the cost-effectiveness of the service provision.

5. *Statistical Abstract of the United States: The National Data Book* (Washington, DC: U.S. Department of Commerce, 1997).

6. *Occupational Outlook Handbook*, 1996–97 Edition. U.S. Department of Labor.

7. Casper, Lynne, "What Does It Cost to Mind Our Preschoolers?" (1995). Current Population Reports 70–52.

8. *Statistical Abstract of the United States*, Table 631. There were 7.7 million married women with children under 6 in the labor force. 61.7 percent of all women in that category were in the labor force. The remaining 38.3 percent would be 4,779,741. Calculated by ([1-participation rate]/participation rate)* number of married mothers with children under six in the labor force.

9. This is simply the annual wage earnings times the number of workers.

10. Ibid.

11. Ibid.

12. Scott Derks, ed., *The Value of a Dollar: 1860–1999* (Lakeville, CT: Grey House Publishing, 1999).

13. Gomby, Deanna S., Mary B. Larner, Donna L. Terman, Nora Krantzler, Carol Stevenson, and Richard Behrman, "Financing Child Care: Analysis and Recommendations," in *The Future of Children*, 6/2 (1996), pp. 5–25.

14. *Statistical Abstract of the United States*, Table 520. In 1994, federal outlays for the judiciary were $2,552 million, $278,901 million for the Department of Health and Human Services, $281,642 million for national defense (including 34,762 for research and development, testing, and evaluation), and $7,049 million for international development and humanitarian assistance.

15. *Statistical Abstract of the United States*, Table 693. In 1994, the manufacturing, furniture, and fixtures industry was $19 billion, railroad transportation was $24.3 billion, radio and television broadcasting was $39.7 billion, and the movie industry was $24.8 billion.

16. While preschool works as a compensatory intervention helping children from deprived or neglected backgrounds, there is no evidence that it would help other children. See Barnett, W. Stephen, *The Future of*

Children (1995), pp. 3, 5, 31–5, on long–term effects of early childhood programs on cognitive and school outcomes. See also David Elkind, *Miseducation: Preschoolers at Risk* (New York: Knopf, 1987).

17. Robert Rector, "Facts about American Families and Day Care," FYI No. 170 (The Heritage Foundation, 1998).

18. Figures are for 1994. Source: *Statistical Abstract of United States, Occupational Handbook,* and Casper, "What Does It Cost to Mind Our Preschoolers? (1995). SIPP = Survey of Income and Program Participation. Full-time workweek = 2080 hours per year. In 1994, there were 4,779,741 married mothers with children under six out of the labor force. Each family had an average of 1.32 children under six. Median child-care worker income is $260 per week. Hourly price of child care is $1.85.

19. In 1997, the estimate would be $46.6 billion.

20. Data from Rochester's child-care council on actual full-time child-care prices (including both center and family day care) averaged $115.02 per week (more expensive for center care and for younger children), which is the equivalent of $5,521.20 annually per child.

SESSION VI
CONTRACEPTION AND THE CULTURE OF DEATH

CONTRACEPTION AND THE CULTURE OF DEATH
Dr. William E. May[1]

Introduction

The title of this paper will offend many people, both Catholic and non-Catholic, who can see no connection between contraception and the "culture of death." For most people in our society, Catholic and non-Catholic as well, contraception by married persons is regarded as "natural." It is the obvious thing to do if there are good reasons for avoiding a pregnancy; and the suggestion that there is a link between contraception and the "culture of death" is considered outrageous, in particular by married couples who are "pro-life," but who nonetheless believe that there is nothing wrong with contraception.

Many people committed to the culture of life and unalterably opposed to the culture of death – people like Gilbert Meilaender, Philip Turner, James Nuechterlein, and the late, great Paul Ramsey, a Methodist moral theologian to whom I owe much – believe, mistakenly, that contraception is not, as I argue, an anti-life kind of act. I in no way imply that these people and others like them advocate the culture of death. Nor do I pass moral judgment on those married couples, whether Catholic, Protestant, or non-Christian, who practice contraception; nor do I claim that they are champions of the culture of death. But I think that the contraceptive culture in which we live has so affected their way of perceiving reality that they fail to recognize contraception for what it is. They mistakenly believe that its practice is compatible with a love for life. As I hope to show, though, this is not true; and it is not true precisely because contraception *is* an anti-life kind of act, incompatible with a love for life and inextricably linked logically to the culture of death.

The denial that contraception is related to the culture of death is illustrated by some of the contributors to the December 1998, symposium on contraception in the journal *First Things*. Gilbert Meilaender, a Lutheran theologian known widely for his opposition to abortion, and Philip Turner, an Anglican theologian also "on the side of life," in their joint contribution, expressed the view that "contraceptive intercourse may sometimes be a fitting means by which husband and wife aim to nourish simultaneously the procreative and unitive purposes of their marriage."[2]

Similarly, the editor of *First Things*, James Nuechterlein, reflecting on the symposium in a subsequent number of the journal, began by observing that he and his wife did not want children immediately because of their circumstances, although, had she become pregnant, "we would not for a moment have considered abortion. But," he continued,

> Neither for a moment did we morally hesitate to practice contraception. . . . We no more debated whether we would use contraception than we debated whether we would, in the fullness of time, have children. Of course we would someday, God willing, have children; in the meantime we would practice (non-abortifacient) contraception. This was not, for us, a matter of presuming on God's providence. It seemed rather a right use of reason in fulfilling the various goods of our marriage. . . . We intended both the unitive and the procreative goods of marriage, but not necessarily both in every act of love.[3]

Concluding, Nuechterlein said:

> The point of this self-revelation is . . . to suggest how utterly typical that view was and is. There is nothing singular in our experience. I believe it is, *mutatis mutandis*, the experience of most Protestant couples of our generation and after.[4]

Note that Nuechterlein refers to the common experience of contemporary *Protestants* (and this, seemingly, was also in the mind of Meilaender and Turner). However, it is no doubt true that a great majority of Catholic couples completely agree with these writers. On reading their essays, in fact, I was reminded of the views set forth in the celebrated "Majority Papers" of the Papal Commission on Population, the Family, and Natality.[5] Two passages from these papers – to which I will return later for closer examination – seem in particular to express the view articulated by the contributors to *First Things*.

In one passage, the Majority justify contraception by married couples as an intelligent use of reason to control biological nature:

> The true opposition is not to be sought between some material conformity to the physiological processes of nature and some artificial intervention. For it is natural for man to use his skill in order to put under human control what is given by physical nature. The opposition is to be sought really between one way of acting which is contraceptive [in the sense of selfishly excluding children from marriage] and opposed to a prudent and generous fruitfulness, and another way which is in an ordered relationship to responsible fruitfulness and which has a concern for education and all the essential human and Christian values.[6]

In another passage, they justify the use of contraception by married couples by distinguishing between individual acts of sexual union within marriage and the totality of the marriage. According to them,

> When man interferes with the procreative purpose of individual acts by contracepting, he does this with the intention of regulating and not excluding fertility. Then he unites the material finality toward fecundity which exists in intercourse with the formal finality of the person and renders the entire process human. . . . Conjugal acts which by intention are infertile or which are rendered infertile are ordered to the expression of the union of love; that love, however, reaches its culmination in fertility responsibly accepted. For that reason other acts of union are in a certain sense incomplete, and they receive their full moral quality with ordination toward the fertile act. . . . Infertile conjugal acts constitute a totality with fertile acts and have a single moral specification.[7]

The "single moral specification" of such acts, as the Majority makes clear, is "the fostering of love responsibly toward a generous fecundity."

On this view, what married couples who use contraception as a way of spacing children *in* their marriage, and not of excluding them *from* their marriage, are doing is simply using appropriate means for nourishing both the procreative and unitive purposes of marriage. This is their "intention" – as Meilaender/Turner and Nuechterlein indicate in the passages previously cited – and it is surely not an immoral intention.

This way of viewing the use of contraception by married couples who have serious reasons to avoid having children, at least for a time, is quite common in our society. Many, Catholic and non-Catholic alike, who hold it regard abortion with horror, and they also unambiguously judge sex outside of marriage as absolutely immoral. But they can see nothing wrong with the "responsible" use of contraception within marriage; nor do they believe that there is some inexorable link between contraception and the "culture of death," which they also abhor.

This widely held view, however, is mistaken. For centuries Christian writers regarded contraception an "anti-life" kind of act. In fact, one of the contributors to the *First Things* symposium, Alicia Mosier, an editorial assistant of the journal, forcefully expressed this view. She began by emphasizing that the issue does not center on the "artificiality" of the means used to prevent conception, but rather with the nature of contraception itself. As she said, "what is wrong is contraception itself: the deliberate will, the choice, to subvert the life-giving order and meaning of the conjugal act."[8] Commenting on Pope Paul's description of contraception as "every action . . . which proposes . . . to render procreation impossible,"[9] she wrote:

> Proposing to render procreation impossible means, simply put, willing directly against the order of intercourse and consequently against life. . . . Couples who contracept introduce a countermeasure . . . whose sole purpose is to make it impossible for a new life to come to be. Contraception is an act that can only express the will that *any* baby that might result from *this* sexual encounter not be conceived . . . it manifests a will aimed directly against new life.[10]

Mosier's way of expressing this view echoes the argument against contraception mounted by Germain Grisez, Joseph Boyle, John Finnis, and me in 1988.[11] But, as noted already, she articulates a position that was traditional in the Church, both East and West, both Catholic and Protestant, from the early days of Christianity to the mid-twentieth century. It is found in such Church Fathers as John Chrysostom, Ambrose, and Jerome, in medieval theologians such as Thomas Aquinas, in the canon law operative in the Catholic Church from the mid-thirteenth century until 1917, in the thought of reformers such as John Calvin, and in the teaching of the *Roman Catechism*, popularly known as the *Catechism of the Council of Trent*. There is no need here to recapitulate this tradition. In the accompanying note I cite representative witnesses.[12] There is thus a long and respected Christian tradition that judges contraception to be anti-life, expressing a will that is indeed at the heart of the "culture of death."

I intend to show why contraception is intimately related to the culture of death and, indeed, is the gateway to this culture. I will begin by considering Pope John Paul II's thought regarding the roots of the culture of death and his way of relating contraception to that culture. I will then take up his claim that the difference, anthropological and moral, between contraception and recourse to the rhythm of the cycle is enormous and involves ultimately "irreconcilable concepts of the human person and of human sexuality." This section will show that the acceptance of contraception is based on a dualistic anthropology of the human person and a consequentialist/proportionalist understanding of the morality of human acts: an anthropology and moral perspective central to the "culture of death." This section will likewise show how confusing and misleading talk about "intentions" can be. I will follow this with an analysis of the human act of contraception to show that it is and cannot not be anti-life, and that this is *the* reason why contraception is indeed the gateway to the "culture of death." In conclusion, I will consider contraception as an act both anti-love and anti-life, utterly incompatible with the "culture of life" and the "civilization of love."

1. Pope John Paul II on the Roots of the Culture of Death and

Contraception's Relationship to It

In the first chapter of his Encyclical *Evangelium Vitae,* Pope John Paul II identifies two roots of the "culture of death." This culture, he says, is rooted first of all in the "mentality which *carries the concept of subjectivity to an extreme* and even distorts it, and recognizes as a subject of rights only the person who enjoys full or at least incipient autonomy and who emerges from a state of total dependence on others" (No. 19). It is rooted, secondly, in a *"notion of freedom* which exalts the isolated individual in an absolute way" (No. 19).

Of these two roots, the first is most relevant for showing the relationship of contraception to the culture of death. At its heart is the idea that only those members of the human species who enjoy at least "incipient autonomy," i.e., individuals with exercisable capacities of reasoning and will, are *truly* persons with rights that ought to be recognized by society. This mentality, John Paul II points out, "tends to *equate personal dignity with the capacity for verbal and explicit,* or at least perceptible, *communication"* (No. 19). On this view, a "person" is preeminently a subject aware of itself as a self and capable of relating to other selves; and not all members of the human species are persons on this understanding of "person." This idea, as will be seen later, fits in well with the anthropology underlying the acceptance of contraception.

In the first chapter of *Evangelium Vitae,* John Paul II also discusses the relationship between contraception and abortion, whose justification and legalization is, of course, a hallmark of the "culture of death." To the common claim that contraception, "if made safe and available to all, is the most effective remedy against abortion," John Paul II replied:

> When looked at carefully, this objection is clearly unfounded. It may be that many people use contraception with a view to excluding the subsequent temptation of abortion. But the negative values inherent in the "contraceptive mentality" – which is very different from responsible parenthood, lived in respect for the full truth of the conjugal act – are such that they in fact strengthen this temptation when an unwanted life is conceived. . . . Certainly, from the moral point of view contraception and

abortion are *specifically different* evils: the former contradicts the full truth of the sexual act as the proper expression of conjugal love, whereas the latter destroys the life of a human being; the former is opposed to the virtue of chastity in marriage, the latter is opposed to the virtue of justice and directly violates the divine commandment "You shall not kill" (No.13).

It is important to emphasize that here John Paul II does *not,* as did the long Christian tradition noted above, identify contraception as an "anti-life" kind of act, akin to murder. He rather characterizes it as an "anti-love" kind of act, one that, as he says elsewhere, "falsifies" the meaning of the conjugal act as one in which the spouses give themselves unreservedly one another.[13] But he nonetheless insists that despite their differences "contraception and abortion are often closely connected, as fruits of the same tree"; and he points out that the close link between the two "is being demonstrated in an alarming way by the development of chemical products, intrauterine devices and vaccines which, distributed with the same ease as contraceptives, really act as abortifacients in the very early stages of the development of the life of a new human being" (No.13).

John Paul II obviously sees a real and substantive link between contraception and abortion – and, through it – to the "culture of death." But he does not here *directly* relate contraception to the culture of death. For him, contraception directly violates marital chastity and not the good of human life. I will return to John Paul II's thought on this matter later.

2. Contraception vs. "Recourse to the Rhythm of the Cycle": Their Anthropological and Moral Difference, One Ultimately Entailing "Irreconcilable Concepts of the Human Person and of Human Sexuality"

In his apostolic exhortation on the *Role of the Christian Family in the Modern World (Familiaris Consortio),* Pope John Paul II made the following bold claim:

In the light of the experience of many couples and the data provided by the different human sciences, theological reflection is

able to perceive and is called to study further *the difference,
both anthropological and moral,* between contraception and
recourse to the rhythm of the cycle: it is a difference which is
much wider and deeper than is usually thought, one which
involves in the final analysis *two irreconcilable concepts of the
human person and of human sexuality* (No. 32).[14]

Many people who *practice* contraception – and many who *practice* periodic abstinence – perhaps are not consciously aware of the
difference between these two ways of exercising responsible parenthood, but the difference is profound. I will show this by examining
the rationale used to defend the legitimacy of contraception in order
to disclose its underlying anthropology and moral methodology. I
will then contrast this by presenting the anthropology and moral
methodology on which the practice of natural family planning or
periodic abstinence or what John Paul II calls here "recourse to the
rhythm of the cycle" is based.

A. Contraception: Its Underlying Anthropology and Moral Methodology

A dualistic understanding of the human person and of human
sexuality is at the heart of the defense of contraception. This anthropology regards the body as an instrument of the person, a good for
the person insofar as it is a necessary condition for goods and values
intrinsic to the person; the latter, so-called personalistic goods and
values, are those whose existence depends on their being consciously experienced. This anthropology underlies several key arguments
given to support contraception, in particular, the argument defending
contraception as the exercise of intelligent human dominion over
nature and that justifying it on the basis that it is in harmony with the
nature of *human* sexuality.

Several passages from the Majority documents of the Papal
Commission illustrate the first line of reasoning, based on
humankind's dominion over the world of nature. I cited one of these
at the beginning of this paper, in which the authors stressed that "it
is natural for man to use his skill in order to put under human control what is given by physical nature."[15] In another passage they
declare that, "in the matter at hand," namely, contraception,

There is a certain change in the mind of contemporary man. He feels that he is more conformed to his rational nature, created by God with liberty and responsibility, when he uses his skill to intervene in the biological processes of nature so that he can achieve the institution of matrimony in the conditions of actual life, than if he would abandon himself to chance.[16]

In yet another passage the majority emphasized that "it is proper to man, created in the image of God, to use what is given in physical nature in a way that he may develop it to its full significance with a view to the good of the whole person."[17]

These passages make it clear that those defending contraception consider the biological fertility of human persons and the biological processes involved in the generation of new human life as physical or biological "givens." Human fertility, in other words, is part of the world of subhuman or subpersonal nature over which persons have been given dominion. The majority theologians of the Papal Commission, in fact, assert that "biological fertility . . . ought to be assumed into the human sphere and be regulated within it."[18] Obviously, if the biological fecundity of human persons is intrinsically human, it does not need to be "assumed into the human sphere." Nothing assumes what it already is or has of itself. This passage is a clear assertion of dualism.

In other words, on this view, the fertility of human persons is in and of itself a biological given belonging to the physical, not human, world over which the person has been given dominion. Biological givens, such as fertility, confront the person who is to control and regulate them by "assuming" them into the human and personal, i.e., by making use of them when they serve "personalist" goods and by suppressing or impeding them when their continued flourishing inhibits participation in these goods, whose existence, as noted already, depends on their being consciously experienced.

The notion that human biological fertility is, of itself, subhuman and subpersonal is closely related to the understanding of human sexuality central to the defense of contraception. One of the major reasons for changing Church teaching on the matter, the majority theologians argued, is the "changed estimation of the value and meaning of human sexuality," one leading to a "better, deeper, and more correct understanding of conjugal life and the conjugal act."[19] According to this understanding, *human* sexuality, as distinct from *animal* sexuality, is above all relational or unitive in character. As one theologian put it, "the most profound meaning of human sexuality is that it is a relational reality, having a special significance for the person in his relationships."[20] Human sexuality, as some other theological defenders of contraception contend, "is preeminently. . . the mode whereby an isolated subjectivity [=person] reaches out to communion with another subject. Embodied subjectivity reaches out to another body-subject in order to banish loneliness and to experience the fullness of being-with-another in the human project."[21]

Proponents of this understanding of human sexuality acknowledge that human sexual union can be procreative – or, to use the term that the more secularistic of them prefer, "reproductive." Yet in addition to these "biological" needs, sexual union serves other, more personal values, namely, those whose existence depends on their being consciously experienced. The fact that such union, at times, results in the conception of a new human being has, in the past and even today, frequently inhibited the realization of these more personal purposes. But today – and this is *the* important consideration – it is possible through efficient methods of contraception to sever the connection between the procreative and unitive or relational dimensions of human sexuality.

The more radical, secularistic proponents of contraception sever this connection totally. As George Gilder so perceptively observed over a quarter of a century ago:

> The members of the sex coalition go well beyond a mere search for better contraceptives. They are not satisfied merely to control the biological tie between intercourse and childbirth. They also want to eliminate the psychological and symbolic connections. . . . By far the most frequent and durably important long-term use of sex, they would say, is the fulfillment of the physical and psychological need for orgasmic pleasure and the communication of affection. For these purposes, sex is most adaptable if it is not connected with procreation, if it is regarded as a completely separate mode of activity.[22]

It cannot be denied that many people in the Western (and increasingly the non-Western) world regard the emergence of contraceptive technologies as a truly liberating event. They believe that the effective use of contraceptives enables human persons to liberate the *personal* and *human* purposes of sexuality and of genital intercourse from the tyranny of biology. Many today would agree with the claim of the well-known British writer, Ashley Montagu, that:

> The pill provides a dependable means of controlling conception. . . . [T]he pill makes it possible to render every individual of reproductive age completely responsible for both his sexual and his reproductive behavior. *It is necessary to be unequivocally clear concerning the distinction between sexual behavior and reproductive behavior.* Sexual behavior may have no purpose other than pleasure . . . without the slightest intent of reproducing, or it may be indulged in for both pleasure and reproduction.[23]

The majority theologians of the Papal Commission as well as Protestant authors such as Meilaender, Turner, and Nuechterlein, would not go as far as Montagu and other secular supporters of contraception and sever completely the bond between the unitive and procreative meanings of human sexuality. Nonetheless, they deem its relational or unitive meaning its *personal,* as distinct from its procreative or *biological,* significance, which requires to be assumed into consciousness in order to become human and personal. Coupling this understanding of human sexuality with the dominion that human persons have over their biological fertility, they contend that if the continued flourishing of biological fecundity inhibits the expression of the relational or unitive meaning of sexuality, it is then licit to suppress this "biological given" so that the *personal,* relational good of sexuality can be realized. They do not want to sever the bond between the unitive (personal) and procreative (biological) meaning of our sexuality for the *whole* of the marriage, but they think it proper intentionally to separate them in *individual acts,* if doing so is thought necessary for serving the procreative-unitive meaning of marriage as a whole.

Biological fertility is, for them, a lesser good – a good *for* the person (something like a coat), not a good *of* the person. For them goods *of* the person are goods whose existence depends on being consciously experienced. Since fertility does not so depend, it is not this kind of a good. On the other hand, they consider the union made possible by sexual coition – the unitive or relational aspect of our sexuality – to be a good *of* the person because its existence and flourishing depends on being consciously experienced.

It is worth noting here that Catholic advocates of this defense of contraception contrast the "personalism" it promotes with the "physicalism" allegedly underlying the Church's rejection of contraception. One of these "personalist" theologians illustrated the contrast between the Church's "physicalism" and the "personalism" of revisionists by saying: "Birth control was, for a very long time, impeded by the physicalistic ethic that left moral man at the mercy of his biology. He had no choice but to conform to the rhythms of his physical nature. . . . Only gradually did technological man discover that he was free to intervene creatively and to achieve birth control by choice."[24]

The foregoing has, I believe, clearly shown the dualistic anthropology and understanding of the human person and of human sexuality crucial to major arguments used to justify contraception. This anthropology distinguishes the person, i.e., the conscious subject of experiences (or, as John Paul II noted in *Evangelium Vitae*, 19, the subject having "the capacity for verbal and explicit, or at least perceptible, communication"), from the *body* that this person uses, now for this purpose, now for that. If the person is really not his or her own body, then the person's sexuality can be "liberated" from regulation by merely biological laws and used for "interpersonal communication" or the "fostering of conjugal love."

This anthropology or understanding of the human person is central to the "culture of death." For, if the person is not his or her own body, then, as Germain Grisez has noted, "the destruction of the life of the body is not directly and in itself an attack on a value intrinsic to the human person." Continuing, Grisez notes:

> The lives of the unborn, the lives of those not fully in possession of themselves – the hopelessly insane and the "vegetating" senile – and the lives of those who no longer can engage in praxis or problem solving, become lives no longer meaningful, no longer valuable, no longer inviolable.[25]

The dualistic anthropology that has led to the justification of abortion on the grounds that the life thus taken, while "biologically" human, is not "meaningfully" human or the life of a "person," and to the justification of euthanasia on the grounds that it serves the needs of the "person" when biological life becomes a burden, is thus definitely operative in the ideology behind contraception, even if this is not acknowledged by many.

I turn now to consider the *moral methodology* employed in the justification of contraception, in particular, contraception by married couples. This methodology is clearly evident in the argument based on the distinction between individual or "isolated" marital acts and marriage as a whole or totality. This argument acknowledges (as Montagu and most secular advocates of contraception do not) that procreation is indeed a good of marriage, and that marriage and children go together. But, this argument claims, the procreative good of marriage is properly respected and honored even when individual acts of marriage are deliberately made infertile, so long as those acts are ordered to the expression of love and to a generous fecundity within the marriage as a whole.

It will be useful here to review this very illuminating passage from the Papal Commission Majority. It reads:

> When man interferes with the procreative purpose of individual acts by contracepting, he does this with the intention of regulating and not excluding fertility. Then he unites the material finality toward fecundity which exists in intercourse with the formal finality of the person and renders the entire process human. . . . Conjugal acts which by intention are infertile or which are rendered infertile are ordered to the expression of the union of love; that love, however, reaches its culmination in fertility responsibly accepted. For that reason other acts of union are in a certain sense incomplete, and they receive their full moral quality with ordination toward the fertile act. . . . Infertile conjugal acts constitute a totality with fertile acts and have a single moral specification.[26]

The "single moral specification" or moral object of this totality is the fostering of love responsibly toward a generous fecundity.

Note that this passage considers "recourse to the rhythm of the cycle" or periodic abstinence as simply another way of contracepting; it equates "acts which by intention are infertile," that is, marital acts chosen while the wife is not fertile, and acts "which are rendered infertile." The authors, in other words, see absolutely no *moral* difference between contraception and "recourse to the cycle." The latter is simply another way of contracepting.[27] They do so because they consider the moral "intentions" to be the same in both cases. Their "intention" is to avoid a pregnancy, perhaps for very serious and good reasons. I will return to this issue below.

The central claim of this passage is that the moral object specifying what couples who "responsibly" contracept individual acts of marital congress are doing is "fostering love responsibly toward a generous fecundity." Their aim, their "intention," as Meilaender and Turner later put it in their *First Things* essay, is to "nourish simultaneously the procreative and unitive purposes of their marriage."

This claim is rooted in the idea that we can identify the moral object specifying a human act *only* by considering the act in its "totality." According to this method of making moral decisions, it is not possible to determine the moral species of an action – its "moral object" – without taking into account the "intention," or end for whose sake the choice is made, along with the foreseeable consequences for the persons concerned. If one does this, so the argument goes, one can conclude that, if the choice to contracept individual acts is directed to the end of nourishing conjugal love so that the good of procreation can also be served, then one can rightly say that *what* the spouses are doing – the *moral object* of their choice – is to foster conjugal love toward a generous fecundity, obviously something good, not bad.

But this reasoning is specious. It is so because it *re-describes* the contraceptive act, in fact, a whole series of contraceptive acts, in terms of hoped-for benefits. The *remote* or *further* end for whose sake the couple contracepts individual acts of sexual union may indeed be to nourish simultaneously the unitive and procreative goods of marriage. This end is indeed "intended." And this end, this "intention," is good. But "intended" also is the *choice* to contracept – and the couple cannot *not choose*, cannot *not intend*, to contracept. And this specious moral reasoning conceals this "moral object."

This reasoning, moreover, relies on a faulty understanding of the marital *act*. According to this reasoning, which re-describes the spouses' behavior in terms of hoped-for benefits, the marital act is intended to foster love between spouses, to unite them. But it is not, as such, intended to be open to the gift of life; rather it is the marriage *as a whole* in which particular acts occur that is so intended. Its proponents would surely hold that spouses ought not, in choosing to unite genitally, freely intend to set aside its unitive dimension. Why, then, do they hold that they can freely intend, in uniting genitally, to set aside its procreative dimension? They can do so only because, as we have seen, they regard this dimension as merely "biological," a "lesser" good than the "personal" good of being sexually united.

The moral methodology used, in other words, is consequentialistic. It fails to recognize that the morality of human acts, as John Paul II has so correctly said, "depends primarily and fundamentally on the 'object' rationally chosen by the deliberate will."[28] With respect to contraception that object is *not* "to foster love responsibly toward a generous fecundity" or to nourish simultaneously the unitive and procreative goods of marriage. Precisely what this object is will be taken up below. My point here, however, is that the consequentialist moral reasoning used in this central argument to justify contraception is plausible only because it re-describes the object of choice – contraception – in terms of the hoped-for benefits of contracepting individual acts of sexual union.

We have now seen the anthropology and moral methodology underlying the defense of contraception. The anthropology, a dualistic one, regards the person primarily as a subject of enduring experiences who uses his or her body now for this purpose, now for that. It likewise locates the *human* and *personal* meaning of human sexuality in its *relational* significance, i.e., its ability to allow two subjects of enduring experiences to enter into deep interpersonal union, while regarding the *procreative* meaning of human sexuality as of itself subpersonal, part of the subhuman world of nature over which the person has been given dominion. This anthropology, as has been shown, is central to the "culture of death."

The moral methodology employed here is a form of consequentialism or proportionalism, one that re-describes chosen deeds in terms of their hoped-for benefits, and by doing so conceals their true nature. This moral methodology is also central to the specious rationalizations used to justify the killings characteristic of the "culture of death." Thus abortion is not recognized as the intentional killing of an unborn child, but is rather re-described as an act protecting the mother's health or the family's stability or something of this kind; rather than being called killing, euthanasia is re-described as helping persons to die with dignity, etc.

B. Recourse to the Rhythm of the Cycle: Its Underlying Anthropology and Moral Methodology

The anthropology supporting the practice of periodic continence as the way to harmonize the requirements of conjugal love with respect for the good of procreation is holistic, i.e., it regards the human person as a unity of body and soul. The person is, in the unity of body and soul, the subject of moral actions.[29] On this anthropology, the body and bodily life are integral to the person, goods *of* the person, not merely goods *for* the person.

Human persons are, in other words, body persons. When God created man, he did not, as some dualistic-minded defenders of contraception claim, create "an isolated subjectivity" who experiences existence in [either] a female body-structure . . . [or] a male body-structure."[30] Quite the contrary, God, in creating *human* persons, created bodily, sexual persons: "male and female he created them" (Gen 1:27). The human body expresses the human person; and since the human body is inescapably either male or female, it expresses a man-person or a woman-person. Precisely because of their sexual differences, manifest in their bodies, the man-person and the woman-person can give themselves to one another bodily. Moreover, since the body, male or female, is the expression of a human person, a man and a woman, in giving their bodies to one another, give their *persons* to one another.

The bodily gift of a man and a woman to each other is the outward sign, the sacrament, of the *communion of persons* existing between them. The body is, therefore, the means and the sign of the gift of the male-person to the female-person. Pope John Paul II calls this capacity of the body to express the communion of persons the *nuptial meaning* of the body.[31]

In addition, human fertility or fecundity is *not* some subhuman, subpersonal aspect of human sexuality. As Vatican Council II clearly affirms, "Man's sexuality and the faculty of generating life wondrously surpass the lower forms of life" (Pastoral Constitution on the Church in the Modern World *Gaudium et Spes,* 51). Pope John Paul II pointedly observes that human fertility "is directed to the generation of a human being, and so by its nature it surpasses the purely biological order and involves a whole series of personal values" (Apostolic exhortation *Familiaris Consortio,* 11). The procreative meaning of human sexuality, in this non-dualistic anthropology, is *not* subhuman or subpersonal; nor is it in need of "being assumed" into the human. It is human and personal to begin with.

The rationale supporting recourse to the rhythm of the cycle does not judge the morality of human acts in terms of hoped-for results or of the anticipated overall proportion of good and evil that will come about. It holds, rather, that the morality of human actions depends on both the *end intended* and the *object chosen* and, because chosen, also *intended.* It distinguishes between the ulterior or remote end for whose sake one chooses to do *this,* and the proximate or immediate end, which is precisely the freely chosen object. Both end intended and object chosen must be morally good, i.e., in conformity with right reason; if either is not in accord with the truth, then the entire action is vitiated.

But the primary source of the morality of the act is, as noted above, the "object" freely and rationally chosen by the acting subject. This is precisely *what one chooses to do.* The moral methodology underlying the practice of contraception ignores this object, the immediate end of one's choice to do *this* here and now; and it focuses on the remote end or further intention of the act, i.e., the reason why one chooses to do this here and now. As we have seen, this consequentialist methodology conceals and keeps hidden from view the precise object of one's freely chosen act and *re-describes* it in terms of its hoped-for benefits, the remote end intended by the acting person, the object of one's "further" intention.

The non-consequentialist way of making moral judgments on which recourse to the rhythm of the cycle is based recognizes, as Pope John Paul II emphasizes, "that there are objects of the human act which are by their nature 'incapable of being ordered' to God, because they radically contradict the good of the person made in his image." Continuing, the pope says:

> These are the acts which, in the Church's moral tradition, have been termed "intrinsically evil" *(intrinsece malum);* they are such *always and per se,* in other words, on account of their very object, and apart from the ulterior intentions of the one acting and the circumstances (*Veritatis splendor,* 80).

We need now to examine the moral object specifying the act of contraception in order to show that it is indeed an anti-life kind of act.

3. Contraception: An Anti-Life Act

In order to pass moral judgment on contraception, it is first necessary to know precisely what we are speaking of. It is essential to provide an accurate description of the kind of human act an act of contraception is and then to judge whether or not it is a human act in accordance with right reason, with the truth, and, if not, why not.

We have seen already that human acts are specified primarily by the "object" freely and rationally chosen by the deliberate will. But what is the "object" freely chosen in contraception? Pope Paul VI offers a good description when he says that what the Church's teaching on the immorality of contraception excludes is "every action, whether in anticipation of the conjugal act, or in its accomplishment, or in the development of its natural consequences, proposes [the Latin text reads *intendat*], either as end or as means, to impede procreation [here the Latin text reads: *ut procreatio impediatur*]" (*Humanae Vitae,* 14). Paul here refers to the conjugal act, since his encyclical was concerned with contraception by married couples. But, if "conjugal act" is changed to "genital act," Paul's description accurately identifies the "object" morally specifying an act as contraceptive, whether within marriage or not.

As this description shows, the object freely chosen and willed by someone who engages in an act of contraception is precisely to impede the beginning of a new human life or to impede procreation. It is reasonable to think that a certain kind of behavior – genital behavior – is the kind of behavior in and through which new human life can come to be. If one does not want that life to come to be, perhaps for very good reasons (e.g., the woman's health, inability properly to care for a new baby, etc.), one therefore chooses to do something to impede the beginning of the new human life that one believes that genital behavior might initiate. If one did not reasonably think that this kind of behavior – genital behavior – could result in the beginning of a new human life, one would have no reason to contracept. If one wanted that life to come to be, obviously one would not contracept in order to impede its beginning. Contraception makes sense, i.e., is an *intelligible* human act, only because one does not want new human life to come into existence as a result of another kind of human activity, namely genital activity. As Mosier so well put it in the essay cited early in this paper, "contraception is an act that can only express the will that *any* baby that might result from *this* sexual encounter not be conceived . . . it [thus] manifests a will aimed directly against new life."[32]

This analysis of the object specifying an act as one of contraception makes it clear that contraception, although related to genital/sexual acts, is not itself a sexual or genital act. Fornication, adultery, masturbation, and marital coition are sexual/genital acts. But if a fornicating couple, an adulterous couple, or a married couple contracept, they choose to do something distinct from the genital act they likewise choose to engage in. In other words, they choose to (a) engage in genital coition and (b) to do something prior to, during, or subsequent to their freely chosen genital coition precisely to impede procreation, i.e., to impede the beginning of the new human life that they reasonably believe could begin in and through the freely chosen genital coition.

The act specified by the second choice, (b), is the act of contraception. It is not even necessary for the person who contracepts to engage in genital coition. For instance, suppose a father provides a home for his newly married daughter and her husband. His daughter and her husband abhor contraception, deeming it a grave moral evil. They would never contracept, although perhaps they plan to practice periodic continence until they can move into their own quarters. But the girl's father, in order to make sure that she does not conceive while living in his house, regularly puts contraceptive pills into his daughter's cereal in the morning. He is the one who is choosing to contracept, not his daughter.[33]

Since the contraceptive act is distinct from any sexual act to which it is related, it cannot be considered a part or element of a sexual act and justified on the alleged grounds that it is merely a part of a larger whole, for instance, the marital or conjugal act. This, in essence, is what the specious argument considered above seeks to do, namely, to justify contraception as simply an aspect of a totality of marital acts that nourish both the unitive and procreative goods of marriage. But, as has now been made clear, contraception is not a part or aspect of any marital act or series thereof; it is a distinct kind of human act, specified by the choice to impede the beginning of new human life, either as an end or as a means to some further end, one perhaps good in itself.

Since contraception is specified precisely by the choice to impede the beginning of new human life, it is an anti-life kind of act, one expressing a contra-life will. It is precisely because contraception is specified by a contra-life will that it was, as we saw earlier, regarded for centuries as analogous to homicide by Christian writers. This analogy, a contemporary author rightly says, "no longer surprises us if we look not exclusively at the material nature of the behavior in the two cases [contraception and homicide], but rather at the intention or movement of the will that has recourse to contraception. Ultimately, in fact, the decision is rationalized and motivated by the judgment: 'It is not good that a new human person should exist.'"[34] Contraception is always seriously wrong because it is always gravely immoral to adopt by choice the proposal to damage, destroy, or impede the good of human life.

If the contraception fails and a child is conceived despite the steps taken deliberately to prevent its life from beginning, the child comes to be as an "unwanted child." This does not mean that those who sought to prevent his or her conception will now resort to abortion – for they may resolutely have set their hearts and minds against abortion, as did Nuechterlein and his wife, as we have seen. But one can hardly say that a child conceived despite efforts to prevent its conception is a "wanted child." Its initial status is that of an unwanted child and this is so because its parents have intentionally done something to "unwant" it, namely, to contracept, to impede the beginning of its life.

This is not true of couples who have "recourse to the rhythm of the cycle" or to periodic abstinence, and who avoid irresponsibly causing a pregnancy by abstaining from the marital act at times when they believe that the wife is fertile and hence could conceive.[35] It is true that, like a contracepting couple, they do not "want" to have a child in the sense that they do not, for good reasons, want to cause a pregnancy. But not wanting to have a child in this sense is quite different from not wanting to have the child one could have as a result of *this freely chosen act of sexual union,* and then freely choosing to do something to *impede that prospective child's coming into being.* Couples who contracept do not "want" a child in this, second sense, and hence if it does come to be despite their contraceptive efforts to prevent it from coming to be, it comes to be as an "unwanted child."

But a child conceived by a couple having recourse to the rhythm of the cycle does not come to be as an "unwanted" child because they have done nothing to "unwant" this particular child. He or she may be a "surprise" baby, but not an "unwanted" baby.[36]

Contraception: Both Anti-Love and Anti-Life

As we have seen, the principal argument proposed by John Paul II as pope against contraception is that it violates marital love and falsifies the language of the body: the natural dynamism of the conjugal act, which is ordered to the procreation and education of children and the mutual love of the spouses, is overlaid with an objectively contradictory language: a refusal to give oneself fully to the other (see Pope John Paul II, apostolic exhortation *Familiaris Consortio,* 32).[37] For John Paul II contraception directly violates marital love and marital chastity and only indirectly is opposed to the good of human life.

This argument, which has featured prominently in John Paul II's teaching on marriage and on the malice of contraception, was well expressed by Paul Quay, S.J., in the early 1960s and has been developed by Dietrich von Hildebrand, Mary Joyce, and others.[38] I believe it true that, by contracepting, a married couple fail to give themselves to one another fully and unreservedly. Yet the "not-giving" entailed is *not* the object specifying the choice to contracept, and most married couples who do contracept would vehemently deny that they are refusing to give themselves to one another. Nuechterlein, in his *First Things* article, illustrates this. He says that "if someone had told us [his wife and himself] . . . that we were 'withholding our fertility' from one another . . . [or 'not giving themselves to one another'] he would have met with blank incomprehension."[39] The "not-giving" is *praeter intentionem* or outside the scope of the intentions of the married couples who are contracepting. It is, I believe, an *effect* or *consequence* of their contracepting their sexual union, but for the most part they do not consciously recognize this. It is surely *not* "the proximate end of a deliberate decision which determines the act of willing on the part of the acting person," as John Paul II himself describes the object morally specifying a human act in *Veritatis Splendor*, 78. Indeed, contracepting married couples commonly attempt to justify their choice to contracept by claiming that contraception *is necessary* in order for them to express their love for one another. I will return to this issue later.

Although the argument summarized here is the principal one used by John Paul II to show that it is wrong for married couples to contracept, in some of his writings he has focused attention on the anti-life character of contraception. Thus, in a homily during a Mass for youth in Nairobi, Kenya, he pointed out that the fullest sign of spousal self-giving occurs when couples willingly accept children. Citing *Gaudium et Spes*, 50, he said: "That is why *anti-life* actions such as contraception and abortion are wrong and are unworthy of good husbands and wives."[40] Moreover, writing as the philosopher Karol Wojtyla, Pope John Paul II had earlier written that the ultimate end served by the sexual urge in human persons, men and women "is the very existence of the [human] species. It follows therefore that that urge, on account of its very own nature, aims at the transmission of life, because on that depends the good of the human species."[41]

In addition, the human sexual urge aims at transmitting *personal* life, and the love of husband and wife, the philosopher Wojtyla argued, is shaped by this good. Indeed, as he says:

Looked at more closely and concretely, these two persons, the

man and the woman, facilitate the existence of another concrete person, their own child, blood of their blood, and flesh of
their flesh. This person is at once an affirmation and a continuation of their own lives. The natural order of human existence
is not in conflict with love between persons but in strict harmony with it.[42]

Thus John Paul II clearly recognizes the anti-life nature of contraception. It is both *anti-love* and *anti-life*. In his papal writings on
marriage and the family, John Paul II has obviously concluded that
he can best persuade married couples to reject contraception by
stressing its character as an act incompatible with conjugal love.
And, if we think clearly about things, this is true, even if the precise
"object" of contraception is to impede the beginning of new human
life and *not* the "not-giving of spouses to one another."

Spouses cannot contracept merely by taking thought. They do so
by choosing to do something to their body-persons, and different
contraceptives work in different ways to "impede procreation." I
here omit discussion of devices allegedly "contraceptive" that are
either definitively abortifacient (e.g., after-morning pills, Norplant)
or that may "work" by preventing implantation in the event that conception occurs (e.g., the pills in use today and, for the most part,
IUDs as well). I hence limit consideration to the so-called "barrier"
methods (condoms, diaphragms, etc.) and "chemical" (spermicidal
jellies and the like).

Now consider this. A person does not put on gloves to touch a
beloved one tenderly, unless one thinks that some disease may be
communicated. But is pregnancy a disease? And is not the use of
condoms, diaphragms, spermicidal jellies and the like similar to putting on gloves? Do husband and wife really become "one flesh" if
they must arm themselves with protective gear before "giving"
themselves to one another genitally? The answers to these questions
are obvious, and they help us see why the argument that contraception is anti-love and a falsification of the "language of the body" is
true. Spouses who must "protect" themselves from one another in
such ways are "not giving" themselves unreservedly to one another
as bodily, sexual beings, even if this "not giving" is "outside the
scope of their intention."

Contraception is thus anti-love as well as anti-life. It is utterly incompatible with the "culture of life" and the "civilization of love." It is rather the gateway to the "culture of death." This is implicit in the slogan frequently on the lips of those who defend our contraceptive culture by saying that "No unwanted child ought ever to be born." This banal slogan typifies the "culture of death," which seeks to avert the tragedy of an "unwanted child" by preventing its coming into being through contraception; and, should this fail, by abortion. It is utterly opposed to the truth that "no person, i.e., no human being, whether born or unborn, male or female, young or old, a genius or demented ought ever to be unwanted, i.e., unloved." And the only way to build a civilization in which every human person is indeed wanted is to respect both the love-giving (unitive) and life-giving meanings of human sexuality and marriage.

Notes

1. Dr. William E. May is the Michael J. McGivney Professor of Moral Theology at the John Paul II Institute for Studies on Marriage and the Family in Washington, DC. He is the author of many articles and books, including *An Introduction to Moral Theology, Catholic Sexual Ethics*, and *Marriage: The Rock on Which the Family Is Built.* He is a past president of the Fellowship of Catholic Scholars and a past recipient of the Fellowship's Cardinal Wright Award.

2. Gilbert Meilaender and Philip Turner, "Contraception: A Symposium," in *First Things*, 88 (December 1998), p. 24.

3. James Nuechterlein, "Catholics, Protestants, and Contraception," *First Things*, 92 (April 1999), p. 10.

4. Ibid.

5. Pope John XXIII established this Commission, whose function was exclusively to offer advice to the pope, in 1963. After Pope John's death, Pope Paul VI ordered that it continue its work. The Commission's original charge was to determine whether the newly discovered "anovulant" pill was indeed a contraceptive (as Pope Pius XII had judged in an address given to a Congress of Hematologists on September 12, 1958, less than a month before he died); but it soon began to open up the entire issue of contraception. The Commission

soon divided into a "minority," which held that the Church's teaching on the immorality of contraception is true and cannot change, and a "majority," which held that contraception by married couples can be justified. The Commission completed its work in 1966. Although its findings were supposed to have been given *only* to the Holy Father, the Commission's papers were leaked to the press in July 1967, and published in the United States in the *National Catholic Reporter.* The Commission issued four documents; all of them can be found in *The Birth-Control Debate: Interim History from the Pages of the National Catholic Reporter,* ed. Robert Hoyt (Kansas City: National Catholic Reporter, 1969). One of them, expressing the minority view, was entitled in Latin *Status Quaestionis: Doctrina Ecclesiae Eiusque Auctoritatis,* and is given the title "The State of the Question: A Conservative View." Three documents set forth the majority position: (1) a rebuttal of the minority view (*Documentum Syntheticum de Moralitatis Nativitatum* in Latin; entitled "The Question Is Not Closed: The Liberals Reply"); (2) the final theological report of the majority (*Schema Documenti de Responsabili Paternitate* in Latin and called "On Responsible Parenthood: The Final Report"); and (3) a pastoral paper, written in French under the title *Indications Pastorales* ("Pastoral Approaches").

     An interesting account of the Commission and its work, written by one fully in agreement with the "majority" position, is provided by Robert McClory: *Turning Point: The Inside Story of the Papal Birth Control Commission, and How Humanae Vitae Changed the Life of Patty Crowley and the Future of the Church* (New York: Crossroad, 1995).

6. "On Responsible Parenthood," in Hoyt, p. 88.

7. "The Question Is Not Closed," in Ibid. p. 72.

8. Alicia Mosier, "Contraception: A Symposium," *First Things,* 88 (December 1998), p. 26.

9. A better translation of the Latin text of *Humanae vitae* to which Mosier refers is "to impede procreation" insofar as the Latin reads "*ut procreatio impediatur.*"

10. Mosier, "Contraception," pp.26–27.

11. See Germain Grisez, Joseph Boyle, John Finnis, and William E. May, "Every Marital Act Ought To Be Open to New Life: Toward a Clearer Understanding," *The Thomist,* 52 (1988), pp. 365–426; reprint-

ed in *The Teaching of Humanae Vitae: A Defense* (San Francisco: Ignatius Press, 1988), pp. 33–116.

12. See, for instance, the following:

(1) St. John Chrysostom, *Homily 24 on the Epistle to the Romans, PG* 60, pp. 626–27: "Why do you sow where the field is eager to destroy the fruit? Where there are medicines of sterility? Where there is murder before birth? You do not even let a harlot remain only a harlot, but you make her a murderess as well. Do you see that from drunkenness comes fornication, from fornication adultery, from adultery murder? Indeed, it is something worse than murder and I do not know what to call it; for she does not kill what is formed but prevents its formation. What then? Do you contemn the gift of God, and fight with his law? What is a curse, do you seek as though it were a blessing? Do you make the anteroom of birth the anteroom of slaughter? Do you teach the woman who is given to you for the procreation of offspring to perpetuate killing?" Cited by John T. Noonan, Jr., in his *Contraception: A History of Its Treatment by Catholic Theologians and Canonists* (Cambridge, MA: The Belknap Press of Harvard University, 1965), p. 98. On pp. 91–94 of this work, Noonan shows that contraception, along with abortion, was considered equivalent to murder in such early Christian writings as *The Didache* and *The Epistle to Barnabas.* As Noonan shows in later sections of his work, e.g., pp. 146, 232–37, this tradition perdured in the Church for centuries.

(2) St. Thomas Aquinas, *Summa contra gentiles,* 3. 122: "Nor, in fact, should it be deemed a slight sin for a man to arrange for the emission of semen apart from the proper purpose of generating and bringing up children . . . the inordinate emission of semen is incompatible with the natural good of preserving the species. Hence, after the sin of homicide whereby a human nature already in existence is destroyed, this type of sin appears to take next place, for by it the generation of human nature is impeded."

(3) The *Si aliquis* canon, which was integrated into the canon law of the Church in the *Decretum Greg. IX* (lib. V, tit., 12, cap. V) and was part of the Church's canon law from the mid–thirteenth century until 1917, clearly likened contraception to murder. It declared: "If anyone for the sake of fulfilling sexual desire or with premeditated hatred does something to a man or a woman, or gives something to drink, so that he cannot generate or she cannot conceive or offspring be born, let

him be held as a murderer." Text in *Corpus iuris canonici,* eds. A. L. Richter and A. Friedberg (Leipzig: Tauchnitz, 1881), 2. 794.

(4) In its treatment of marriage, the *Roman Catechism* declared: "Whoever in marriage artificially prevents conception, or procures an abortion, commits a most serious sin: the sin of premeditated murder" (Part II, Chap. 7, No. 13). It should be noted that Pope Paul VI explicitly refers to this text in footnote No. 16 to No. 14 of *Humanae Vitae,* precisely where Paul defines contraception as every act prior to intercourse, during it, or in the course of its natural effect that proposes (the Latin text reads *intendat*), either as end or as means, to impede procreation (*ut procreatio impediatur*).

(5) John Calvin, in his commentary on the sin of Onan recorded in Genesis 38, had this to say: "Onan not only defrauded his brother of the right due him, but also preferred his semen to putrefy on the ground. . . . The voluntary spilling of semen outside of intercourse between man and woman is a monstrous thing. Deliberately to withdraw from coitus in order that semen may fall on the ground is doubly monstrous. For this is to extinguish the hope of the race and to kill before it is born the hoped-for offspring. . . . If any woman ejects a foetus from her womb by drugs, it is reckoned a crime incapable of expiation, and deservedly Onan incurred upon himself the same kind of punishment, infecting the earth by his semen in order that Tamar might not conceive a future human being as an inhabitant of the earth." *Commentaries on the First Book of Moses Called Genesis,* Ch. 38: 9,10; quoted in Charles D. Provan, *The Bible and Birth Control* (Monongahela, PA: Zimmer Printing, 1989), p. 15. Provan points out that the editor of the *unabridged* series of Calvin's *Commentaries,* published by Baker Book House, has omitted the commentary on these two verses of Genesis.

13. See, for instance, his apostolic exhortation *Familiaris Consortio (The Role of the Christian Family in the Modern World),* 32.

14. On this see Paul F. DeLadurantaye, "'Irreconcilable Concepts of the Human Person' and the Moral Issue of Contraception: An Examination of the Personalism of Louis Janssens and of Pope John Paul II," in *Anthropotes: Rivista di Studi sulla Persona e la Famiglia* 13.2 (1997), pp. 433–56. This essay is a summary of DeLadurantaye's 1997 S.T.D. dissertation under the same title at the John Paul II Institute for Studies on Marriage and Family, Washington, DC.

15. See endnote 5, above.

16. "The Question Is Not Closed," in Hoyt, p. 69.

17. "On Responsible Parenthood," in Hoyt, p. 87.

18. "The Question Is Not Closed," in Hoyt, p. 71.

19. "On Responsible Parenthood," in Hoyt, p. 89.

20. Louis Janssens, "Considerations on *Humanae Vitae*," *Louvain Studies*, 2 (1969), p. 249.

21. Anthony Kosnik, et al., *Human Sexuality: New Directions in American Catholic Thought* (New York: Paulist; 1977), p. 83.

22. George Gilder, *Sexual Suicide* (New York: Quadrangle Books, 1973), p. 34.

23. Ashley Montagu, *Sex, Man, and Society* (New York: G. P. Putnam's, 1969), pp. 13–14; emphasis in the original.

24. Daniel C. Maguire, "The Freedom to Die," in *New Theology # 10*, eds. Martin Marty and Dean Peerman (New York: Macmillan, 1973), p. 188. It is instructive to note that in this essay Maguire goes on to justify "death by choice" as also serving personalist values.

25. Germain Grisez, "Dualism and the New Morality," *Atti del congresso internazionale Tommaso d'Aquino nel suo settimo centenario*, Vol. 5: *L'agire morale* (Naples: Edizioni Domenicane Italiane, 1977), p. 325.

26. "The Question Is Not Closed," in Hoyt, p. 72.

27. In fact, some Catholic advocates of contraception, for instance, Rosemary Ruether and Louis Janssens, claim that with barrier methods of contraception one puts a "spatial" barrier between ovum and sperm, whereas with the use of periodic abstinence one puts a "temporal" barrier between ovum and sperm. Thus Ruether writes: "sexual acts which are calculated to function only during the times of sterility are sterilizing the act just as much as any other means of rendering the act infertile. *It is difficult to see why there should be such an absolute moral difference between creating a spatial barrier to procreation and creating a temporal barrier to procreation*" ("Birth Control and Sexuality," in *Contraception and Holiness: The Catholic Predicament*, Introduction by Thomas D. Roberts, S.J. [New York: Herder and Herder, 1964], p. 74; emphasis added).

28. Pope John Paul II, Encyclical *Veritatis Splendor*, 78.

29. See Ibid., 48. In this section of his encyclical, Pope John Paul II explicitly refers to defined Catholic teaching on the unity of the human person as a unity of body and soul, namely, the Council of Vienne, Constitution *Fides Catholica, DS* 902; Fifth Lateran Council, Bull *Apostolici Regiminis, DS* 1440; and Vatican Council II, Pastoral Constitution on the Church in the Modern World *Gaudium et Spes,* 14. See footnotes 66 and 67 (at 48).

30. Anthony Kosnik, et al., *Human Sexuality: New Directions in American Catholic Thought,* pp. 83–84.

31. The "nuptial meaning" of the body is developed in many of the addresses of Pope John Paul II on the "theology of the body." See in particular, "The Nuptial Meaning of the Body" (General Audience of January 9, 1980) in John Paul II, *The Theology of the Body: Human Love in the Divine Plan* (Boston: Pauline Books and Media, 1997), pp. 60–63; "The Man-Person Becomes a Gift in the Freedom of Love" (General Audience of January 16, 1980), in Ibid., pp. 63–66; "Mystery of Man's Original Innocence" (General Audience of January 30, 1980), in Ibid., pp. 66–69. On this issue see my essay, "Marriage and the Complementarity of Male and Female," Chap. 2 of my book *Marriage: The Rock on Which the Family Is Built* (San Francisco: Ignatius, 1995), pp. 39–66.

32. Mosier, "Contraception: A Symposium," p. 27.

33. In criticizing an earlier version of the argument given here (see endnote 10, above, for bibliographical details of the Grisez, et al., argument), Janet Smith accused the authors of "subjectivism" and of failing to recognize that "what one intends to do is defined as good or bad *independently of any act of the will*" (Janet Smith, *Humanae Vitae: A Generation Later* [Washington, DC: The Catholic University of America Press, 1991], p. 355). This criticism overlooks the fact that Paul VI, in order to reject every sort of contraception, had to define it in terms of the intention to impede procreation. Smith's critique, in fact, completely misunderstands the Grisez, *et al.,* argument; nowhere in her critique does she even report on the *arguments* given by Grisez, *et al.,* to show why it is always wrong to have an anti–life will. For a response to her criticisms, see William E. May, "A Review of Janet Smith's *Humanae Vitae: A Generation Later,*" *The Thomist,* 57 (1993), pp. 155–61.

34. Carlo Caffarra, "*Humanae Vitae Venti Anni Dopo,*" in "*Humanae*

Vitae: 20 Anni Dopo: Atti del II Congresso Internazionale di Teologia Morale (Milan: Edizioni Ares, 1989), p. 192; English translation in *Why Humanae Vitae Was Right: A Reader,* ed. Janet Smith (San Francisco: Ignatius, 1993), p. 267.

35. I acknowledge that some individuals *can* abuse "recourse to the rhythm of the cycle," regarding it merely as another way of impeding new human life. Such individuals have, in fact, a "contraceptive mentality," and may decide to impede new life by this means rather than by barrier or chemical means for aesthetic or hygienic reasons. St. Augustine, who used a primitive form of "fertility awareness" (refraining from having sex with his mistress during certain periods), testifies to this, for in his *Confessions* he acknowledges that his son Adeotatus "was conceived against our wills," but that, once born, he forced Augustine and his mistress to love him (see Book 4, Chap. 2). Such individuals are, in effect, putting a "temporal barrier between sperm and ovum" (as Rosemary Ruether claims) precisely in order to impede procreation. But for those who have "recourse to the rhythm of the cycle," choosing to abstain, not as a means of impeding procreation but of not causing a pregnancy when it would not be prudent to do so, do not have this anti-life will. If told that they "are putting a temporal barrier between sperm and ovum," they would rightly find the charge incomprehensible. Augustine would not find it so.

36. The argument briefly set forth in this section is developed at much greater length by Grisez, *et al.*, in the essay referred to in endnote 10 above. It is masterfully presented in by Grisez in Volume 2 of his *The Way of the Lord Jesus: Living a Christian Life* (Quincy, IL: Franciscan Press, 1993), pp. 506–19.

37. Pope John Paul II develops this argument in many of his papal writings. Janet Smith provides an excellent synthesis of his thought on this matter in her *Humanae Vitae: A Generation Later,* pp. 98–129. See also Fr. Paul DeLadurantaye's work cited in note 13, above.

38. See Paul Quay, S.J., "Contraception and Conjugal Love," *Theological Studies,* 22 (1961), pp. 18–40. See also Mary Joyce, *The Meaning of Contraception* (Collegeville, MN: The Liturgical Press, 1969); Dietrich von Hildebrand, *The Encyclical Humanae Vitae: A Sign of Contradiction* (Chicago: Franciscan Herald Press, 1969); and John Kippley, *Sex and the Marriage Covenant: A Basis for Morality* (Cincinnati: Couple-to-Couple League, 1991), pp. 50–76. In *Contraception and the Natural Law* (Milwaukee: Bruce, 1964), pp.

33–35, Germain Grisez offers an appreciative critique of this argument as expressed by Paul Quay.

39. Nuechterlein, "Catholics, Protestants, and Contraception," p. 10.

40. Pope John Paul II, "Homily at Mass for Youth, Nairobi, Kenya," *L'Osservatore Romano*, English Edition, 8 (August 26, 1985), p. 5; emphasis added. In saying this, John Paul II was in some ways also reaffirming the thought of Pope Paul VI who referred to *Humanae Vitae* as a defense of life "at the very source of human existence"; and, citing the teaching of *Gaudium et Spes*, 51, on abortion and infanticide, added: "We did no more than accept this charge when, then years ago, we published the Encyclical *Humanae Vitae*. This document drew its inspiration from the inviolable teachings of the Bible and the Gospel, which confirms the norms of the natural law and the unsuppressible dictates of conscience on respect for human life, the transmission of which is entrusted to responsible fatherhood and motherhood" (Paul VI, "Homily on the Feast of Sts. Peter and Paul," *L'Osservatore Romano*, English Edition, 2 [6 July 1978], p. 3).

41. Karol Wojtyla, *"Instynkt, Milosc, Malzenstwo,"* *Tygodnik Powszechny*, 8 (1952), p. 39. Quoted in John M. Grondelski, *Fruitfulness as an Essential Dimension in Acts of Conjugal Love: An Interpretative Study of the Pre-Pontifical Thought of John Paul II* (New York: Fordham University Press, 1986), p. 49. I am indebted to Fr. Paul DeLadurantaye for calling this text to my attention. This entire section of my paper owes much to the final portion of DeLadurantaye's unpublished S.T.D. dissertation, *"Irreconcilable Concepts of the Human Person" and the Moral Issue of Contraception: An Examination of the Personalism of Louis Janssens and Pope John Paul II*, especially pp. 259–80. As noted in endnote 13 above, a summary of this excellent study is provided in the journal *Anthropotes*.

42. Karol Wojtyla, *Love and Responsibility*, trans. H. Willetts (New York: Farrar, Straus, Giroux, 1981), pp. 53–54. See also *Evangelium Vitae*, 81: "The meaning of life is found in giving and receiving love, and in this light human sexuality and procreation reach their true and full significance."

RESPONSE TO WILLIAM MAY'S PAPER "CONTRACEPTION AND THE CULTURE OF DEATH"
Dr. Monica Migliorino Miller[1]

Professor William May has made an extremely bold, I would say courageous – others might say audacious – claim that indeed those who practice and or support the practice of contraception contribute to the culture of death – for contraception is the gateway to the anti-life culture! Professor May has corroborated by high scholarship what many pro-life activists have understood by experience – that a real connection exists, for example, between contraception and abortion. Fr. Paul Marx, founder of Human Life International, who has traveled to countries all over the globe to prevent the legalization of abortion, noted many years ago that, once a nation accepts contraception, legalized abortion inevitably follows.

But Professor May is making an even bolder claim. Not only is abortion the fruit of contraception, but the entire contemporary quest to deny the good of human life as seen in infanticide, assisted suicide, and euthanasia is the fruit of the same tree. Professor May has gored an important and significant ox when he argues that many of those who are opposed to the current culture of death are contributors to it by practicing and justifying contraception. Indeed, several people who consider themselves very pro-life, if they read William May's paper, would gnash their teeth. I'm glad I happen to agree with him!

Professor May is correct in showing that both contraception and the culture of death reside on a dualistic anthropology and consequentialist ethic, and that these two things are related insofar as the consequentialist argument attacks the anthropological good of the human person.

It is true that, in the Catholic tradition, contraception is immoral because it is an attack on life. More contemporary theologians, however, while not ignoring natural law arguments, tend to view contraception as immoral based upon anthropological considerations. When William May observes that the culture of death is rooted in a view of man which says that the fully human person is an autonomous isolated self and that such a self is capable of conscious exercise of his will, this anthropology is indeed the very backbone of the *Roe v. Wade* abortion decision in which persons, even married persons, are not inherently related. Indeed, in *Roe* human beings are inherently *unrelated* – and in this isolation the woman in a discovery of selfhood exercises her will to destroy her unborn child whom she says she is not in relation to – nor the child to her. It is the triumph of the mind and will over nature – a human nature that ever threatens to pull us into communion, but instead our new and false understanding of freedom insists that this communion be resisted, lest my selfhood and the ability to determine myself be compromised.

Certainly, control over the forces of nature that threaten to swallow me up is the driving force behind the campaign to legalize euthanasia. In the face of death, human dignity is protected when the person can willfully choose how and when he will die, and not have to wait for the impersonal disposition of his fleshly self to dictate the moment and manner of his demise.

Let me articulate in another way William May's thesis: when the communion of persons is broken, beginning with contraception, this brokenness unleashes a dynamic that causes human life to be unwanted, perhaps even annihilated. Contraception is justified because its use strengthens and enhances the personal unitive good of marriage. Yet how ironic it is that the personal unitive good of marriage is equally foregone when a couple engages in artificial reproduction. At this point, the bringing about of a baby is the result of the mind and will over nature. Children need not be related to any personal bodily act of love between married couples except the love expressed in a united intention to reproduce. As William May states: "If the person really is not his or her own body, then the person's sexuality can be 'liberated' from regulation by merely biological laws and used for 'interpersonal communication.'" But the contraceptive ethic, in its divorce of the unitive and procreative meanings

of sex, leaps even this boundary and leads to having children outside
of bodily interpersonal communication. Once new human lives are
thus separated from us, as we see in artificial reproduction, they are
subject to all sorts of injustices, dangers, and indignities – as when
so called "surplus" embryos are kept frozen, or experimented upon
and destroyed. These atrocities take place because, in the contraceptive ethic, procreation is isolated and distant from the personal self;
and thus, in artificial reproduction, the underbelly of contraception,
human life is also isolated and distant from the personal self. And,
once placed in such isolation, human beings become subject to
atrocities.

The contraceptive ethic shows us that, beginning with the contracepting couple, mind, reason and spirit are what is valued in persons. Human beings who lack reason, whose reason is seriously
compromised, or whose reason is threatened, are considered less
human, perhaps completely non-human – and who may then be dis-
pensed with. This is because the human body and all matter is
deemed to be merely raw biological stuff with no inherent moral
order or meaning. It is the free and autonomous reasoning human
mind that must put order into such a disordered biologically impersonal world. Contrary to the title of a famous feminist tome "Our
Bodies, Ourselves," the culture of death is driven by the ethic "our
bodies are *not* ourselves"! The body is not constitutive of the human
person, including masculinity and femininity and the power to procreate.

The pro-contraception position rests upon a dualistic anthropology and consequentialist ethic but, of course, those who argue that
contraception is justified do not recognize that they are consequentialist. They do not recognize it because they believe procreation is
sub-personal, and thus is not a good that is being attacked for the
sake of another good. Much theological work needs to be done to
demonstrate how the bodily nature of man, including procreation,
are true human goods.

William May begins to develop a response to this problem when
he touches upon the sacramental aspects of human sexuality. But, of
course this theology of the body needs more elaboration. May refers
to *Familiaris Consortio* which affirms that the procreative meaning
of the body is not sub-human or sub-personal. As May says: "It is

human and personal to begin with." But why is this so?

That contraception violates the meaning of conjugal love resides in the theological significance of the human body. Man as male and female forms the very basis of marriage. Genesis 1:27 teaches that man as male and female is created in God's image and likeness. Man and woman not only image God through their spiritual endowments. Man and woman image God through their communion. That two distinct and different beings can freely enjoy communion forms the basis of marriage as a sacramental sign of God's own union with his people. This union – indissoluble and definitive – exists in the union between the Second Adam, Christ and his Bride, the Church. The Letter to the Ephesians states that the union of man and woman in marriage is a sign of Christ's love for the Church, and Adam and Eve serve as the prototype of this love. Husbands are admonished to love their wives as they do their own body – "no one ever hates his own flesh." These verses confirm that the bodies of man and woman are good. St. Paul calls married couples to affirm the goodness of the body. Spouses are to affirm – love – the concrete reality of their masculinity and femininity. To love one's body as male or female means rejecting no part of it, including the body's procreative powers which are given to man by God as a blessing.

In the conjugal act each spouse makes a statement about themselves and one another. The husband makes a statement that he affirms, loves, himself as God created him as a male; the woman too affirms (loves) herself as a female. In their marriage they are to love (accept) each other as they do their own bodies. The word of love spouses speak through their bodies in the conjugal act is God's own language. When husbands and wives affirm the masculinity and femininity of their bodies in conjugal love, they perform an act worthy of participation in the mystery of the unconditional union between Christ and the Church.

When spouses use contraception, though, they express the idea that there is something wrong, evil, or undesirable about their bodies as male and female. A sacred quality about the body is rejected – and what is rejected is part of one's personal word. Consequently, complete union is not achieved because the integrity of the body as a sacred word has been broken. Contraception desecrates conjugal love as a sacramental sign because the spouses fail to affirm themselves and each other in their masculinity and femininity; and thus they fail to express Christ's affirmation of himself and his Bride, the Church.

God created man male and female to participate in this reality. To reject one's power to procreate violates one of the most fundamental (if not the most fundamental) meanings of masculinity and femininity. This refusal to love the body is a "no" uttered to God in the very act which sacramentally is meant by God to be a resounding "yes."

In the conjugal act, spouses perform a true liturgy founded by God himself. In this act spouses ratify their own union, and thus they ratify before God the sacred meaning of their marriage, which, according to his law, includes the good of one's procreative powers.

Masculinity derives its meaning as a sacramental symbol of God who generates life – a begetting principle which, of course, is perpetually present in God the Father. God the Father never rejects his generative role as Father. In imaging God to his creation, the husband likewise needs to affirm, and never reject or destroy, his own God-given generative powers. Christ too possesses generative power in relation to the Church. Christ fills the Church with his presence – his Word. The Church as his Bride truly receives him. She thus germinates what has been given to her. She brings the presence of Christ to fullness in the world. The Church rejects nothing from her Divine Spouse. She joyfully receives him and gives herself to him – holding back nothing. This living and eternal dynamism of love wherein Christ is affirmed as Bridegroom and the Church as Bride has its sacramental image in the one-flesh union of Christian spouses. Christian spouses have been taken up into this covenantal reality and thus serve as its liturgical expression in the celebration of their own bodily love. This liturgy precludes the use of contraception.

When spouses practice contraception surely they may will to become one flesh, and, in intercourse, they have at least superficially reproduced the outward appearance of union. But they have failed to fully give and receive one another. In failing to fully accept one another as male and female, they actually assault the liturgical significance of their married love.

It appears that we are dealing with a mystery. A connection exists between this failure to fully give of oneself in conjugal love and a will to not accept the lives of others in the beginning of life and even at the end. As William May so rightly argues, the attitude that the human body is a mere biological entity, sub-human, sub-personal to the mind, will and spirit, begins in contraception and ends in the chapels of alienation of the abortion and euthanasia chambers.

The cure for this ethics of isolation is the authentic Christian view that creation itself, and in some special way the human body in its power to create, is a sacrament of God's presence and love. If we can convince Christians of this truth, the culture of death will be overcome and the culture of life will flourish.

I wish to thank Professor May for his insight into the connection between contraception and the culture of death, his illustration of the anthropological and consequentialist dimensions of this problem, and also for pointing the way to the healing which lies in the liturgical and sacramental understanding of the human body as given by God. I hope that my few comments have shed some light on an essential aspect of this very troubling and very controversial subject.

Note

1. Monica Migliorino Miller, Ph.D., teaches theology at Marquette University in Milwaukee; she is also well known for her work in the pro-life movement. She has authored two books: *Sexuality and Authority in the Catholic Church* (University of Scranton Press) and *The Authority of Women in the Catholic Church* (Crisis Books).

APPENDIX

CRITERIA FOR POLICIES ON MARRIAGE, FAMILY, AND LIFE
Carl A. Anderson[1]

Politics has been defined as the art of the possible. In the most superficial way of thinking, this view of politics suggests that the fundamental criteria for public policy is attainability: can the law-maker through persuasion, compromise, and consensus succeed in reaching a predicted policy objective? Such political pragmatism may be normative in the day-to-day policy making of the world's democracies. However, that should not prevent us from asking two basic questions of a more philosophical nature: what is it that defines what is possible in politics, and how is it that what may be possible changes over time?

These questions point us in the direction of considering the relationship between culture and politics because, in so many ways, it is the culture of a particular society that defines what is politically possible within its democratic institutions. Moreover, consideration of the relationship between culture and politics is absolutely necessary because we are concerned with public policies affecting fundamental cultural institutions, namely, marriage and the family.

Thus, consideration of public policies that affect fundamental cultural institutions go beyond politics narrowly defined. Indeed, such consideration must go beyond narrow definitions to the consideration of a form of cultural politics that by its very nature must implicate profound cultural values. This is in part what I think Vaclav Havel was intimating when he wrote, "We must not be afraid of dreaming the seemingly impossible if we want the seemingly impossible to become a reality."[2]

It may be that in this case the "seemingly impossible" is absolutely necessary if fundamental change in regard to family and

marriage policies can become reality. Moreover, there is an anthropological basis for this hope in the realization of the "seemingly
impossible." As Pope John Paul II writes in *Veritatis Splendor*, "the
very progress of cultures demonstrates that there is something in
man which transcends those cultures. This 'something' is precisely
human nature: this nature is itself the measure of culture and the
condition of ensuring that man does not become prisoner of any of
his cultures, but asserts his personal dignity by living in accordance
with the profound truth of his being" (53). Thus, the "seemingly
impossible" should be attainable when what is sought is consistent
with and indeed mandated by the dignity and nature of the human
person.

Beyond this anthropological foundation, there is also a theological one regarding the reality of the evangelization of culture. Pope
Paul VI made clear in *Evangelii Nuntiandi* that in the mission of
evangelization, cultures are to be evangelized "not in a purely deco-
rative way, as it were, by applying a thin veneer, but in a vital way,
in depth and right to their very roots" (19). As the Pontifical Council
for Culture recently observed, "faith has the power to get to the core
of every culture and to purify it, to make it fruitful, to enrich it and
to make it blossom." And in this sense, the Pontifical Council for
Culture concludes, "faith's encounter with different cultures has created something new . . . it creates an original culture."[3] In this light
then I would like to propose criteria for policies on marriage, family, and life that address both the cultural and political dimensions of
these questions.

1. Hope as Cultural Criteria for the Family

There are at least three fundamental cultural impediments to
hope as an informing principle in contemporary Western societies.

The first is a form of Kafkaesque devaluation of the self that perhaps has been best described by Vaclav Havel. In a speech at
Hebrew University in 1990, Havel described his own experience of
the world as "a profound, banal, and therefore utterly vague sensa-
tion of culpability, as though my very existence were a kind of sin.
Then there is a powerful feeling of general alienation, both my own
and one that relates to everything around me that helps to create such
feelings; an experience of unbearable oppressiveness, a need con-

stantly to explain myself to some, to defend myself, a longing for an unattainable order of things . . . I find myself essentially hateful, deserving only mockery" (30).

The second, is the sensibility described by Jean-Francois Lyotard when he wrote "there is a sort of grief in the *Zeitgeist*" of modern culture. Moreover, Lyotard emphasizes this point when he cites Auschwitz as the symbol of a modernity that has failed in its moral promise and of the fundamental impoverishment of the West. It is a sensibility closely attached to that found in the writings of Elie Wiesel and especially of the horrific account of his experience at Auschwitz. Some may consider that these views of Havel, Lyotard, and Wiesel are the product of personal experience of the horrors of this century's totalitarian cruelties or obsession with them. Yet it seems to me that there is more here than just personalities wounded by ideological violence. It seems rather that the sensibilities reflected in by Havel, Lyotard, and Wiesel, each in their own way, point to the loss of hope as a cultural ideal throughout the West.

There is another cultural phenomena that has also undermined hope per se throughout the West but from the opposite direction. I would describe it as a form of historical optimism almost bordering upon a kind of determinism. It was recently expressed in the writing of Francis Fukuyama. In his work, *The End of History and the Last Man*, Fukuyama argues that the end point of history and human consciousness is Western liberal democracy. In this cultural milieu, hope as a Christian virtue becomes lost. Its place has been taken over by an uncritical view of progress that guarantees that everything will gradually evolve for the best, including the arrangement of marriage and the family. Given the inevitability of Western progress, what need is there of hope?

This has profound effects upon the family since it is the family as a cultural institution that most concretely embodies hope as a cultural imperative. It is the family in its role as begetting, nurturing, and developing each successive generation that projects a culture's commitment to the future and expresses most concretely a society's hope. A society without hope will soon become a society without families. As Pope John Paul II has said, "the future of humanity passes by way of the family." A society unsure or despondent about its future will be unable to muster the cultural resources sufficient to preserve and defend the family. Thus, the first criteria for policies on marriage, family, and life are the restoration of hope as a cultural value.

2. Marriage as a Principle of Reconciliation between Man and Woman

Historically, the effects of industrialization in the West accelerated the displacement of the family based upon marriage as a central cultural institution that was an essential aspect of the Enlightenment's assault upon Christian cultural norms. The sacramental and permanent character of marriage was viewed by the Enlightenment *philosophes* as a reflection of the "irrationality, cruelty, and unnaturalness of Catholic society."[4] Rousseau's view of monogamous, sacramental marriage as essentially oppressive of human freedom became legally, and shortly thereafter, culturally, normative in France with the Constitution of 1791 and the divorce law of 1792. These legal developments were premised on the principle that "any indissoluble tie is an infringement of individual liberty and that therefore the principle of individual liberty presupposes a natural right to divorce."[5]

This undermining of family stability was greatly increased through substantial incorporation of women and children into the workforce outside the home by industrialization. To this general view of the institution of marriage as oppressive, and the exploitation of women and children in industrialized societies, Marxism introduced a further development in regard to exploitation within the family structure. Writing in *The German Ideology*, Marx and Engels maintained that "The first class antagonism which appears in history coincides with the development of the antagonism between man and woman in monogamous marriage, and the first class oppression with that of the female sex by the male."[6]

In this view, later developed by Engels and other Marxist theorists, the principle of dialectic was introduced into the heart of the family. Marxism treated the husband as the oppressive bourgeois and the wife was viewed as the oppressed proletariat. This notion of class oppression and therefore class struggle carried over into the dynamics of the family has, of course, been taken up as a regular theme of much recent feminist theory.

At this theoretical point, Marxist ideology, feminist theory, and libertarian philosophy find themselves as unlikely allies in the destabilization of the family based upon marriage. Libertarian philosophy espousing individual autonomy and freedom as the greatest social good also tended toward the view that the indissolubility of marriage is a limitation on individual freedom and personal development. This philosophy tends to view marriage as a joint venture between two individuals not dissimilar from other contractual undertakings for mutual benefit. Thus, individual interests and development rather than that of the common good of the marital community tend to take precedence in this view. When commitment to the common good of the marital community is further undermined by so-called "no-fault" divorce laws, sacrifices by a spouse of his or her own individual interest for the good of the marital community or family are made at his or her own risk. The introduction of laws throughout the West providing for the relatively easy dissolution of marriage, supported by socialist, feminist, and libertarian ideologies, has introduced a subtle yet substantial form of competition between the spouses within the institution of marriage that has further de-stabilized marriage as a permanent institution.

A second criterion for marriage and family policies must be to move beyond the ideologies of Marxism, feminism, and libertarianism, and their consideration of marriage as a principle of conflict, oppression or competition, to a view of family which understands marriage as a form of reconciliation between man and woman.

3. The Family as a Principle of Moral Consciousness

From what has just been said, it should be obvious that the role of the family as a moral influence within society has been dramatically undermined. Today the family is too often viewed as a set of relationships defined by contract principles imposed by the state with little or no regard for the inherent character of those relationships. Moreover, the moral foundation of the family has been further reduced by an essentially *laissez-faire* understanding of contract itself, which sees a contract as nothing more than the structuring of differing sets of self-interest among parties. Viewed in this light, marriage is aptly summed up by the editors of one American law school textbook as follows: "Perceived as neither a sacrament nor a status necessarily assumed for life, the relationship contemplated by parties is not dissimilar from that of other long-term contracts."[7]

The unique position of marriage in Western culture arose as a consequence of the Christian insight that the commitment of the spouses to one another was faithful and exclusive until death. Although the application of certain contract principles are essential to marital stability, this Christian view of marriage is essentially a covenant rather than contract understanding of marriage. It is this covenant understanding of marriage that is foundational to our understanding of the sacramental nature of marriage. The effort by theologians and canon lawyers since the Middle Ages to bring greater clarity to our understanding of marriage has benefited greatly from the application of contract principles to questions involving when and how a marriage comes into existence. But this application of contract principles should not change the basic covenant nature of the institution of marriage. It is time to recover the understanding of marriage as essentially a covenant relationship and with it the understanding of covenant as essentially a *moral* relationship.

4. The Family as a Principle of *Communio Personarum* and thus as Foundational to Society

It has long been recognized in international human rights documents that the family as an institution is foundational to society. The United Nations Declaration of Human Rights observes that "the family is the natural and fundamental group unit of society." The American Declaration of the Rights and Duties of Man recognizes the family as "the basic element of society." The European Social Charter states that the family is "a fundamental unit of society."

However, while these documents do speak of the family as the "fundamental group unit" or "basic element" of society, none actually defines what is "fundamental" or "basic" about the family. Absent from this international recognition is the recognition of the family as a community which possesses inherent and inalienable rights, or even a definitive character which is independent of the state and outside of its control.

The Charter of the Rights of the Family presented by the Holy See in 1983 recognizes a criterion that is fundamental to all public policies regarding marriage and family, namely, that as "a natural society" the family "exists prior to the state or any other community and possesses inherent rights which are inalienable." This is an absolutely essential first criterion for family policy; otherwise the family may too easily become simply another instrumentality for the realization of state power.

The assertion that the family "exists prior to the state" and that it "possesses inherent rights, which are inalienable" rests upon the realization that the family also possesses an identity, which is independent of both the state and of individuals. It is this "identity" of the family which is the subject of the profound analysis undertaken by Pope John Paul II in *Familiaris Consortio,* and which allows him to conclude, "family, become what you are!"

Obviously the question of criteria for marriage and family policies must cross the threshold question: just what constitutes this social entity entitles it to respect? The definition provided by the American Home Economics Association approximately three decades ago is increasingly normative in American and European policy-making. It states: "We describe it as a unit of two or more persons who share resources, share responsibilities for decisions, share values and goals, and have a commitment to one another over time. Family is that climate that one 'comes home to' and it is this network of sharing and commitments that more accurately describes family, regardless of blood, legal ties, adoption or marriage."[8]

The logical consequence of such a view of marriage and family can be seen in the 1973 revision of the Swedish marriage law. During its preparation, the Swedish Ministry of Justice set out this guideline: "New legislation ought as far as possible to be neutral in relation to the different forms of living together and different moral views . . . one should try to see that family law legislation does not contain provisions which create unnecessary hardships or inconveniences for those who have children and build families without marrying."[9] By reducing formal marriage to merely one form of voluntary cohabitation among several alternatives, and then combining this legal structure with an extensive government commitment to welfare benefits structured to effect "the decrease in mutual dependence between the spouses," Swedish law has successfully deprived couples of the idea that they are doing something unique in marrying. This principle of Swedish family law has become the model for the treatment of the institution of the family based upon marriage among many Western democracies.

As the definition of family proposed by the American Home Economics Association suggests, once the traditional view of marriage is abandoned, there is simply no principled way to limit the ever increasing level of generality that seeks to subsume more and more unconventional forms of conduct within the protection of the law. This tendency is enhanced in the legal systems of many Western countries by principles of individual liberty and equality. This is especially the case when liberty and equality have been applied to protect a broad range of intimate non-coercive sexual actions. As one American legal scholar puts it, the question then is "to define the liberty at a high enough level of generality to permit unconventional variants to claim protection along with mainstream versions of protected conduct."[10]

In the face of such a widely accepted reductionist view of the family, it is essential to propose in response an anthropology of the family which is adequate to support public policies centered on the family based upon marriage. Much of the analysis of *Familiaris Consortio* and Pope John Paul II's "Letter to Families" is precisely the presentation of such an anthropology; yet much remains to be done in structuring the relationship between this anthropology, and the wide variety of public policies affecting the family. The "Charter of Family Rights" proposed in *Familiaris Consortio* and the later "Charter of the Rights of the Family" are important steps in establishing guidelines for family policies consistent with a Christian anthropology. But more needs to be done to develop specific links between public policies and, especially, the Trinitarian dimension of family life.

5. Human Dignity as Constitutive of the Family and Foundational of its Anthropology

The contingent nature of human existence may lead some to view human dignity as itself conditional. The emphasis placed on this point in *Evangelium Vitae* regarding the unconditional nature of human dignity is an absolutely necessary criterion for the development of public policies and laws regarding the inviolability of all human life. Pope John Paul II makes this point very clear in the encyclical. But this point is also vitally important in understanding the nature of the family and the responsibility of the state in protecting and promoting family life based upon marriage. As the Holy Father writes in *Evangelium Vitae*, "It is . . . urgently necessary . . . to rediscover those essential and innate human and moral values which flow from the very truth of the human being and express and safeguard the dignity of the person: values which no individual, no majority and no state can ever create, modify or destroy, but must only acknowledge, respect, and promote" (71). This principle has vital application to public policies related to the family.

It is precisely because human dignity within the context of the family must be regarded as unconditional that the permanence of the relationship between the spouses and their responsibilities regarding the transmission of human life must be free from the manipulations of ethical relativism. Respect for the human dignity of each spouse demand that the dignity of each not be treated in a qualified or conditional manner. Each person within the context of marriage and the family has the right to be treated in a manner consistent with human dignity. Therefore each person has the right not to be subjected to laws which treat the relationship between the spouses, or between parents and children, as morally relative – as do laws that permit divorce and abortion. Certainly great attention has been given to the demands of human dignity in relation to the questions of abortion, euthanasia and the transmission of human life. Both *Humanae Vitae* and *Evangelium Vitae* have proposed a means of analysis that finds a personalistic approach centered on the dignity of the human person foundational.

But unfortunately it is not equally true that such a comprehensive analysis has been provided regarding laws which permit divorce or which recognize non-marital co-habitation. They similarly undermine human dignity. Such laws do this by treating a relationship between men and women, which is by its very structure inherently unqualified in a way, which seeks to make marriage only a qualified and conditional relationship.

More now needs to be done to broaden the analysis of marriage centered on the dignity of the human person from the perspective of public policy. Such analysis should include the basic structure and nature of the family so as to better understand and support the rights of family members to the permanence of the family structure and its unique role in society.

6. The Family as the Paradigm of Public Policy

As the rationale of the Swedish family law makes clear, in contemporary public policy the operating paradigm is the autonomous individual. The fundamental difficulty with this approach to public policy-making is that it rests upon a fiction. The isolated individual who lives his life in autonomy does not exist. To the extent that a minority of individuals may approach such a lifestyle, they are usually regarded as in some important sense suffering from a personal or social pathology. The great majority of persons are born into families and are raised and educated within the family, and within communal extensions of the family, such as the neighborhood school. They continue their familial relationships throughout their lives, and they live and work in communal environments that in many ways are extensions of the family. The recovery of a domestic public policy free of illusion and focused upon this reality would be a public policy that recognizes the essentially familial character of human existence. A realistic public policy would therefore seek to measure economic, social, and legal policies by the standard of how laws and government programs support the family.

Adopting the family as the paradigm of public policy means something considerably more than the rather meager family allowances that have been implemented in some European nations and proposed at various times in the United States. It also means the reconsideration of such government services and benefit programs that have become substitutes for functions traditionally performed by families in the past. Certainly, there are short-term advantages to such government initiatives. However, too little attention has been given to the long-term effect of substituting government action for family action. When coupled with high rates of taxation needed to pay for such services, the long-term effect of government intervention may be to drain the family of the ability to perform for itself the social and economic functions which give the family social meaning and purpose.

However, the shift to viewing the family as a public policy paradigm raises the additional and in some ways more profound issue of the treatment of motherhood. Pope John Paul II from the early days of his pontificate has argued that due regard for motherhood is a fundamental criterion for public policy. During his 1979 trip to Poland he stated: "The family is one of the fundamental factors determining the economy and policy of work. These keep their ethical character when they take into consideration the needs and rights of the family. Through work the adult human being must earn the means to maintain his family. Motherhood must be treated in work policy and economy as a great task in itself. For with it is connected the mother's work in giving birth, feeding, and rearing, and no one can take her place. Nothing can take the place of the heart of the mother always present and always waiting in the home. True respect for work brings with it due esteem for motherhood. It cannot be otherwise. The moral health of the whole of society depends on that."[11]

What is at issue here is not the rather insignificant child allowances made available in some European countries, or the insufficient child federal tax exemption in the United States. What is at issue is whether motherhood and the support system which nature has built around it, namely, the family, will be at the center or at the margin of the governmental decision-making process. In the United States, at least, such consideration of the family would result in radical and far-reaching change in the traditional approach of government to the family. Time permits only one example.

In the United States, the work of economist Henry Simons in the 1930s was foundational to the development and the approach of the American system of federal taxation. In regard to the economic importance of the family, the following was Simons' view: "It would be hard to maintain that the raising of children is not a form of consumption on the part of parents."[12] To the contrary, it would not be hard to maintain that the raising of children is a contribution to the good of society and is an activity that deserves community reward and support.

7. Human Dignity as the Fundamental Criterion for Pro-Life Policies

Because the actions and responsibilities surrounding the begetting and bearing of children remain essential to the character of marriage and the family, much of what has already been said concerning the fundamental criteria for polices affecting marriage and family apply to pro-life policies. For example, hope as a cultural criteria for marriage is also a fundamental cultural criteria for pro-life policies since, obviously, hope in the future is required for the commitment necessary to beget and bear children, and thus to extend society into the future.

Also, what was just said about the dignity and centrality of motherhood would, if realized, do much to alleviate the pressure many women believe they feel to forego motherhood by means of abortion in order to continue career objectives outside the home. *Evangelium Vitae* summarizes this point when the encyclical states that "a family policy must be the basis and driving force of all social policies" (90).

In *Evangelium Vitae*, Pope John Paul II proposes very specific criteria for pro-life policies, both from the standpoint of culture and from that of governmental action. The time remaining is not adequate to do justice to the profound analysis presented by the Holy Father in this encyclical. Nonetheless several broad observations are necessary.

First, the Holy Father understands the fundamental questions concerning human life today to be a cultural project. Indeed, nearly a fourth of the encyclical deals with the question of "a new culture of human life" (Chapter 4). In this section, the Holy Father calls on the Catholic people to be "a people of life and a people for life" (78). This "people of life" are called to "proclaim life," evangelize culture in favor of life, and in so doing to build a "culture of life." Moreover, he sees this cultural project as one that is tied inseparably to the common good. As the encyclical states towards its conclusion, "to be actively pro-life is to contribute to the renewal of society through the promotion of the common good. It is impossible to further the common good without acknowledging and defending the right to life, upon which all the other inalienable rights of individuals are founded and from which they develop" (101).

Considering the jurisprudence of abortion, especially as it has developed in the United States, the rationale for the legalization of abortion has evolved. This rationale has evolved from the articulation of a new doctrine of privacy in the 1973 case of *Roe v. Wade* to one of liberty in the 1992 case of *Planned Parenthood v. Casey*. The unique historical elements within the American constitutional tradition that gave rise to the doctrine of privacy in matters related to procreation are not essential to our discussion. It is sufficient to observe that while privacy was discussed in terms of the expectation of secrecy or confidentiality, that understanding of privacy was only secondary. What was central to the United States Supreme Court's functional understanding of privacy as a constitutional doctrine was that it operated to create a zone of autonomous decision-making free from governmental supervision, regulation or control. In other words, the constitutional doctrine of privacy in the United States was essentially a doctrine related to personal liberty first and confidentiality second.

In the case of *Planned Parenthood v. Casey*, the Supreme Court made clear that this abortion "liberty" was linked to the Court's understanding of the dignity of the person. The Court stated that this liberty "involving the most intimate and personal choices a person may make in a lifetime, choices central to personal dignity and autonomy, are central to the liberty protected by the [Constitution]. At the heart of liberty is the right to define one's own concept of existence, of meaning, of the universe, and of the mystery of human life. Beliefs about these matters could not define the attributes of personhood were they formed under compulsion of the state."[13]

In 1973, the Supreme Court in *Roe v. Wade* held that "We need not resolve the difficult question of when life begins. When those trained in the respective disciplines of medicine, philosophy, and theology are unable to arrive at any consensus, the judiciary, at this point in the development of man's knowledge, is not in a position to speculate as to the answer."[14] By asserting such ambiguity into the discussion about the beginning of a person's life, the Supreme Court defined the scope of the abortion debate to consider the biological and other facts regarding the life of the human person before birth. But as those facts with time overwhelmingly pointed to the autonomy and humanity of the child before birth, the Court shifted discussion of personhood away from the unborn child to the personhood of the mother. Regardless of the effect of the abortion liberty on the human rights and dignity of the child in the womb, the Supreme Court in *Planned Parenthood v. Casey* now argued that what was essential was the effect of the abortion liberty on the dignity of the woman. With the Supreme Court's opinion in the *Casey* decision, the question of personhood and human dignity has shifted to include the woman as the principal, if not exclusive focus.

Promulgated nearly three years after the *Planned Parenthood v. Casey* case, *Evangelium Vitae* makes a profound response to the Supreme Court's decision precisely on the grounds of human dignity. In doing so, the encyclical sets forth three essential criteria for pro-life policies. The Holy Father states first that society must recognize the equal dignity of every human being regardless of age, condition, or race. This is especially true of the poor, the weak, and the defenseless. Second, he maintains that it is always a violation of human dignity to treat a person like an instrument or a means to an end: Every person must be seen as worthy in himself and never as an object of manipulation. Third, he insists that the deliberate killing of an innocent human being, whatever the circumstances, is always morally wrong. This is a vision of the dignity of the human person strong enough to counter that put forward by those who would distort the concept of human dignity to shield the intentional killing of the innocent.

The concept of liberty inherent within the abortion jurisprudence articulated in *Planned Parenthood v. Casey* unhinges human autonomy and free decision-making from moral responsibility to other human beings. Responsibility to "the other" person is essentially non-existent in the Supreme Court's understanding of the exercise of liberty in the abortion context. In *Casey* we read, in regard to the abortion decision, that "the liberty of the woman is at stake in a sense unique to the law. The mother who carries a child to full term is subject to anxieties, to physical constraints, to pain that only she must bear. . . . Her suffering is too intimate and personal for the State to insist, without more, upon its own vision of the woman's role, however dominant that vision has been in the course of our history and our culture. The destiny of the woman must be shaped to a large extent on her own conception of her spiritual imperatives and her place in society" (at p. 2807). In the Court's view, then, the liberty to make the abortion decision is a central dimension of the liberty which is constitutive of its understanding of the person.

To the contrary, in *Evangelium Vitae*, the Holy Father relates human dignity directly to human freedom. This linkage of human

dignity and human liberty rests upon a respect for the human dignity of the other as inherent in any concept of freedom – not only in
regard to the exercise of liberty by the other, but also in regard to
human dignity itself and to the fact that that respect entails an obligation of service. The exercise of liberty cannot be an isolated event
purely within the domain of the autonomous individual. Thus for
Pope John Paul II the "gift of self" is implicit within any ordered
exercise of personal liberty. "It is therefore urgently necessary,"
writes the Holy Father in *Evangelium Vitae*, "for the future of society and the development of a sound democracy, to rediscover those
essential and innate human and moral values which flow from the
very truth of the human being and express and safeguard the dignity of the person: values which no individual, no majority and no
state can ever create, modify or destroy, but must only acknowledge,
respect, and promote" (71).

This means that the exercise of freedom cannot be cut off from
"the task of accepting and serving life"; and that this is a task that
"must be fulfilled above all towards life when it is at its weakest"
(43). This means that if human dignity is to be the fundamental criterion for pro-life policies, then our commitment to liberty must
include a commitment to an understanding of freedom that acknowledges service to others as a necessary pre-condition to the adequate
recognition of human dignity.

Permit me one final observation in conclusion. Because of the
global nature of the Pontifical Institute for Studies on Marriage and
the Family, and its worldwide mission, we cannot avoid the implications of our work in supporting the mission of the Church in a new
evangelization and in the Church's mission *ad gentes*. Working with
families is dealing with the challenge of inculturation *par excellence*. As the Holy Father wrote in *Redemptoris Missio*, "the
Church's insertion into people's cultures is a lengthy one. It is not a
matter of purely external adaptation, for inculturation means the intimate transformation of authentic cultural values through their inte-
gration in Christianity and the insertion of Christianity in the various
human cultures" (52). This process requires that the Church accept
and build upon what is already good within an existing culture; and
that process in turn requires that the Church avoid both the uncritical alienation and acceptance of particular existing cultures and cul-

tural values (54). The process of cultural discernment is of utmost importance to the work of the Institute, just as it has implication for all aspects of our work and, especially, those related to the concrete proposals concerning policies affecting family, marriage, and pro-life questions.

Notes

1. Carl A. Anderson is Supreme Secretary, Knights of Columbus, and Dean, John Paul II Institute for Studies on Marriage and Family in Washington, DC. He has served as a member of the Board of Directors of the Fellowship of Catholic Scholars. This address was delivered at an International Study Week on Marriage and the Family in Rome in August 1999, just prior to the Fellowship convention on the same subject, and is printed here as an Appendix because of its pertinence to the theme of the FCS convention.

2. Vaclav Havel, *The Art of the Impossible: Politics as Morality in Practice* (New York: Fromm International, 1998), p. xi.

3. Pontifical Council for Culture, "Towards a Pastoral Approach to Culture," *L'Osservatore Romano,* English Edition (9 June 1999).

4. Max Rheinstein, *Marriage Stability, Divorce and the Law* (University of Chicago Press: Chicago, 1972), p. 267.

5. Mary Ann Glendon, "The French Divorce Reform Law of 1976," *American Journal of Comparative Law,* 24 (1976), pp. 199–200.

6. See Karl Marx and Frederick Engels, *Selected Works* (International Publishers: New York, 1968), p. 468.

7. Walter Weyrauch and Sanford Katz, *American Family Law in Transition* (Bureau of National Affairs: Washington, DC, 1983), p. 1.

8. See Hearings on the White House Conference on Families before the Senate Subcommittee on Child and Human Development, 95th Congress, 2nd Session, February 2 & 3, 1978, at p. 432.

9. Sundberg, "Recent Changes in Swedish Family Law," *American Journal of Comparative Law,* 24 (1975), p. 41.

10. Lawrence Tribe, *American Constitutional Law* (Milwaukee: West Law Book Company, 1978), p. 945.

11. *L'Osservatore Romano*, English Edition (16 June 1979).

12. See Henry Simons, *Personal Income Taxation* (Chicago: University of Chicago Press, 1938).

13. *Planned Parenthood v. Casey*, 112 S. Ct. 2791, 2807 (1992).

14. *Roe v. Wade*, 410 U.S. 113, 181 (1973).

FELLOWSHIP OF CATHOLIC SCHOLARS

Membership Information
http://www4.allencol.edu/~philtheo/FCS/

Statement of Purpose

(1) We Catholic scholars in various disciplines join in fellowship in order to serve Jesus Christ better by helping one another in our work and by putting our abilities more fully at the service of the Catholic faith.

(2) We wish to form a fellowship of scholars who see their intellectual work as expressing the service they owe to God. To Him we give thanks for our Catholic faith and for every opportunity He gives us to serve that faith.

(3) We wish to form a fellowship of Catholic scholars open to the work of the Holy Spirit within the Church. Thus we wholeheartedly accept and support the renewal of the Church of Christ undertaken by Pope John XXIII, shaped by Vatican II, and carried on by succeeding pontiffs.

(4) We accept as the rule of our life and thought the entire faith of the Catholic Church. This we see not merely in solemn definitions but in the ordinary teaching of the Pope and those bishops in union with him, and also embodied in those modes of worship and ways of Christian life, of the present as of the past, which have been in harmony with the teaching of St. Peter's successors in the See of Rome.

(6) To contribute to this sacred work, our fellowship will strive to:

     * Come to know and welcome all who share our purpose;
     * Make known to one another our various competencies and interests;
     * Share our abilities with one another unstintingly in our efforts directed to our common purpose;
     * Cooperate in clarifying the challenges which must be met;

* Help one another to evaluate critically the variety of responses which are proposed to these challenges;
* Communicate our suggestions and evaluations to members of the Church who might find them helpful;
* Respond to requests to help the Church in its task of guarding the faith as inviolable and defending it with fidelity;
* Help one another to work through, in scholarly and prayerful fashion and without public dissent, any problem which may arise from magisterial teaching.

(7) With the grace of God for which we pray, we hope to assist the whole Church to understand its own identity more clearly, to proclaim the joyous Gospel of Jesus more confidently, and to carry out its redemptive mission of all humankind more effectively.

To apply for membership, contact:

Rev. Thomas F. Dailey, O.S.F.S.
FCS Executive Secretary
Allentown College of St. Francis de Sales
2755 Station Avenue
Center Valley, PA 18034–9568
Tel.: (610) 282–1100, Ext. 1464
E-mail: tfdO@email.allencol.edu

Member Benefits

FCS Quarterly – All members receive four issues annually. The 50-page publication includes:
* President's page
* Scholarly articles
* Documentation
* Bulletin Board (news)
* Book Reviews

Membership Directory – All members receive the annually updated listing of FCS members in the U.S.A. and abroad.

National Conventions – All members are invited to participate in the annual gathering. The typical program includes:

* Daily Mass
* Six scholarly Sessions
* Keynote Address
* Banquet and Awards

Regular members receive a copy of the *Proceedings* of each convention.

National Awards – The Fellowship grants the following awards, usually presented during its annual convention:

> * The *Cardinal Wright Award* is given *annually* to a Catholic adjudged to have done an outstanding service for the Church in the tradition of the late Cardinal John J. Wright, Bishop of Pittsburgh and later Prefect, Congregation for the Clergy. Previous recipients are:

1979 – Rev. Msgr. George A. Kelly
1980 – Dr. William E. May
1981 – Dr. James Hitchcock
1982 – Dr. Germain Grisez
1983 – Rev. John Connery, S.J.
1984 – Rev. John Hardon, S.J.
1985 – Dr. Herbert Ratner
1986 – Dr. Joseph P. Scottino
1987 – Rev. Joseph Farraher, S.J. & Rev.
          Joseph Fessio, S.J.
1988 – Rev. John Harvey, O.S.F.S.
1989 – Dr. John Finnis
1990 – Rev. Ronald Lawler, O.F.M. Cap
1991 – Rev. Francis Caravan, S.J.
1992 – Rev. Donald J. Keefe, S.J.
1993 – Dr. Janet E. Smith
1994 – Dr. Jude P. Dougherty
1995 – Rev. Msgr. William B. Smith
1996 – Dr. Ralph McInerny
1997 – Rev. James V. Schall, S.J.

1998 – Mr. Kenneth D. Whitehead & Rev.
    Msgr. Michael Wrenn
1999 – Dr. Robert P. George

* The *Cardinal O'Boyle Award* is given *occasionally* to an
individual whose actions demonstrate a courage and witness for the Catholic Church similar to that exhibited by the
late Cardinal Patrick A. O'Boyle, Archbishop of
Washington, in light of dissenting pressures in our society.
    1988 – Rev. John C. Ford, S.J.
    1991 – Mother Angelica, P.C.P.A., EWTN
    1995 – John and Sheila Kippley, Couple to
        Couple League
    1997 – Rep. Henry J. Hyde, (R-IL)